Semiotics with a Conscience

Bloomsbury Advances in Semiotics

Series Editor: Paul Bouissac

Formerly Continuum Advances in Semiotics.
Bloomsbury Advances in Semiotics publishes original works applying semiotic approaches to linguistics and non-verbal productions, social institutions and discourses, embodied cognition and communication, and the new virtual realities of the digital age. It covers topics such as socio-semiotics, evolutionary semiotics, game theory, cultural and literary studies, human-computer interactions, and the challenging new dimensions of human networking afforded by social websites.

Editorial Board

Zuanglin Hu, Peking University, Beijing
Marcel Kinsbourne, New School for Social Research, New York City, USA
Franson Manjali, Jawaharlal Nehru University, India
Mihai Nadin, University of Texas at Dallas, USA
Kay O'Halloran, National University of Singapore, Singapore
Jerzy Pelc, Warsaw University, Poland
Goran Sonesson, Lund University, Sweden
Jef Verschueren, University of Antwerp, Belgium
Anne Wagner, Universite du Littoral Cote d'Opale, France and China University of Political Science and Law, China
Ruth Wodak, Lancaster University, UK
Hiroshi Yoshioka, Kyoto University, Japan

Titles published in the series:

Developing a Neo-Peircean Approach to Signs, Tony Jappy
The Social Semiotics of Populism, Sebastián Moreno Barreneche
Systemic Semiotics, Piotr Sadowski
The Semiotics of Architecture in Video Games, Gabriele Aroni
Semiotics of the Christian Imagination, Domenico Pietropaolo
Computational Semiotics, Jean-Guy Meunier
Cognitive Semiotics, Per Aage Brandt
The Semiotics of Caesar Augustus, Elina Pyy
The Social Semiotics of Tattoos, Chris William Martin
The Semiotics of X, Jamin Pelkey

The Semiotics of Light and Shadows, Piotr Sadowski
Music as Multimodal Discourse, edited by
Lyndon C. S. Way and Simon McKerrell
Peirce's Twenty-Eight Classes of Signs and the Philosophy of Representation,
Tony Jappy
The Semiotics of Emoji, Marcel Danesi
Semiotics and Pragmatics of Stage Improvisation, Domenico Pietropaolo
Critical Semiotics, Gary Genosko
The Languages of Humor, edited by Arie Sover
Semiotics of Happiness, Ashley Frawley
Warning Signs, Marcel Danesi
Semiotics of Religion, Robert A. Yelle
Computable Bodies, Josh Berson
The Semiotics of Clowns and Clowning, Paul Bouissac
The Semiotics of Che Guevara, Maria-Carolina Cambre
The Visual Language of Comics, Neil Cohn
The Language of War Monuments, David Machin and Gill Abousnnouga
A Buddhist Theory of Semiotics, Fabio Rambelli
Introduction to Peircean Visual Semiotics, Tony Jappy

Semiotics with a Conscience

Decoding Dangerous Discourses

Marcel Danesi

BLOOMSBURY ACADEMIC
LONDON • NEW YORK • OXFORD • NEW DELHI • SYDNEY

BLOOMSBURY ACADEMIC

Bloomsbury Publishing Plc, 50 Bedford Square, London, WC1B 3DP, UK
Bloomsbury Publishing Inc, 1359 Broadway, New York, NY 10018, USA
Bloomsbury Publishing Ireland, 29 Earlsfort Terrace, Dublin 2, D02 AY28, Ireland

BLOOMSBURY, BLOOMSBURY ACADEMIC and the Diana logo
are trademarks of Bloomsbury Publishing Plc

First published in Great Britain 2024
Paperback edition published 2025

Copyright © Marcel Danesi, 2024, 2025

Marcel Danesi has asserted his right under the Copyright,
Designs and Patents Act, 1988, to be identified as Author of this work.

For legal purposes the Acknowledgments on p. xv constitute
an extension of this copyright page.

Cover design: Elena Durey
Cover image © Oleksandr BerezkoEyeEm/Getty

All rights reserved. No part of this publication may be: i) reproduced or transmitted in any form, electronic or mechanical, including photocopying, recording or by means of any information storage or retrieval system without prior permission in writing from the publishers; or ii) used or reproduced in any way for the training, development or operation of artificial intelligence (AI) technologies, including generative AI technologies. The rights holders expressly reserve this publication from the text and data mining exception as per Article 4(3) of the Digital Single Market Directive (EU) 2019/790.

Bloomsbury Publishing Plc does not have any control over, or responsibility for, any third-party websites referred to or in this book. All internet addresses given in this book were correct at the time of going to press. The author and publisher regret any inconvenience caused if addresses have changed or sites have ceased to exist, but can accept no responsibility for any such changes.

A catalogue record for this book is available from the British Library.

A catalog record for this book is available from the Library of Congress.

ISBN: HB: 978-1-3503-6208-6
PB: 978-1-3503-6212-3
ePDF: 978-1-3503-6209-3
eBook: 978-1-3503-6210-9

Series: Bloomsbury Advances in Semiotics

Typeset by Integra Software Services Pvt. Ltd.

For product safety related questions contact productsafety@bloomsbury.com.

To find out more about our authors and books visit www.bloomsbury.com
and sign up for our newsletters.

Contents

List of Figures		viii
Preface		ix
Acknowledgments		xv
1	Semiotics, Ethics, and Dangerous Discourses	1
2	Words, Symbols, and Images of Conflict	31
3	Denial Discourses	61
4	Decoding Big Lies	83
5	False Narratives	103
6	Semiotics with a Conscience	129
References		152
Index		170

Figures

1.1	A Semiotic Network	12
1.2	#MeToo Emoji	14
1.3	Nazi Propaganda Poster (1941–5)	27
2.1	The Blood Drop Cross	45
2.2	KKK Triangle Symbol	46
2.3	Othala Rune	47
2.4	Nazi Flag	49
2.5	Poster of a Nazi Youth	55
2.6	Tweet from the Ukrainian Government, February 24, 2022	59
3.1	Image from *Popular Mechanics*, 1912	80
5.1	Nazi Election Poster, 1932	106
6.1	Connectionist Model	134
6.2	Inter-Codability Model	141

Preface

Times of severe international difficulties, upheavals, and military dangers have always existed—times beset by wars, famine, dystopias, insurgencies, riots, and other ordeals. Searching for the underlying psychological and historical motivations behind the turmoils has typically involved framing them in philosophical, political, economic, ideological, and social terms. Rarely has the search been guided by the identification and analysis of the dangerous discourses that ignited them in the first place—namely, the mendacious, deceptive, and false verbal and nonverbal discourses constructed via the manipulation of the meaning-bearing signs and structures characterizing "normal truthful discourses," distorting them for self-serving purposes. Today, such discourses are everywhere in the digital global village, eroding truth, upsetting norms of ethical behavior, and generating emotional, social, and cultural mayhem across the world.

The objective of this book is to examine the strategies deployed in the construction of the dangerous discourses, using semiotics as the theoretical tool to do so, which allows for a decipherment of how they are interlinked linguistically, visually, symbolically, and in other sign-based ways. Given the many conspiracy theories and big lies that are now spread throughout cyberspace, which negatively impact the emotional well-being of individuals and entire societies, the need for a "semiotics with a conscience," as it can be called, has become a pressing one in my view. By unraveling the meaning-distorting strategies used to create the unethical discourses, a complementary aim of this book is to show that semiotics can be enlisted to help solve, or at least deconstruct, the many ethical problems we now face, raising awareness of the deleterious effects that meaning collapses can bring about. Such discourses have, of course, been used throughout history as a propaganda technique, grossly distorting or misrepresenting objective facts and ethical norms, in order to turn sentiments against targeted groups and then exercising emotional control over people by spreading and embedding the falsehoods via different channels and forms, from words and symbols to pictures and films. Political tyrants even create intelligence services and "truth ministries" to spread lies and sow discord, aiming to defeat truth by replacing it with "alternative truth," as Orwell so keenly understood in his novel, *Nineteen Eighty-Four* (1949), written after Nazism had been defeated (temporarily).

Social media platforms have come forth to allow anyone to spread disinformation, conspiracism, and other unethical forms of discourse, which are becoming ever more prominent. Propaganda has always existed, of course. But never before the advent of social media has it become so widespread, utilized by random conspiracy groups and nefarious political actors alike. Disinformation is now one of the most powerful discourse weapons that is literally at everyone's fingertips, constituting its own ecosystem, of more accurately "semiosystem," in which false narratives, big lies, and other falsehoods are concocted regularly to strategically advance one's particular goals. The Internet has led to the crystallization of a "firehose of falsehoods," as it is called, aptly describing the enormous number of false messages that are broadcast rapidly and repeatedly over multiple communicative channels. An extension of Soviet propaganda techniques, the firehose model is the overarching strategy of propaganda under the Russian President Vladimir Putin, who has used it successfully during his campaign against Georgia in 2008 and Ukraine during both his 2014 annexation of Crimea and his 2022 invasion of the same country. The idea behind the term recalls Ray Bradbury's 1953 novel, *Fahrenheit 451*, which revolves around the activities of a fireman, Guy Montag, in a dystopian world where books are banned and firemen create fires rather than put them out so as to protect society from the purported dangers of reading.

Why semiotics, one might legitimately ask? To preface an answer to this question, it is relevant to note that there are two widely held negative perspectives with regard to semiotics itself. First, semiotics is perceived by some (perhaps many) as an abstruse, formalistic practice that is academically inward-looking, with little or no regard for the real world or Realpolitik; that is, as an intellectually solipsistic and even presumptuous enterprise that claims to explain all aspects of human communication within its small set of notions and methodological principles. Second, semiotics has been critiqued for having been applied to commercial enterprises such as advertising and marketing, which some see as helping manipulators enhance the persuasiveness of their messages, thus adding to the rampant "pollution" of mind and of the environment. Even the current author has engaged in such applications, perhaps unaware of the reach that semiotics has had in this domain. But, then, as the late Umberto Eco (1984: vi) pointed out, describing the uses of a discipline as "good" or "bad" is a value judgment, since one cannot really know what the consequences of a certain approach may entail, especially since notions such as objectivity and naturalness are themselves steeped in arbitrary opinions within a discipline:

> Good or bad are theoretical stipulations according to which, by a philosophical decision, many scattered instances of the most different facts or acts become the same thing. It is interesting to remark that also the notions of 'object', 'phenomenon', or 'natural kind', as used by the natural sciences, share the same philosophical nature. This is certainly not the case of specific semiotics or of a human science.

Attempts have been made to rectify such negative images of semiotics, but with scattered success, which is truly unfortunate, given that semiotics does indeed provide powerful analytical tools that can be used to shed light on pressing ethical issues and on questions of species survival, from climate change to the negative impacts on human sanity posed by the spread of hate speech throughout cyberspace. Roland Barthes was perhaps the first semiotician to argue that semiotics had implications for understanding and promoting ethical behavior (or lack thereof)—an argument he made during his last lectures (in Pieters and Pint 2008). But even before then, Barthes showed how it can be used to unravel the meanings hidden in popular culture representations and thus in how the marketplace used sign structures to manipulate beliefs and attitudes (Barthes 1957). However, Barthes's intention to make semiotics a true voice of ethical behavior has rarely (if ever) been realized. Moreover, as Chela Sandoval (2000: 201) has acerbically stated, "Barthes's discovery and articulation of the 'new' liberatory category of perception and deciphering, semiotic-mythology, belongs to the praxis of his heroic mythologist, alone. This unfortunate theoretical strategy makes the articulation of a coalitional consciousness in social struggle impossible to imagine or enact."

More recently, the so-called "semioethic" movement has come forth to argue that bringing about a "semiotic consciousness" is the key to solving world problems. But as important as this movement is, it has rarely looked at the actual discursive practices behind the problems and how these affect belief systems. Its laudable goal, however, needs to be pursued in more focused ways, which is the main objective of the present book—namely, to show in a concrete, non-ideological way how semiotics can be used as a tool to decode the sign structures and strategies behind unethical representations in specific semiotic media (from deceitful language to false mythological discourses), fleshing them out into the open so that they can be seen in the light of "semiotic reason" (so to speak). Issues of serious concern today, such as climate change denials, anti-science discourses, mind-manipulating political tactics, and the like can be framed and analyzed in terms of basic semiotic theory—hence the designation of a *semiotics with a conscience*. I have tailored the book for a general public, which may still envision semiotics as an impractical, self-serving academic enterprise, or worse, a servant of those who would use it for material gain. Hopefully, I can allay such apprehensions, by showing concretely how semiotics can actually help raise awareness about critical issues today and, hopefully, help promote more robust ethical attitudes and behavior.

It is relevant to note that the greatest mind-manipulators of history have always been keenly aware of the power of discourse to alter people's belief systems by simply twisting the meaning mode. The term *big lie* was, actually, coined by Adolf Hitler in his 1925 book, *Mein Kampf*, to describe a lie so "colossal" that no one would believe that the perpetrator "could have the impudence to distort the truth so infamously." He cunningly used this term to characterize a supposed Jewish cabal operating behind the social scenes. But it was Hitler who was the "big liar," with his fabricated narrative of a racially pure race and the need to eliminate inferior people, such as the Jewish "big liars," who he claimed were threatening German society with their deceptions. To back up his big lie, which was the only colossal one, he used techniques that have now become almost routine on social media—conspiracy theories (against the Jews), propaganda (to keep his audiences misinformed, claiming that Germany was not defeated in 1918, but betrayed internally), and false myths (such as the one of a superior race destined by history to rule the world)—which accumulated in people's minds through constant repetition, inspiring the overthrow of Germany's political system at the time, opening the way for the Nazis to take over. Big lies are everywhere today, used to justify conflicts, such as invasions into national territories, as is the case of Putin's invasion of Ukraine, which he justified as a purification operation, much like the purification of Jews from society by Hitler. Decoding semiotically how the tactics of mendacity work in manipulating minds, in order to come up with counter-strategies for obviating or stemming their deleterious influence, is an urgent objective—and that is the goal of a "semiotics of conscience."

Big lies have fascinated us since the dawn of history, from the biblical lie of Satan and the story of the Trojan horse to the propaganda perpetrated by autocrats and nefarious political actors. A primary aim of this book is to argue that a semiotic analysis of the "system" underling how distortions of truth are encoded discursively will hopefully shed light on why they have the power to affect beliefs and disrupt the normal process of meaning-making. Bolstering and spreading unethical behavior today is the rise of all kinds of conspiracy theories, which are not the same as actual conspiracies—they are hypothesized or concocted conspiratorial narratives with a specific objective, such as opposition to a political ideology or some scientific view (including climate change and vaccination). The emergence of such discourses lends credence to the theory that belief and cognition can be shaped or rewired (so to speak) by different semiotic systems, from language to visual art—called the semiotic relativity hypothesis (Lucy 1997). Conspiracy theories resist counter-argumentation because they cannot be disproved—only believed or disbelieved. Moreover, as Hofstadter (1964) has aptly remarked, whoever spins such false stories becomes a protagonist in them, seeing the world in apocalyptic terms and living constantly on edge:

> The paranoid spokesman sees the fate of conspiracy in apocalyptic terms—he traffics in the birth and death of whole worlds, whole political orders, whole systems of human values. He is always manning the barricades of civilization. He constantly lives at a turning point. Like religious millennialists he expresses the anxiety of those who are living through the last days and he is sometimes disposed to set a date for the apocalypse. As a member of the avant-garde who is capable of perceiving the conspiracy before it is fully obvious to an as yet unaroused public, the paranoid is a militant leader. He does not see social conflict as something to be mediated and compromised. Since what is at stake is always a conflict between absolute good and absolute evil, what is necessary is not compromise but the will to fight things out to a finish. Unlike the rest of us, the enemy is not caught in the toils of the vast mechanism of history, himself a victim of his past, his desires, his limitations.

Single words or symbols in themselves, as hateful as they might appear in isolation, cannot shape false beliefs. To do so, they must be incorporated strategically into discourse-symbolic-imagistic frames that can surreptitiously spread biases and prejudices. The term *code* will be used in this book to describe how the frames are organized semiotically and how the elements within them are interlinked to produce a cohesive "semiotic network" of meanings, from which there is little or no escape, once caught up in it. Terms such as "intertextuality" and "inter-codability" will also be used throughout, not because they are self-serving (as might be presumed), but because, when explained and illustrated concretely, they will be able (in my view) to pinpoint where the power of codes lies. Reference to Hitler's speeches, for instance, figures prominently in hate discourses, creating belief in a cause by virtue of the fact that it resounds with "mythic authority." Studying the discourse code behind such speech involves examining how it has spread to influence and structure conversations and pertinent nonverbal forms (such as insignias), so as to be able to deliver a constant and consistent hateful meaning.

The current era is sometimes called a "post-truth" one, because of the spread of falsehoods and conspiracy theories broadly, especially through the Internet. It may be better described, however, as an unethical era. While this book does not offer concrete practical advice on what to do about protecting oneself against the unethical distortions, it will hopefully have implications for "immunization" against them, by deconstructing the tactics on which disinformation and lies are implanted and spread. Semiotics does not (and really should not) put forth "remedies" or "antidotes"; it can only raise awareness of the meanings behind the words, the symbols, and the other representational forms that are injecting falsehoods into groupthink, leading to meaning breakdowns throughout the world. I will attempt to show, overall, how semiotic theory can be used as a potentially powerful science of conscience with the exact same techniques that have allowed marketers to use it for self-serving commercial purposes. Hopefully, it will shed constructive light on the following warning issued by Hannah Arendt, who was the first to propose that Nazism and Stalinism had common roots and who, if alive today, would discern these roots in many other areas: "A people that no longer can believe anything cannot make up its mind. It is deprived not only of its capacity to act but also of its capacity to think and to judge. And with such a people you can then do what you please."

Marcel Danesi
University of Toronto, 2023

Acknowledgments

Every effort has been made to trace copyright holders and to obtain their permission for the use of copyright material. However, if any have been inadvertently overlooked, the publishers will be pleased, if notified of any omissions, to make the necessary arrangement at the first opportunity.

1

Semiotics, Ethics, and Dangerous Discourses

Prologue

As mentioned in the preface, semiotics is often perceived as an overly formalistic inward-looking academic exercise in the analysis of the supposed codes involved in culture and mind-states, with little or no relevance to helping solve the ethical problems of the world, many of which are imprinted in the very signs and meanings it analyzes. In other words, semiotics may still be viewed as intellectually self-centered—semioticians talking to other semioticians in recondite ways—and thus as part of a self-serving discursive practice. Also as mentioned, another negative critique of semiotics concerns how it has been appropriated by marketers and advertisers who use it (with the help of semioticians) to enhance the persuasiveness of their consumerist messages, in the service of the profit motive rather than human well-being, and thus adding to the world's problems, rather than attempting to solve them—a critique to which the present author has been rightly subjected (for example, Beasley and Danesi 2002, Danesi 2008). As Anne Johnson (2020) has aptly phrased it:

> You can't consume commercially sponsored video or audio without encountering semiotic symbols and signs. They invade your thoughts and encourage you to respond, and they're everywhere. Advertisers use symbolism to represent a service or product and tempt consumers to purchase it. They create a story that ... makes you feel that their product should be important in your life. It goes beyond just the motivation to purchase. Semiotics in advertising often encourages you to believe that a product or service will somehow enhance your prestige or lifestyle. It creates an emotional response.

Attempts to rectify such negative images of semiotics have met with little success overall because, often, the justifications themselves are abstruse and poorly articulated. Lacking are practical illustrations of how the analytical tools of semiotics can actually be used practically by anyone to grasp "what is going on" in human interactions and discourses. Also as mentioned, it was Roland Barthes who was among the first to argue that semiotics had concrete implications for understanding and promoting ethical behavior, deconstructing the hidden mythic meaning structures in popular culture representations and spectacles (Barthes 1957). It is no coincidence that of all the works produced by semioticians in the last century, Barthes's book has been the one used most by researchers in other fields and read by the public at large. Barthes showed, in effect, that it is not necessary (or even useful) to engage in a technical jargon that few understand (including semioticians themselves); all that is needed is to show how semiotics can be used to unravel the meanings of everyday things in ways that make sense to anyone, not just to those versed in semiotic theory. Admitting that there is always a subjectivity in semiotic analysis, Barthes states explicitly in his preface to *Mythologies* that the reader can still be an active participant in the semiotic process itself (Barthes 1957: xi):

> And what I sought throughout this book were significant features. Is this a significance which I read into them? In other words, is there a mythology of the mythologist? No doubt, and the reader will easily see where.

Barthes also made the explicit claim during his last lectures at the Collège de France that semiotics must develop an ethical conscience itself, which can then be used for the better good (in Pieters and Pint 2008). His main suggestion, which he termed as the "Neutral," was the elimination of the binarism built into the concepts within language and other semiotic systems (good-versus-evil, us-versus-them, etc.), which will be discussed in the final chapter of this book. The goal was eliminating "either-or" forms of understanding which, in turn, might lead to the spread of unfortunate and dangerous dichotomies of mind and society, such as us-versus-them. It would have been interesting to see how Barthes would have applied this notion to ethical discourses concretely and practically. Unfortunately, he passed away shortly after his Collège lectures.

An attempt to follow up on Barthes's suggestion, making semiotics relevant to ethical analysis, is the "semioethic" movement (e.g., Petrilli 2014). The stated objective of the movement is articulated by Ponzio and Petrilli (2007: 29) as follows: "the aim in a semioethic perspective is to show how a semiotic consciousness is not only integral to understanding developments in the world today, but that it is crucial to the future of the planet." Carrying out this laudable goal is still in its fledgling stages (at the time of writing this book); it is however slanted toward specific stances both within semiotics and in the political sphere that appear to shape its overall intellectual thrust. Moreover, it is not a descriptive or illustrative approach, but rather a generic philosophical form of argumentation based on semiotic notions. It has been fashioned in line with the bioethics movement, which studies the ethical issues that arise in the trends in biomedical research; semioethics analogously studies the ethical issues that arise in political and social trends with regard to the perception of otherness. In her book *Signs, Language and Listening: Semioethic Perspectives* (2019), Susan Petrilli defines semioethics as the "semiotics of otherness ... with the capacity for criticism, social awareness, and responsible behavior as central issues" (Petrilli 2019: 25). As such, semioethics shares a similar overall objective of what has been called here, *semiotics with a conscience*, namely, to critically address what can be called "sign diseases" occurring throughout the world, whereby sign systems are being used in "unhealthy" ways to engender abnormal and corrupt modes of interaction.

The purpose of this chapter is to present an overview of how semiotics can be used concretely as a theoretical instrument for decoding the linguistic, artistic, symbolic, and narrative strategies that are used to represent meanings in the various media (language, visual art, etc.) and how these can be applied to understanding current discourses. The aim here is to put a semiotic lens on the sign-based sources utilized to construct dangerous discourses (verbal and nonverbal), from climate change anti-science discourses, to conspiracy theories and hate symbols created to target specific groups—hence the designation *semiotics with a conscience*, that is, a semiotics whose ultimate goal is to promote ethical discourses and interactions. To allow this kind of approach to gain traction beyond semioticians, it is tailored primarily for a general public, which may still envision semiotics as an impractical exercise based on abstruse notions. By exemplifying how dangerous discourses and representations can be decoded from a semiotic angle, albeit subjectively by the present author, the objective is that this whole line of inquiry and analysis may lead to a broader understanding of the nexus between semiotic codes and understanding, and hopefully raise awareness of the danger that unethical discourse practices pose in areas such as climate change, social justice, communication dysfunctions, crises of meaning, and the like.

One of the greatest dangers we face today involves the perpetration and perpetuation of falsehoods throughout the social media sphere, spilling over into other systems of communication. These have the ability to spread and reinforce biases and even old hatreds more broadly than at any other time in history. An example is that of Holocaust denial—namely the false discourse that the Holocaust did not take place or, at the very least, that it was not as bad as it is claimed, despite evidence to the contrary. This denial discourse has become even more embedded today because of its incorporation in radical social media platforms, where it is repeated over and over, having become a "hate meme." This has ensconced anti-Semitism more deeply than at any other time in the past, simply because the hate meme is repeated endless times in cyberspace. The goal of a semiotics with a conscience is to peel off the different layers of meaning distortions with which this kind of hateful discourse is constructed, which has the ability to alter responses to truthful information and thus diminish the capacity for people to interact fluidly and meaningfully (Genosko 2016).

The premise adopted in this book is that the mind is highly susceptible to the hidden meanings of "coded" words, symbols, and images used intentionally to create hate memes and discourses more generally. Any sign taken in isolation can, of course, be studied in terms of the communally established meanings it encompasses and the range of interpretations it can evoke, which has always been the primary goal of semiotics. It is when the same sign is used to distort or redirect the interpretive range that it alters mind states. This type of mind manipulation cannot be underestimated, as the effects of dangerous discourses such as the Holocaust denial one shows. As per a 2022 report by the United Nations, titled *Social Media Feeds Holocaust Denial and Distortion*, with the advent of social media, it has become ever more urgent to assail such discourses, with any means possible, including the use of semiotics. Below is a relevant excerpt from the report:

> The review finds that nearly half of Holocaust-related content on Telegram either denied or distorted its history. On moderated or regulated platforms, the review found that nearly 10 per cent of posts on Facebook and 15 per cent of posts on Twitter, which discussed the Holocaust, contained denial or distortion content ... Holocaust denial and distortion as part of antisemitic discourse, shifts in form in new contexts, and is entwined with other types of online harms, fueling racism, misogyny, xenophobia, and homophobia. The report concludes that reducing such harmful content largely depends on the willingness of social media platforms to take effective action.

The Method of Decoding

As Daniel Chandler (2022) has perceptively noted, a weakness of semiotics as a discipline is that "there is relatively little agreement amongst semioticians themselves as to the scope and methodology of semiotics." Ironically, a major aim of one of its modern-day founders, Ferdinand de Saussure (1916: 16), was to lay the groundwork for developing a scientific consensus on "what constitutes signs, what laws govern them." Saussure put forth a set of notions that came to constitute the methodology of structuralism, uniting semiotics, psychology, and linguistics (Bouissac 2010). For example, the idea that words and other sign structures did not possess meaning in themselves, but in relation to other structures within a system such as language, and that these reflected patterns below a superficial diversity, became a core principle in these disciplines. As Blackburn (2008: 353) has aptly remarked, the methods of structuralism were forged on the "belief that phenomena of human life are not intelligible except through their interrelations [and that] behind local variations in the surface phenomena there are constant laws of abstract structure."

A common set of principles for semiotics and linguistics was established further with the founding of the Prague School in 1926, which developed an agenda of research for the systematic study of language and other semiotic systems (Toman 1995). The lack of agreement that Chandler identifies surfaced in the late 1960s, when structuralism came under attack from a new wave of semioticians, called post-structuralists, who saw its whole theoretical apparatus as useless, rejecting the core principle that culture has a structure that is modeled on language (Derrida 1967, 1972, Foucault 1978). As post-structuralism spread in certain disciplinary circles, such as literary criticism and cultural analysis, semiotics started losing its identity as a unified science, becoming viewed more and more as a critical tool that could be applied to study anything and everything in various and often divergent ways. As John Sturrock (1986: 89) has aptly observed, the "dramatic extension of the semiotic field, to include the whole of culture, [was] looked on by those suspicious of it as a kind of intellectual terrorism, overfilling our lives with meanings." The starting point for post-structuralism is traced to a 1966 lecture titled "Structure, Sign, and Play in the Discourse of the Human Sciences," given by the late Jacques Derrida at John Hopkins, and published a year later in his book, *Writing and Difference* (1967), in which he assailed structuralism as misguided because the meaning of signs cannot be pinned down with the techniques of structuralism. Aware of the challenge that such views posed, Roland Barthes published *Elements of Semiology* in 1968, where he laid out a set of abstract principles of sign study that he claimed would put semiotics on a more solid theoretical footing.

However, the damage was done, as those from outside started to question its legitimacy. John Searle (1990) summarized the disenchantment bluntly as follows: "The spread of 'poststructuralist' literary theory is perhaps the best-known example of a silly but non-catastrophic phenomenon." Semiotics regained some of its reputation as a scientific enterprise in the 1980s, after the publication of a report written for the American government by Thomas Sebeok (1984), in which he used a blend of traditional structuralist notions with Peircean ideas, illustrating practically how semiotics could be used to enhance the sense of danger in creating the warning signs located at nuclear waste sites. Sebeok showed that semiotics could be used practically and methodically to help solve specific social problems (Bouissac 1985, 1989, Danesi 2022). Since then, the view of semiotics as a broad mode of systematic inquiry (based on an amalgam of Saussurean and Peircean approaches) has increased. This is evidenced today by the breadth of application of semiotics exemplified by the books in the *Bloomsbury Advances in Semiotics* series, edited by Paul Bouissac, the four-volume encyclopedia, *Bloomsbury Semiotics*, edited by Jamin Pelkey and Paul Cobley (2023), and other such enterprises.

Despite such strides in making semiotics a practicable method for research on all kinds of current-day problems, from social injustices to the meaning structures in online hate discourses, there is still a lingering sense that it is a "general-purpose" critical method, as Sturrock noted. A primary goal of this book is to show that semiotics allows for a "specific-purpose" coherent method that can be used concretely to help *decode* dangerous discourses. The term *code* is used to designate a "core meaning" pattern delivered by different types of sign structures—verbal and nonverbal—which cohere into what can be called semiotic networks that are implanted on the code. This definition dovetails somewhat with the term *symbolic code*, which is used broadly in reference to the meaning beneath the surface of what we see, hear, or perceive. In this framework, Holocaust denial discourses would be described as grounded in an amalgam of several anti-Semitic codes, called *inter-codability* in this book. So, the anti-Semitic hate memes that are spread today throughout the Internet are seen as being motivated by several interlinked codes, including the cabal code, whose core meaning revolves around a purported Jewish cabal aiming to take over and control the world, as evidenced by online hate tropes such as "Jewish world order," and a stereotypical greed code, as exemplified by hate caricatures of Jewish people as "grubbers." This definition of code is intended to avoid many of its overly technical designations within semiotics (Corner 1980, Cook 1992, Messaris 1994), while still retaining its essential usefulness as a key concept. The main claim made in this book is that by decoding dangerous discourses semiotically—fleshing out the code or amalgam of codes below the surface into the open—a better understanding of the psychological and historical sources of hate speech and other dangerous discourses can be attained. The primary method of identifying the code(s) involves examining the different verbal and nonverbal signs and texts that are used to deliver its meaning, as will be discussed and illustrated throughout this book.

As Krampen (2010: 340) has asserted, the term *code* "was first introduced into semiotics by Ferdinand de Saussure in his 3rd Course of lectures at the University of Geneva on April 28, 1911" to denote a system of shared meanings within a specific medium, although in his *Cours de linguistique générale* (1916), Saussure never really pinned down what he intended with this term. The closest he comes to a definition can be seen in the following excerpt (1916: 25):

> Language is apparently governed by a code; the code itself consists of a written set of strict rules of usage, orthography; and that is why writing acquires primary importance. The result is that people forget that they learn to speak before they learn to write, and the natural sequence is reversed.

As Umberto Eco (1976) pointed out, the notion of code has become an intuitive, axiomatic one, which dovetails somewhat with Peirce's notion of the *interpretant*, or the meaning we extract from signs within a specific context, that is, the meaning that a sign elicits cognitively, emotionally, historically, and socially. Barthes (1964, 1968, 1970) used the notion of code to make a distinction between denotative (literal) and connotative (extended) meanings in specific texts, based on earlier work by Benveniste (1939), Hjelmslev (1959), and Jakobson (1960). So, even a simple print advertisement works semiotically on two levels—an uncoded one where the advertisement presents relevant information denotatively (literally), so as to identify and promote a product, and a coded level, where connotative meanings, based on culturally shared codes of meaning, unfold with regard to the social interpretations of the product. While this approach has been criticized on several counts, such as the fact that it ignores that the advertisement can be understood across cultures in ways that do not involve coded meanings (Kress and Van Leeuwen 1996), the main thrust of Barthes's analysis is a valid one—namely, meaning occurs at different levels, which are coded in differential ways.

The phrase "decoding advertisements" was first used by Judith Williamson in her 1978 book as a term to designate how advertisements are coded for meaning, following Barthes's model (Williamson 1978: 100):

> The assumption of pre-existing bodies of knowledge allows reference to take the place of description, connotation of denotation, in ads: this reference must inevitably take place on the formal level, by pointing at another structure, since

the 'content' or substance of the reference is the product itself. So the 'referent system' is always a connotation because what is denoted is the product. However, there is a circular process involved because having introduced the referent system by means of connotation, it is then made to denote the product—'place' it in a system of meaning.

Williamson's term "referent system" is analogous to what is called a "semiotic network" here; that is, a network of sign structures (verbal and nonverbal) that deliver the code in actual expressions, communications, and representations via a cohesive system of interlinked references. Williamson's approach was adopted broadly in the collection of studies in marketing semiotics edited by Umiker-Sebeok (1987) and used in this field to this day (Oswald 2012, 2015). Given the demonstrated efficacy of the decoding method in analyzing marketing and advertising texts, there is no reason to believe that it would not be just as effective, if not more so, in other domains of meaning-making, such as decoding dangerous discourses. The key psychological feature of semiotic codes, as the advertising studies have demonstrated, is that they are not just mediators of thought, but also its shapers. In decoding dangerous or hateful political and conspiratorial discourses, semiotic network theory can expose the unconscious codes that underlie them, casting light on how referent systems can shape false beliefs and unethical behaviors. As such, semiotics can thus have implications for what can be done to reinforce the ethical discourses and behaviors that have been impugned by hate speech and other dangerous discourses.

Ethics and Semiotics

Before Saussure, semiotics came to be primarily associated with philosophical inquiry ever since John Locke introduced it into the discipline in his *Essay Concerning Humane Understanding* (1690), defining *semeiotics* as "the doctrine of signs." Significantly, Locke saw it as a branch of his tripartite division of science: (1) natural philosophy (*physica*), which is concerned with the nature of things in themselves and "their manner of operation"; (2) ethics (*practica*), which is concerned with what "man himself ought to do, as a rational and voluntary agent, for the attainment of any end, especially happiness"; and (3) sign study (*semeiotics*), whose field of study is "the ways and means whereby the knowledge of both [natural philosophy] and [ethics] are attained and communicated" (Locke 1650: 442). However, as far as can be told, semiotics has rarely included the direct study of ethics within it, with some recent exceptions (e.g., Herdy

2014, Duits 2017, Liszka 2022, Barreneche 2023). Projecting the study of ethical behavior directly into the semiotic domain would arguably liberate it from abstruse philosophical discourses, allowing it to ask a concrete question: What is the relation between semiotic codes and ethical-unethical behaviors? Examining this question involves, as claimed here, the use of a method for unraveling the sign-based codes and sign structures that underlie the kinds of discourses that are used to shape thought unethically.

As mentioned in his final lectures at the Collège de France (1977–1980), Roland Barthes discussed the possibility of using semiotics concretely to promote ethical behavior in human interactions (in Pieters and Pint 2008, O'Meara 2013). As a master practitioner of semiotic analysis, having shown how it could be used in concrete and understandable ways (Barthes 1957), it is unfortunate that Barthes did not live long thereafter to put forth an "ethical semiotics," as a branch centered on studying how semiotic structures undergird both ethical and unethical ideas. *Semiotics with a conscience* falls under this methodological rubric, constituting a specific method for identifying such ideas, and exposing the habits of thought that they ensconce. Scattered research in neuroscience has been showing, in fact, that when discursive practices are used routinely they become embedded in habitual thinking (Silvera-Roig and López-Varela Azcárate 2019). By extension, it can be assumed that when these practices are designed to generate unethical behaviors, deleterious effects on habits of mind may crystallize which, in turn, may lay the foundations for radical or extreme political and social movements.

As mentioned in the preface, a movement aiming to locate the study of ethics within a semiotic framework is the semioethic one, introduced and developed primarily by Susan Petrilli and Augusto Ponzio of the University of Bari (Deely 2005, Petrilli and Ponzio 2005). Their approach is based on using semiotic arguments in a generic way to promote ethical behavior, arguing that semiotic cognition can help evaluate meaning structures in the context of current global communication practices and crises. Theoretically, it is based on an amalgam of the ideas of Charles Peirce, Lady Victoria Welby, Thomas Sebeok, Mikhail Bakhtin, Ferruccio Rossi-Landi, and various scholars in the biosemiotic movement, focusing on how the "action of signs" is central to grasping the essence of ethical-unethical behaviors in terms of political and social power systems. Its goal is to promote what Jürgen Habermas (1973) called "discourse ethics." This highly laudable movement has not, however, put forth a concrete methodology for decoding the sign structures that underlie, and may even shape, discursive behaviors. The same type of goal is espoused by the so-called *social semiotic* movement, which goes a step further by envisioning a direct relation between social power structures and semiotic systems. The starting point for this movement is Michael Halliday's *Language as Social Semiotic* in 1978, developed subsequently by Gunther Kress, Robert Hodge, Theo van Leeuwen, and others (e.g., Halliday 1985, Hodge and Kress 1988, Kress and Leeuwen 1996, Randviir 2004, and Leeuwen 2005). Currently, social semiotics constitutes a self-contained field of inquiry, blending pragmatic linguistics, Peircean theory, and sociological ideas, which it applies to unraveling meaning patterns in communicative systems, such as the mainstream and social media ones.

The urgency of systematically exposing the codes motivating dangerous discourses has been highlighted by international agencies such as the United Nations and the Council on Foreign Relations, which have emphasized that, given the ability of fringe social media sites to reach audiences far broader than their core followers, the peril of random, hate-inspired violence worldwide has increased significantly. As the Council on Foreign Relations has stressed, citing relevant research, such sites have been linked to violent actions, including the following cases-in-point (Laub 2019):

- A correlation between anti-refugee posts by the far-right "Alternative for Germany" party and attacks on refugees in Germany was established by social scientists.
- In the United States, prosecutors discovered that the Charleston church shooter, who killed nine African American clergy and worshippers in June 2015, engaged in what they characterized as a "self-learning process" online, which induced him to believe that violent action was required to ensure the survival of the white race in the country.
- Investigators and prosecutors involved in the 2018 Pittsburgh synagogue shooting found that the shooter was a constant participant in the anti-Semitic discourses on the social media network Gab, which perpetrated the conspiracy theory that Jews sought to bring immigrants into the United States, so as to make whites a minority. This conspiracy is based on the "great replacement" trope, which is one of the more dangerous semiotic codes in anti-Semitic discourses (to be discussed subsequently).
- The same code inspired the perpetrator of the 2019 New Zealand mosque shootings, indicating that the ethnicity involved in the hate code is a variable one.
- In Sri Lanka, the vigilantism inspired by rumors spread online targeting the Tamil minority led to a spate of violence in March of 2018.

The list of such incidences is a lengthy one. Overall, as both the Council and the United Nations have found, through their fact-finding missions, social media have become useful instruments for those seeking to spread hate, mobilizing some people to act out violently against specific groups. As the United Nations put it in 2021:

> Hate speech incites violence and intolerance. The devastating effect of hatred is sadly nothing new. However, its scale and impact are now amplified by new communications technologies. Hate speech—including online—has become one of the most common ways of spreading divisive rhetoric on a global scale, threatening peace around the world.

Semiotic Networks

The method of semiotic analysis used here is based on a two-fold premise: (1) dangerous discourses, such as denial ones, conspiratorial ones, and the like, are coded for meaning, that is, they are grounded in a core meaning (or set of meanings), often carried over from historical biases, prejudices, or skewed beliefs (O'Halloran and Tau 2023); (2) the code is embedded in actual discourses via interlinked, inter-modal sign structures—linguistic, imagistic, symbolic, textual. The linkage system is called a "semiotic network," for the sake of convenience, so as to render the idea that the sign structures that convey the underlying meaning code are not autonomous, but rather semiotically interlinked ones, like the nodes in a topological graph.

This term is not used in any technical sense, although it is somewhat similar to the notion of semantic network in linguistics and artificial intelligence. As a case-in-point, consider the semiotic network that is inherent in anti-Semitic discourses based on a cabal code at the core of the network. In the diagram below, C = code (Jews are part of a cabal), R = specific kinds of rhetorical words, such as metaphors, S = related symbols, I = images, T = (narrative) texts. The subscript numbers indicate specific sign or textual forms emanating from the main nodes (R, S, I, and T), as for example, R_1 = the metaphor of "parasites" (as will be discussed), S_1 = the Star of David, I_1 = a caricature of Jews depicted holding money in their hands, and T_1 = the forged *Protocols of the Elders of Zion* (also to be discussed subsequently) (See Figure 1.1 below).

Semiotic network analysis consists in gathering and analyzing the manifestations of such sign forms in specific discourses, examining how they are linked to each other to deliver the meaning of the core code or codes within

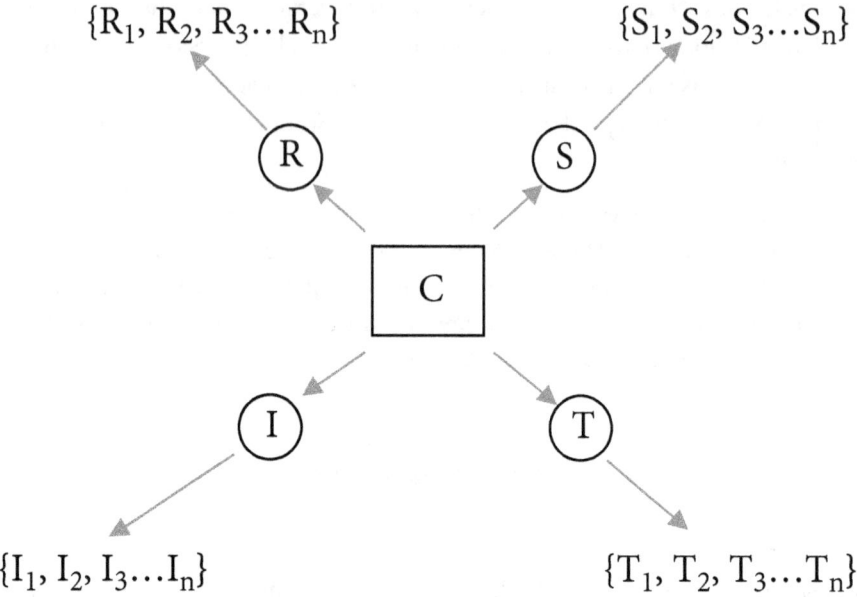

Figure 1.1 A Semiotic Network.

the network. Roland Barthes adopted a similar perspective in his 1957 book *Mythologies*, where he showed how the meanings of contemporary popular spectacles and texts are coded in terms of ancient myths. As he put it a later work, *Elements of Semiology* (Barthes 1968: 5):

> It is true that objects, images and patterns of behaviour can signify, and do so on a large scale, but never autonomously; every semiological system has its linguistic admixture. Where there is a visual substance, for example, the meaning is confirmed by being duplicated in a linguistic message (which happens in the case of the cinema, advertising, comic strips, press photography, etc.) so that at least a part of the iconic message is, in terms of structural relationship, either redundant or taken up by the linguistic system … In more general terms, it appears increasingly more difficult to conceive a system of images and objects whose signifieds can exist independently of language: to perceive what a substance signifies is inevitably to fall back on the individuation of a language: there is no meaning which is not designated, and the world of signifieds is none other than that of language.

In sum, semiotic network analysis involves showing how specific types of discourses reveal sign nodes (R, S, I, T) linked in a network configuration to deliver the meaning code (C). In this framework, meaning can be seen to emanate from an interrelated network in which the boundaries are never clear-cut. Every sign in the network is caught up in a system of references to other signs within a coded center. As soon as one dismantles this unity, the system loses its communicative power, indicating itself—a situation that has implications for counteracting dangerous discourses.

As an illustrative example of how a specific type of discourse manifests a coded meaning that is realized through a semiotic network, consider the #MeToo movement—a movement that emerged to promote sexual justice for women of all backgrounds. In this case, we are dealing with a socially constructive type of discourse, not the opposite, which will be the target of analysis in the remainder of this book. The hashtag #MeToo was first used by activist Tarana Burke (2006), quickly becoming a code, whose meaning was stated explicitly by actress Alyssa Milano on Twitter on October 15, 2017: "If all the women who have been sexually harassed or assaulted wrote 'Me too' as a status, we might give people a sense of the magnitude of the problem" (Milano 2017). The code has allowed women to voice their concerns in a coherent way via the creation of a relevant semiotic network of signs and texts (Buxton 2018, Nicolaou and Smith 2019). For instance, the emoji below, which shows three hands of different races raised up in a "stop gesture" (indicating that sexual abuse and discrimination must stop), became an I-node sign in the network (See Figure 1.2 below).

The different color shades of the hands can be seen to symbolize the equality of the races as well as implying that abuse is found among all races. As an I-sign in the network, it points to the code in a visually suggestive way. Another I-sign that gained prominence for a while in the network was a statue created by Argentinian artist Luciano Garbati, through which he inverted the myth of Medusa, showing Medusa holding the severed head of Perseus, rather than the other way around. It was installed across the street from a courthouse in lower Manhattan, remaining there on display until April of 2021. The original Greek myth portrayed Medusa as a monstrous being with snakes for hair, who was violated in Athena's temple. The goddess punished Medusa by turning her into a Gorgon and exiling her. Perseus was then sent to bring her head back. One night, Perseus crept up on Medusa while she was sleeping, cutting off her head, and then using it as a weapon for turning enemies into stone.

A perusal of #MeToo tweets and posts (Keyword Search 2020) turned up the phrase "Reverse the roles" as a common R-node, which can be seen to be synchronized conceptually with the Garbati I-node and its reversal of the Medusa myth, thus making it a T-node as well. Before the attention it received

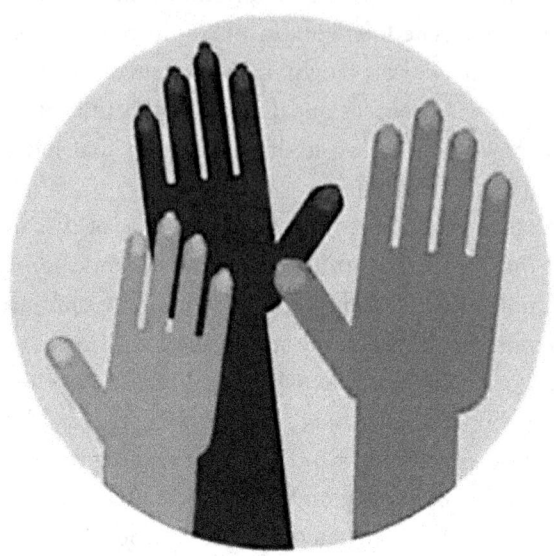

Figure 1.2 #MeToo Emoji.
Source: Twitter.

on social media, Garbati's statue had remained relatively obscure. The starting point occurred when Garbati posted photos of the sculpture to his Facebook page, which prompted a blogger to point out that it reflected a mythological reversal that was consistent thematically with the #MeToo movement. Soon after, the Medusa statue started cropping up all over social media, reinforcing the underlying code of the movement in visual and textual ways.

It is the connectivity of the sign forms within the #MeToo semiotic network that makes the discourse powerful. The racially diverse hands raised up in a stop posture in the Twitter emoji, the powerful connotations of reversing the Medusa myth embedded in the Garbati statue, the use of a phraseology that became associated with the myth, and other kinds of nodes in the semiotic network became interlinked to deliver and reinforce the #MeToo code. Interestingly, this code generated related hashtag codes that expanded its overall discourse range. Among these were "#BelieveWomen" and "#BelieveSurvivors," which revealed what Fairclough (2003: 88) characterizes as a "collapsing [of] difference by 'textualizing' relations of equivalence between them." The choice of "survivors" rather than "victims" is an apt one, highlighting strength, defiance, and courage (as implied by the Garbati statue) juxtaposed against a previous discourse of weakness and victimization. Of course, the semiotic network itself is always open to new nodes, reflecting changing values and interpretations of the original code. But its modifications and expansions will still be tied thematically and semiotically to the central code.

Now, the same type of analysis can be applied to decoding dangerous discourses, which are implanted in hateful, conspiratorial, or outright false codes, which are used in destructive ways, including promoting the hatred of others, false beliefs, and the like. The question becomes: Why are people so susceptible to discursive practices? This question will be addressed more concretely in subsequent chapters. Suffice it to say here that discourses without a code, such as those that characterize everyday conversations, have few if any mind-altering effects; those with a code do, shaping thought and beliefs. Once a coded discourse system is internalized, it becomes a mental filter through which incoming information is either accepted or rejected, according to its content and meaning.

The term *discourse*, as used here, is consistent with the views put forth by Michel Foucault (1969) and Mikhail Bakhtin (1981)—namely, as a form of expression that manifests specific beliefs or worldviews. As such, it delimits the conceptual boundaries about what can be said about something, constituting "any practice (found in a wide range of forms) by which individuals imbue reality with meaning" (Foucault 1972). This definition is traced originally to Bakhtin in the 1920s, who saw discourse as both reflecting and engendering shared values, worldviews, beliefs, interests, and biases in a group. A particularly crucial element in discourse is intertextuality, or the direct or indirect allusion to ideas and texts that have special value to a group. For instance, the citations from, or allusions to, Biblical figures, events, and sayings figure prominently in religious discourse; on the other hand, allusions to acts of violence are part of a generic criminal discourse. Now, for a discourse to be effective it must be based on coded meanings that are delivered by interlinkages of signs. It is argued here that it is the chain of semiotic structures itself which creates belief in a cause (or more specifically a code) by virtue of the fact that it makes the discourse appear to be coherent and unified. Foucault characterized the semiotic chain as "an entity of sequences, of signs, in that they are enouncements," which assign meaning to signs via repeatable themes (Foucault 1972).

Inherent in semiotic network analysis is a consideration of how interpretations of specific discourses vary across cultures and time, while retaining common sign patterns grounded in a meaning core. For example, as the #MeToo discourse spread throughout cyberspace and adopted by non-English-speaking cultures, it became adapted locally. In China, for example, the hashtag faced censorship on social media, so users developed the alternative #RiceBunny, which in Mandarin mimics the sound of #MeToo. As interpretations spread across the globe, they may also mutate into different and more dangerous forms of discourse—as will be discussed subsequently. As Eco (1990: 23) put it in the *Limits of Interpretation*, there is always what he called the danger of a "cancer of uncontrolled interpretation," implying that interpreters may go too far in their use of discourses, thereby destroying their original meaning. A goal of semiotic analysis is to determine if, within the meaning range that a discursive practice covers, there is an interpretive core or limit. A related question is: Are reactions to discourses such as the #MeToo one based on the political-ideological orientation of interpreters? Perhaps the only way a semiotician can approach interpretive divarications in a non-subjective way is to step back and describe them in terms of their semiotic structure and coded meanings.

To paraphrase Lakoff (2004), it is the framing of discursive practices that is key to shaping the interpretive process. So, by framing the need for social justice as a hashtag with attendant sign forms (a hand emoji, the Medusa myth in reverse, etc.) an unconscious image schema of a common cause crystallizes. Neuroscientific research has found (Feldman and Narayan 2004, Boulenger, Shtyrov, and Pulvermuller 2012) that the brain encodes a concept through visual image schemas that form a kind of circuit around the concept, which is an indirect corroboration of the premise adopted here that it is the semiotic network (or circuit) structure of a discourse that influences cognition. The effectiveness varies according to the suggestive ideas generated; the more suggestive, the more effective, as can be seen with the emoji and Medusa statue in the #MeToo semiotic network.

In August of 2021, the *Washington Post* investigated the impacts of #MeToo on social groupthink in America (McCarthy 2021). The survey revealed a mixed picture in this regard. While a smaller percentage of women had experienced unwanted sexual attention at the workplace in comparison to previous years, inappropriate sexual behaviors continued to be evident in the workplace and elsewhere. The survey also noted a backlash to the #MeToo movement, especially from people with a fixed view of gender roles. The gist of the survey was that the movement did indeed have an effect, albeit to varying degrees; and it generated counter-discourses, claiming that the movement may have gone too far in labeling behaviors too loosely and broadly, or that there are few consequences for accusers. The conventional wisdom has been that bringing abuse issues to light would have a deterrent effect. But this has not materialized as expected. A claim of the present book is, actually, that the discourses with the most power to affect change are the dangerous ones, since these tap into beliefs surreptitiously and nefariously. They do not attempt to rectify a social imbalance or a habitual pattern of behavior.

Dangerous Discourses

In his play, *The Babylonians*, the Greek playwright Aristophanes denounced Cleon, the Athenian general and politician, portraying him in a negative way as a promoter of demagogic politics. A major subtext in the play was: How could an unscrupulous politician appeal on some unconscious level to average citizens, who voted enthusiastically again and again to support Cleon, a grifter who did nothing but ruin and steal from those who backed him? Aristophanes's answer was Cleon's forceful, populist, anti-intellectual, charismatic style of oratory—an example of a dangerous discourse based on surreptitiously deceitful language that common citizens could not resist, because it encapsulated their concern that they were disregarded by élite groups. As such, it tapped into the *volonté générale* to eliminate the corrupt élites from government, banishing them into political exile, constituting an ancient example of attacking a "deep state" of intellectuals (as it is called today) who want to control society. As most subsequent populist politicians, Cleon claimed misleadingly that he was a champion of democracy, which catapulted him to the center of Athenian politics. Like any autocrat, he used persuasive discourse to attract obsequious and servile followers, whom he used to help him oppose those who were likely to endanger his ascendancy. The historian Thucydides (431 BCE) described him as "a popular leader of the time and very powerful with the multitude."

One of the first treatises on the power of populist discourse to manipulate the minds of the common citizenry came centuries later—namely, Niccolò Machiavelli's 1532 book, *The Prince*, in which he advises rulers how to acquire power by deceitful discursive methods, almost exactly matching those used by Cleon, as described by Aristophanes and Thucydides. Machiavelli's main premise was that such methods are effective for the simple reason that people are drawn in by lies that tap into their grievances and feelings. So, Machiavelli instructs the ruler to become a "great liar and deceiver" to both gain power and maintain it. In effect, *The Prince* is a psychological-political manual on how deceptive language can be used to garner support from the general populace—a language that emphasizes to them artfully that they need the prince to make things right in the state (Lee 2021).

Machiavelli had previously written an entire book on political discourses, *Discorsi sopra la prima deca di Tito Livio* (1517) ("Discourses on the First Decade of Titus Livius"), which is essentially a treatise on how strategic lies will shape people's beliefs. Once a mendacious leader is in power, moreover, he can remain there indefinitely through further deception, repeating lies over and over to ensure that they will be accepted as truth—a cognitive symptom now called the illusory truth effect, identified in 1977 by Hasher, Goldstein, and Toppino, as the tendency to believe lies after repeated exposure. It has even been found that familiarity with a lie can supersede critical thinking, since it starts to feel correct after a while (Hertwig, Gigerenzer, and Hiffrage 1997, Ozubko and Fugelsang 2011). Constant lying involves suggestibility which activates related information, or misinformation, producing a form of false memory. As Hassan and Barber (2021) summarize: "Repeated information is often perceived as more truthful than new information ... Because fluency and truth are frequently correlated in the real world, people learn to use processing fluency as a marker for truthfulness."

In addition to repetition, Machiavelli put forth some general tactics for effective mendacity, including using clear and simple language, ensuring that the lie tells a plausible story or alludes to something credible, avoiding abstractions and vagueness about details, and incorporating the lie into an otherwise truthful account. But even if a lie sounds plausible, why would anyone set what they know aside just after hearing the lie repeatedly? A significant study by Fazio, Payne, Brashier, and Marsh (2015) provided a likely answer to this question, showing that the illusory truth effect worked just as strongly for known information as for unknown facts, suggesting that prior knowledge does not prevent repetition from swaying our judgments of plausibility. A well-crafted lie is a work of oratorical art, which extracts buried biases and predispositions and brings them out in the open, whereby it is likely to be believed, remembered, and later recalled, even after we learn that it was false.

Given the plausibility of the claims made by Machiavelli in *The Prince*, corroborated centuries later by psychology, it should come as little surprise to find that many autocrats and dictators read Machiavelli carefully, following his advice. Hermann Rauschning (1940), who joined the Nazi movement and then renounced the party, wrote the following in this regard:

> Hitler told me he had read and reread *The Prince* of the Great Florentine. To his mind, the book is indispensable to every political man. For a long time it did not leave Hitler's side. The reading of those unequaled pages, he said, was like a cleansing of the mind. It has disencumbered him from plenty of false ideas and prejudices. It is only after having read *The Prince* that Hitler understood what politics really is.

Hitler had learned from Machiavelli that mind control is language control, because as Socrates observed in antiquity (in Plato 2022): "Whenever people are deceived and form opinions wide of the truth, it is clear that the error has slid into their minds through the medium of certain resemblances to that truth." A dangerous discourse based on mendacity and deception "cleanses the mind," to paraphrase Hitler, of existing truths within it. Hitler also learned from Machiavelli that, once a lie is perpetrated, one must never go back on it, never admit that it was a lie, and never concede to the enemy's rebuttals and accusations. In its psychological profile of Hitler, the Office of Strategic Services (a US intelligence agency during the Second World War) described Hitler's strategy insightfully as follows (in Langer 1972):

> His primary rules were: never allow the public to cool off; never admit a fault or wrong; never concede that there may be some good in your enemy; never leave room for alternatives; never accept blame; concentrate on one enemy at a time and blame him for everything that goes wrong; people will believe a big lie sooner than a little one; and if you repeat it frequently enough people will sooner or later believe it.

The intent of systemic mendacious speech is, in effect, to attack those who do not belong to a preferred group (in the case of the Nazis this was the so-called Aryans), using dehumanizing semiotic forms (metaphors, cartoons, caricatures, conspiratorial narratives, etc.) to enhance believability. Over time, the words, images, and stories accumulate in the unconscious to engender what journalist Walter Lippmann (1922) called "simplified pictures in the mind," influencing how people think and talk about reality. Metaphor in particular plays a powerful role in this mental picturing process. In 1915, for example, newspaper headlines designed to expel Armenians from the Ottoman Empire referred to the uprooting of "malignant weeds" in the land (Kuper 1981: 91). It is no coincidence that this type of speech preceded widespread violence against the Armenians and their mass displacement. Examples such as this abound in the annals of history. As Hobbs and Antonopoulos (2013: 44) have argued, in the case of foreigners or immigrants, hate metaphors are effective because they are based on a code that they call an *alien conspiracy theory*, or the view that foreigners are responsible for endemic social ills.

A classic example of this is the conspiratorial narrative used against Italian immigrants to the United States in the first decade of the twentieth century, which revolved around the Black Hand extortion schemes of the era (Nicaso and Danesi 2020). These consisted of extortion letters sent to victims demanding money; each letter was signed with the picture of a black hand. The newspapers and the movies at the time portrayed such schemes as the result of opening up immigration from Italy to America. This portrayal created a negative picture in the mind, to use Lippmann's phrase, of all Italian immigrants as either part of crime families or as sympathetic to them. They were seen, in effect, as a "dangerous class," a term traced initially to a book by Honoré Antoine Frégier published in 1840, in which he links criminality to Italian character. As Robert Lombardo (2002: 394) elaborates:

> The "alien conspiracy" theory maintains that organized crime in American society evolved in a linear fashion, beginning with the Mafia in Sicily and emerging in the form of the Black Hand in America's immigrant colonies and culminating in the development of the Cosa Nostra in America's urban centers ... Black Hand crimes were often described as the work of the Mafia and the Camorra (Italian crime groups). Whether intentional or not, Black Hand criminals traded on the reputations of these groups. In spite of the popular belief that Black Hand activity originated in Sicily and the south of Italy, however, there is little evidence that Black Hand practices existed there. Although the Black Hand in Chicago was not a secret society, there were many small Black Hand gangs ... [The] historical record indicates that Black Hand extortion was the outcome of conditions that existed within American society. These conditions included the isolation of the Italian community; the Italian immigrant's mistrust of formal authority; the existence of saloons and saloonkeepers with powerful political connections; and a criminal justice system that was ineffective in repressing crime.

As the social media universe expanded in the second decade of the twenty-first century, the use of dehumanizing metaphors to engender hatred of foreigners or of those who are different in some way from the mainstream citizenry has spread worldwide, with depictions of outsiders as pests, parasites, or venomous creatures. The hate-based speech posted beforehand by the white supremacist protestors who were behind the violent unrest that took place in August 2017 in the city of Charlottesville brought out how dehumanizing metaphors can lead to unrest and violence. These included hate slogans such as "Jews will not replace us" and "blood and soil" (a rendition of Nazi Germany's *Blut und Boden*), among others. The same type of speech was used in the January 6 insurrection on the American Capitol—ignited by Donald Trump's big lie that the election was stolen from him and his constant use of slogans such as "save America" and "take it back" from democratic liberal élites. As Alfred Korzybski (1921: 71) noted decades before, such speech is mind poison:

> Humans can be literally poisoned by false ideas and false teachings. Many people have a just horror at the thought of putting poison into tea or coffee, but seem unable to realize that, when they teach false ideas and false doctrines, they are poisoning the time-binding capacity of their fellow men and women. One has to stop and think! There is nothing mystical about the fact that ideas and words are energies which powerfully affect the physico-chemical base of our time-binding activities. Humans are thus made untrue to "human nature." The conception of man as a mixture of animal and supernatural has for ages kept human beings under the deadly spell of the suggestion that, animal selfishness and animal greediness are their essential character, and the spell has operated to suppress their real human nature and to prevent it from expressing itself naturally and freely.

Hitler's big lie of an Aryan race that was superior to all other races showed how a mind-altering false rhetorical strategy, used in his speeches and official pronouncements over and over, can destroy social harmony under the false guise of restoring it. To back up his big lie, he used techniques that have now become routine on social media—conspiracy theories (such as the false theory that the Jews were responsible for world wars), propaganda (Germany was not defeated in 1918, but betrayed internally), and false myths (the Aryan false narrative)—which accumulated in people's minds twisting their interpretation of the world and the players in it. In *Nineteen Eight-Four,* and other works, George Orwell claimed that this kind of manipulative strategy works emotionally and indelibly when it is institutionalized with a Ministry of Truth, an agency that controls language. The Ministry also controls the meaning of history, rewriting it to fit the conspiracy theories and false myths. As Machiavelli understood, this is crucial not only for mind control, but also to silence the opposition and to hold on to power.

Orwell warned that the rise of totalitarianism was more likely to emerge when language is distorted to serve the machinations of the dictator. His description of doublespeak ("Newspeak" in the novel) showed how language can be altered to suppress the normal system of reference it evokes, assigning ambiguous meaning to specific words and phrases which were then adapted to an underlying code, such as the Nazi Aryan myth, a fabricated origin story of a superior race destined to rule the world. The myth actually predated Hitler in the nineteenth century (Dunlap 1944). Archaeological evidence has never come forward to support the existence of a historical Aryan race. There was an Aryan dialect spoken by people in the Indian subcontinent, but never a race as such. Its adoption and promulgation by the Nazis constituted a dangerous big lie that was used to destroy particular ethnic groups. An analogous mythic lie is the MAGA myth (Make America Great Again), perpetrated by Donald Trump, whereby it is assumed that America was founded by a group of white colonists who were able to take over the land because of divine destiny and who are being assailed by a cadre of liberal élites who operate in a deep state planning to overtake America.

It was nineteenth-century political theorist Joseph Arthur de Gobineau (1856) who used the term "Aryan" as a synonym for "white race." His skewed view resonated with the false notion of a master race that was spreading by the end of the century—a notion that gained traction in the first decades of the twentieth century when the Nazi party came to power in Germany, claiming that the Aryan race was "chosen" (by biology and history) to rule over the world; relegating other races to serving the master race or else eliminated if they posed a threat to it. The master race could thus build a harmonious, orderly, and prosperous society. Many believed this mythology, because of the persuasive discourse that the Nazis developed to promote it, which included rhetorical strategies, such as calling the Jews parasites, symbols such as the swastika to connect the Nazis to their supposed divine origins, and forged texts, such as the *Protocols of the Elders of Zion*, to falsely claim that the Jews were planning to rule the world. In effect, the Nazis constructed emotionally powerful semiotic networks to deliver both the code of a superior race and the code of a Jewish cabal. The claim made here is that without this semiotic apparatus, Nazism would not have spread as broadly. It required a control of meaning that was made possible by a construction of the appropriate semiotic networks. But the truth of the matter turned out to be just the opposite of what Hitler promised. His regime brought about terrorism, war, and the Holocaust, instead of harmony and prosperity.

Belief in racial superiority is not exclusive to a particular society or a specific era. It has existed since the dawn of history. Ironically, the ancient Romans saw the Germanic tribes as a race of barbarians that was barely human. This tendency to ascribe superiority to one's own tribe creates a sense of continuity from one era to the next, and thus the need to preserve it from "enemies from the outside." A made-up story such as the Aryan myth gains believability as it spreads through the populace because it is framed as a historical account of the truth—an account controlled by the Orwellian Ministry of Truth. Through constant repetition via semiotic networks, the believability level continues to increase, until the alternative history becomes the accepted truth. As Marcel Proust (1913) so aptly put it, "Time passes, and little by little everything that we have spoken in falsehood becomes true."

Among the nodes in the Nazi semiotic network, the following stand out:

- *Richard Wagner.* Hitler's apparent love of the operas of Richard Wagner led to his adoption of Wagner's music as a T-node (textual node in the network) to help fuel the birth of Nazism, given Hitler's interpretation of the operas as representing the desire for transcendence and racial superiority (the main semiotic code in Nazism). Wagner had died fifty years before Hitler came to power, and yet his music became a kind of "background sound track" for Hitler's megalomania. The "Ride of the Valkyries" (from *Die Walküre*) was played frequently at various Nazi meetings, becoming a kind of battle cry.
- *The Swastika.* The Nazis' principal symbol was the swastika, which the Party formally adopted in 1920. The emblem was black, rotated 45 degrees on a white circle and on a red background. It was used on flags, badges, armbands, posters, and as a logo in official communications. Derived from a spiritual Indo-European tradition, the swastika constituted an S-sign in the semiotic network, reinforcing the underlying Aryan code. Hitler described the symbolism astutely as follows (*Mein Kampf* 1925): "The red expressed the social thought underlying the movement. White the national thought. And the swastika signified the mission allotted to us—the struggle for the victory of Aryan mankind and at the same time the triumph of the ideal of creative work." To avoid clashes of meaning with the semiotic network it had established, the Nazi regime removed competing religious symbolism from society.
- *Runic letters.* The Nazis used the runic alphabet for various symbolic purposes, given that it was the historical alphabet used to write various Germanic languages before the Latin alphabet was adopted. The runes thus became another element of the S-node in the semiotic network.
- *Völkisch Nationalism.* Inspired by the works of Johann Gottlieb Fichte (1808), Hitler developed an alternative history to support his notion of a superior race, which came to constitute a key T-node (textual-narrative) in

the network. During the Napoleonic Wars, Fichte had called for a German national revolution against the French occupiers, using a populist style of oratory and writing, speaking of the need for a *Volkskrieg* (a "People's War') and stressing the need for the German nation to purify itself of foreigners and enemies within, even proposing a purge from the German language of French words, a policy that the Nazis adopted after their rise to power.

- *Blut und Boden*. Nazi *völkisch* thinking was influenced by Wilhelm Heinrich Riehl's work *Land und Leute* (1857) ("Land and People"), in which Riehl argued that "each nation-state was an organism that required a particular living space in order to survive." This was adopted and extended as a *Volk* slogan, *Blut und Boden* ("Blood and Soil"), by the Nazi regime, which came to constitute a powerful R-node (rhetorical node) in their semiotic network, where *Blut* referred to a superior *Volk* as located in a national soil (*Boden*). The slogan has been adopted by radical groups today, including Neo-Nazis and members of the alt-right.
- *Lebensraum*. The Blood and Soil theme became the source (within the network) of the concept of *Lebensraum*, "living space" from which inferior peoples were to be removed. In *Mein Kampf* Hitler identified this as the political will of the Nazis: "And so, we National Socialists consciously draw a line beneath the foreign policy tendency of our pre-War period. We take up where we broke off 600 years ago. We stop the endless German movement to the south and west, and turn our gaze toward the land in the East. At long last, we break off the colonial and commercial policy of the pre–War period and shift to the soil policy of the future."
- *Aryanism*. As mentioned, this is the primary code in the semiotics of Nazism, generating large circuitry within the Nazi semiotic network, rhetorical, symbolic, imagistic, and narrative. The concept of an Aryan race was adopted to draw a distinction between what the Nazis deemed to be "high and noble" Aryan culture versus that of a "parasitic" Jewish culture.
- *Mendelism*. The pioneering work of German biologist Gregor Mendel (1856), establishing genetics as a solid scientific enterprise, was supported by the Nazis in a twisted way. The Mendelian theory of inheritance showed that genetic traits were passed from one generation to another. The Nazis used this theory to argue that it supported their view of a superior genetically based race, claiming a racial nature behind certain general traits such as greediness and criminal behavior.

These and other semiotic nodes associated with Nazism will be discussed in due course. Suffice it to say here that without such interconnected nodes in the overall semiotic network that the Nazis perpetrated and perpetuated, it is unlikely that people would have accepted their view of reality outright, without challenging it. It is in the interconnectivity of meaning that mind-control can be achieved, especially given the illusory truth effect that repetition in various modes and media (rhetorical, symbolic, imagistic, textual) tends to produce, which in cases such as Nazism even rises to the level of a metaphysical truth that is ascribed to words and symbols (Espes Brown 1992). When this is achieved there is virtually no logical argumentation against it—it is either believed or not. Incredibly, the Nazi code has even transcended historical evolution, remaining almost intact to this day, spreading throughout alt-right social media sites and beyond. Once a belief system is embedded into groupthink it becomes almost impossible to eradicate it completely. As Jason Lee (2018: 9) has perceptively observed:

> Despite the killing of over 6 million Jews in the Nazi death camps during World War II, there are still people throughout the world forging identities stemming from Nazi ideology. Recorded incidences of neo-Nazi attacks were increasing even before the rise of Donald Trump, and globally the popularity of neo-Nazi related groups was growing in a variety of forms in different nations. We might conclude with Primo Levi [Jewish-Italian writer] that every age has its own form of fascism.

Epilogue

Interconnected circuits of meaning can be based on truth or falsity. The semiotic network that characterized the #MeToo movement was intended to convey a truth about the treatment of women. On the other hand, the semiotic network constructed by the Nazis was meant to establish a belief in a false code (or set of codes). It accomplished this, arguably, because it possessed its own semiotic logic, based on the connectivity of words, symbols, images, and stories in the network. This claim may not be a far-fetched one, psychologically speaking. The term used to describe a belief in a false connected network of meaning, such as the one used in Nazism, is *apophenia,* a term introduced by psychiatrist Klaus Conrad in 1958 in reference to the "unmotivated seeing of connections" that are accompanied by "a specific feeling of abnormal meaningfulness." Conrad applied the term to describe the early stages of delusional thought emanating from over-interpretations of sensory information and perceptions. The same notion has come to describe the propensity to unreasonably seek patterns in random information, as can be seen in the origins and spread of conspiracy theories, whereby coincidences are woven together into an apparent secret plot.

Conrad used the term *apophany* to characterize the false insight derived from aphophenic thinking, in contrast to the term *epiphany*, or the experience of a sudden realization of the truth of something. He found that those who experienced apophanies started sensing abnormal meanings in their daily life. The over-interpretation of random patterns in non-delusional individuals has been traced to an evolutionary survival instinct. Whatever the truth, apophenia provides direct evidence that semiotic networks, constructed for deceptive purposes, produce belief in the codes they express, making us prone to manipulation by those who harness this very tendency to create unified patterns of meaning, from which there is no cognitive escape other than to reject the whole semiotic network system entirely. Each sign in a network in isolation would not produce a false belief; it is via its connectivity to other signs in the network that makes it resonate with believability. To cite psychologist Bruce Poulsen (2012):

> Our brains are pattern-detection machines that connect the dots, making it possible to uncover meaningful relationships among the barrage of sensory input we face. Without such meaning-making, we would be unable to make predictions about survival and reproduction. The natural and interpersonal world around us would be too chaotic ... So, when our pattern-recognition systems misfire, they tend to err on the side of caution and self-deception.

To reiterate by way of conclusion to this chapter, the claim here is that semiotic networks are psychologically real, affecting beliefs and cognitive states. False beliefs are products of sign-based connective thinking, which forms the emotional power of dangerous discourses. To repeat, what makes both a social justice discourse such as the #MeToo one, and a nefarious discourse like the Nazi one, is the sense of connectivity among the sign forms and structures embedded in the respective discourses. Consider the Nazi propaganda poster below, titled *This Is the Enemy*, which is in a collection created and maintained by the United States Government.

Poster "THIS IS THE ENEMY, 1941–1945." Creator: Office for Emergency Management, Office of War Information. U.S. It can be found at Hennepin County Library, James K. Hosner Special Collections Library, Kirttleson World War II, Collection MPW00520 (See Figure 1.3 below).

Whoever created the poster, it bears Nazi symbolism in a compact visual way. It shows the hand of a Nazi officer brandishing a knife that he thrusts through a copy of the Bible, clearly suggesting that the ideas in this book are dangerous to Nazism (itself a religion) and must be destroyed in their core—hence the

Figure 1.3 Nazi Propaganda Poster (1941–5).

Source: Office for Emergency Management, Office of War Information. U.S. It can be found at Hennepin County Library, James K. Hosner Special Collections Library, Kirttleson World War II, Collection MPW00520.

plunging of the knife through the middle (heart) of the book. The swastika is, of course, a prominent Nazi symbol on the officer's sleeve, implying that he is acting in its service. The red background is symbolic of the *Blut und Boden* theme in the overall semiotic network (to be discussed subsequently). The intent of the poster is encapsulated in its caption ("This Is the Enemy"). This poster manages to enfold anti-Semitic tropes at once, such as the *Blut* background, and the Bible as a symbol of Jewish faith—all of which must be eliminated by a powerful hand holding a quasi-mythical dagger.

It is truly remarkable to consider, retrospectively, how such meaning-based tactics allowed a totalitarian government to gain control over people's minds. Interestingly, Hitler's tactics were first described systematically by literary theorist, Kenneth Burke (1939), who identified the trope of the Jewish "common enemy" and the need to destroy the past to generate a "symbolic rebirth"—both of which can be seen in the poster above. Without identifying an "enemy," who is scheming to destroy everything good and beautiful, the Nazi discourse would come apart. It is the primary code in the network, whereby an enemy in German society—the Jews—is working secretly against it (*Mein Kampf* 1925):

> Therefore, in August, 1914, it was not a people resolved to attack which rushed to the battlefield; no, it was only the last flicker of the national instinct of self-preservation in face of the progressing pacifist-Marxist paralysis of our national body. Since even in these days of destiny, our people did not recognize the inner enemy, all outward resistance was in vain and Providence did not bestow her reward on the victorious sword, but followed the law of eternal retribution … Anyone who picks up a Jewish newspaper in the morning and does not see himself slandered in it has not made profitable use of the previous day; for if he had, he would be persecuted, reviled, slandered, abused, befouled. And only the man who combats this mortal enemy of our nation and of all Aryan humanity and culture most effectively may expect to see the slanders of this race and the struggle of this people directed against him.

The concept of a common enemy became a symbol of the evil against which people must unite, distracting society from the politically inconvenient issues that they faced every day by relating them to the common rhetorical enemy. As Burke notes, this trope produced an us-versus-them system of belief, which was used to legitimize Hitler's divide-and-conquer tactic—a tactic that was emphasized by Machiavelli himself. In this context, opposing voices are seen as antithetical to unity—without a united voice, the purported enemy would gain the upper hand.

Burke also identified a geo-location trope in the network, encapsulated by the proverb, "All roads lead to Rome," which, as Burke argues, in Ancient Rome was literally and metaphorically true. All roads radiated from the capital outward to the areas of the Roman Empire, and all authority was located there. It was a form of power mapping, connecting geo-location with strong leadership. Hitler promoted Munich as the place to which all roads must lead, and where authority should be implanted. The symbolic rebirth trope, Burke claimed, was a way to cast even more negative light on the enemy within. It was in this semiotic framework that Hitler proposed the concept of a pure superior Aryan race. When the inferior scapegoat is identified a symbolic rebirth will occur—it will occur only once in a lifetime (*Mein Kampf* 1925):

> For their whole activity leads the people away from the common struggle against the common enemy, the Jew, and instead lets them waste their strength on inner religious squabbles as senseless as they are disastrous. For these very reasons the establishment of a strong central power implying the unconditional

authority of a leadership is necessary in the movement. By it alone can such ruinous elements be squelched. And for this reason the greatest enemies of a uniform, strictly led and conducted movement are to be found in the circles of these folkish wandering Jews. In the movement they hate the power that checks their mischief ... Everything on this earth is capable of improvement. Every defeat can become the father of a subsequent victory, every lost war the cause of a later resurgence, every hardship the fertilization of human energy, and from every oppression the forces for a new spiritual rebirth can come—as long as the blood is preserved pure.

The Nazis converted these themes into all kinds of sign structures that composed their discursive network using slogans, symbols, images, and false narratives to indoctrinate society, employing different media to get the overall message repeated consistently on a daily basis. Headed by Joseph Goebbels, the Nazis used an Orwellian Propaganda Ministry to control discourses and meanings, spreading their own propaganda through films, theater, music, the press, and radio broadcasts. The carefully crafted messages were designed to mobilize the German population to support all Nazi efforts, including the deportation of Jews and others to concentration camps. It is alarming to note that current neo-Nazi and white supremacist groups are using the exact same kind of dangerous discourse and its coded network of meanings.

In *Origins of Totalitarianism* (1951), Hannah Arendt saw the regimes of Hitler and Stalin as based on propagandistic techniques like the ones described in this chapter, which had the ability to activate "a curiously varying mixture of gullibility and cynicism with which each member is expected to react to the changing lying statements of the leaders ... [whereby people would] believe everything and nothing, think that everything was possible and nothing was true." As Machiavelli had understood centuries earlier, instead of deserting the leaders who had lied to them, the people would protest that they had known all along that they were correct and would thus admire the leaders for their superior tactical cleverness. The result of a consistent and total substitution of lies for factual truth is not that the lies will be accepted as truth and truth will be defamed as a lie, but that the sense by which we take our bearings in the real world is destroyed. Arendt concluded: "politics is a game of cheating and that the 'first commandment' of the movement; 'the Fuehrer is always right,' is as necessary for the purposes of world politics, that is, world-wide cheating, as the rules of military discipline are for the purposes of war."

2

Words, Symbols, and Images of Conflict

Prologue

In late February of 2022, Russian Federation President Vladimir Putin announced that he was going to conduct a "special military operation" in neighboring Ukraine (Putin 2022), giving as his reason that there were Nazi sympathizers in the government which he wanted to remove from power so that the country could be liberated from the dangers posed by its leaders. He described his mission as one of "denazification." His choice of the word was hardly a convenient figure of speech; it was a coded word, despite the irony that the Ukrainian President Volodymyr Zelenskyy was Jewish and had lost three family members in the Holocaust. It alluded at one level to the Second World War, when some Ukrainian nationalists fought along with the Nazis. But there was no evidence of any residue support for Nazism in modern-day Ukraine. Putin's strategy behind the word was, clearly, to stoke a historically based resentment that he believed lingered in the country. But it did not stop there. At another level, the word recalled how it was used at the Nuremberg trials, which held Nazi leaders to account, and how post-war Germany eliminated Nazi elements within it. In semiotic terms, it was a key R-node in the network of meanings that Putin was aiming to construct to justify his invasion. Benjamin Tromly (2022) perceptively describes the strategy behind this term as follows:

> Putin might believe his own rhetoric of "denazification," but he also finds it politically useful ... [as] patriotic memory of World War II remains a powerful tool for holding Putin's domestic base together ... mobilizing Russia behind war through manipulation of the powerful symbols of fascism and Nazism.

The word can be connected geo-politically to a contemporary Lebensraum code (Chapter 1), which, as Brian Czech (2022) perceptively notes, differs from the Nazi one in terms of cardinal direction, "coming from the east instead of the west." In a similar vein, Igor Torbakov pointed to Putin's reference to Ukraine as part of "historical Russia," and to the concept of a "larger Russian nation" as a geo-political code to validate his imperialist ambitions, using an intentional misrepresentation of the historical past, which subsumes Ukrainians as part of a single ethnic Russian identity—an idea that goes back to the Bolshevik movement around 1917 when "the Russian grand narrative championing the 'one and indivisible Russian state' and a 'single, indissoluble Russian nation' became so pervasive that the upsurge of Ukrainian nationalism triggered by the First World War and revolutionary upheavals caught the Russian educated public off guard."

It is not a coincidence that the term denazification (German *Entnazifizierung*) was used after the Second World War to describe an initiative to rid German society and politics of Nazi ideology, carried out by removing Nazi Party members from positions of power and influence, and disbanding institutions, practices, and organizations associated with Nazism, as well as trying prominent Nazis for war crimes. Ironically for Putin, the term *denazification* was first coined as a legal term in 1943 by the US military. Aware of this etymological anomaly in using the term, his adoption is hardly a semantic malapropism. It is a calculating Machiavellian rhetorical strategy of deflection by projection—blaming others of employing his own tactics, namely, NATO and the United States in particular for encroaching on "Russia's historical borders" (which included Ukraine for Putin) for which, as a consequence, he felt impelled to act militarily. Putin thus projects his own Nazi-like politics onto Ukraine, making the country a scapegoat for his tactics. In effect, Putin's use of the term *denazification* produces a form of gaslighting that he maintained in place in his own country via strict totalitarian controls of media messaging, in line with an Orwellian Ministry of Truth ploy. In his 2008 book, *State of Confusion*, Bryant Welch has aptly remarked that political gaslighting has become highly effective today because it enlists modern technologies and persuasive-type marketing techniques amalgamated with the traditional methods of propaganda—all of which have been used by Putin throughout his invasion of Ukraine, thus perpetrating and perpetuating an illusion of truth within a large portion of Russian society.

The question becomes: How can a single word enlist so much unconscious meaning? As research on the psychology of rhetorical language has shown (Shapiro 1984, Musolff 2004, Lakoff 2004, 2008, 2016, Joseph 2006, Yu 2013, Hanne, Crano, and Mio 2014), a single metaphor can spark a conflict or encapsulate a cause and the reason is that it branches out to encode a system of interrelated concepts. In terms of semiotic network method, a term such as *denazification* would work psychologically in this way, given that it is a node in the Lebensraum code network. This pattern has occurred throughout history.

For example, the French national motto was based on the metaphorical power of three words—*liberté, égalité, fraternité* ("liberty, equality, brotherhood")—which acquired meaning in the context of the French Revolution. A famous 1796 letter, written by British marine officer Watkin Tench, who was being held prisoner on a ship at the time, succinctly explains the rhetorical power of these words (Tench 1796: 15):

> The republican spirit is inculcated not in songs only, for in every part of the ship I find emblems purposely displayed to awaken it. All the orders relating to the discipline of the crew are hung up, and prefaced by the words Liberté, Égalité, Fraternité, où la Mort, written in capital letters.

It is somewhat surprising to find that this type of rhetorically coded discourse has been examined only sporadically from the semiotic angle (Moeschberger and DeZalia 2014, Jacob 2020). In the present framework, the focus is on the connectivity between politically charged words and their nonverbal counterparts, such as the symbols and images used to reinforce the verbal code. It is no coincidence that Putin introduced the letter "Z" to symbolize his code of denazification, as will be discussed below. Even at an orthographic level, it can be seen to stand iconically for one of the letters in the English word *Nazi*, likely suggesting to users of the English alphabet (such as countries within NATO) that its removal from the word symbolizes the goal of his operation—the removal of supposed Nazism from Ukraine.

The lexical, symbolic, and imagistic strategies that are utilized to construct "discourses of war" will be investigated semiotically in this chapter, focusing on how one word leads to another, one symbol to another, and so on. In one speech, Putin in fact reinforced his underlying imperialist code by employing phraseology such as "protection of Russia" from "those who took Ukraine hostage and are trying to use it against our country and its people," to build an image of victimization as a ploy to justify his real victimization of another country, even blaming the whole situation on "hostage takers" (namely NATO). Putin's speeches on the invasion, disguised rhetorically as a special operation, are replete with coded metaphorical allusions, such as "comrades" (evoking the previous Soviet Union's rejection of the Nazis during the Second World War), "Motherland," "junta," and others that are derivatives of the core semiotic code. Below is an excerpt from one such speech (Putin 2022):

> Dear comrades! Your fathers, grandfathers, great-grandfathers did not fight the Nazis, defending our common Motherland, so that today's neo-Nazis seized power in Ukraine. You took an oath of allegiance to the Ukrainian people, and not to the anti-people junta that plunders Ukraine and mocks these same

people. Don't follow her criminal orders. I urge you to lay down your weapons immediately and go home.

The premise adopted in this book is that political conflict works successfully if it is based on such coded language, designed to foster false beliefs and thus to gain control over people's minds. As Prometheus stated in Aeschylus's *Prometheus Bound*, this strategy ensures that "rulers would conquer and control not by strength, nor by violence, but by cunning." One of the first manifestos on political and military warfare, written around 500 BCE by Chinese military strategist and philosopher, Sun Tzu, identifies a set of principles on which war is based. In it, Sun Tzu suggests that the best victories are those won without actually fighting, but through the deployment of a "dangerous rhetoric," which affects people's minds and thus will impel nations to act violently (Sun Tzu 2002: 42).

Dangerous Rhetoric

A concrete example of how dangerous rhetoric can ignite violence was, as mentioned previously, the "Unite the Right" rally, organized by Neo-Nazi and white supremacist groups in Charlottesville, Virginia, from August 11 to 12, 2017. The participants screamed anti-Semitic slogans, wearing Nazi symbols, and carrying Confederate battle flags. The goal of the rally was, purportedly, to unify the American white nationalist movement and oppose the removal of the statue of General Robert E. Lee from Charlottesville's former Lee Park. It sparked confrontations between the Neo-Nazis and opponents, ending in tragedy when one of the white supremacists deliberately rammed his automobile into a crowd of counter-protesters, killing a woman and injuring thirty-five other people.

A slogan repeated over and over by the mainly young white male rallyists as they marched in unison was "Blood and Soil," followed by "Jews will not replace us." The referential domain of that phraseology was unmistakable—it pointed indexically to the Nazi Aryan code (Chapter 1). *Blut und Boden* was, as discussed, the slogan that the Nazis used to assign rhetorical force to the mythic code. *Blut* stood for "blood purity" (Trueman 2015), which was claimed to ensure the survival of the Aryan race and the "1000 Year Reich." Anyone deemed to not be racially pure could be imprisoned for *rassenschande*, a "racial crime." In *Mein Kampf*, Hitler laid out his reasons why blood purity was critical to ensuring that the "good race" would prevail (Hitler 1925):

Blood mixture and the resultant drop in the racial level is the sole cause of the dying out of old cultures; for men do not perish as a result of lost wars, but by the loss of that force of resistance which is contained only in pure blood. All who are not of good race in this world are chaff. And all occurrences in world history are only expression of the races' instinct for self-preservation. What we must fight for is to safeguard the existence and reproduction of our race and our people, the sustenance of our children and the purity of our blood, the freedom and independence of the fatherland, so that our people may mature for the fulfilment of the mission allotted it by the creator of the universe. Those who are physically and mentally unhealthy and unworthy must not perpetuate their suffering in the body of their children.

The Nazi government even decreed that any Aryan who had a romantic relationship with a non-Aryan would be considered guilty of "blood treason," a clear reference to the link between race and duty to the nation. The *Blut* term specifically targeted the Jews, who were labeled as "blood eaters" of children. In the early days of Nazi rule, such brutal, discriminatory language did not receive wide support. But by the mid-1930s, it became widespread and enshrined into the Nuremberg Laws—the anti-Semitic laws that were enacted in 1935 at a special meeting of the Reichstag during the annual Nuremberg Rally of the Nazi Party. This showed conspicuously how some words are constructed purposively to generate hatred of targeted groups and to generate false beliefs. Rhetorical tropes, such as the *Blut* one, are indexical in intent, in the Peircean sense that they enfold an existential sign function—whereby the sign and the idea are linked existentially in the mind, like smoke with fire. The *Boden* term in the Nazi slogan was also designed to reinforce the Aryan myth, indexing a mystical relationship between Aryans and (sacred) land. In sum, the *Blut und Boden* trope became a powerful metaphorical justification for the Nazi land seizures in Eastern Europe and the expulsion of local populations in favor of ethnic Germans (the Lebensraum ideology), as well as a rationalization of the Holocaust. In other words, a rhetorical structure had the ability to activate all kinds of semiotic nodes in a dangerous discourse network, which, together, delivered the overall Nazi code.

It is unlikely that Nazism would have spread so broadly in German society (and beyond) without such manipulative rhetoric. The reason why it is so emotionally powerful may have a neurological basis—it has been found that it directly affects the emotional centers in the brain (Boulenger, Shtyrov, and Pulvermüller 2012). Metaphorical constructs in particular activate different neural circuits, because they arise from a blending of different neural regions involved in emotional processing, including the processing of belief (Lakoff 2014, Feldman 2006). This assures that core beliefs are self-sustaining, since a particular metaphor acts, as Padesky (1991) observes, as a kind of mental magnet that attracts corroborative information and rejects disconfirmatory evidence. Moreover, as Telis (2012) remarks, the neuropsychological fMRI evidence indicates that there is a powerful synesthetic effect produced by metaphors, given that they activate regions of the brain, such as the somatosensory cortex, involved in the experience of sensory textures.

The Nazi's awareness of the power of rhetoric to "change minds" was saliently obvious from the outset, prefiguring the relevant neuroscience behind it. As Loebs (2015) points out, this awareness can already be seen in Hitler while he was in prison:

> Hitler understood the indispensable role rhetoric played in his quest for power. While brooding in a minimum security cell in Landsberg in 1924 for leading a failed coup d'état—the "beer hall putsch"—Hitler told a friend, "When I resume work it will be necessary to pursue a new policy. Instead of working to achieve power through an armed coup, we shall have to hold our noses and enter the Reichstag against the Catholic and Marxist deputies. Sooner or later we shall have a majority, and after that—Germany!"

The Nazis bombarded society with anti-Semitic metaphors constantly, some of which reached back to the Middle Ages, including the caricaturization of Jews as "animals," "vampires (blood eaters)," and "child murderers." This rhetorical strategy was very successful psychologically, allowing the Nazis to rationalize their purges of "parasites" from society and thus to justify the Holocaust through the metaphorical strategy of dehumanization. A metaphor such as "parasite" produces a negative physical sensation within us, projecting the body into the metaphorical thought in our minds, thus stimulating the physiological reaction by rhetorical proxy. This then impels us to project the metaphorical image onto the targeted group as being literally parasitic and dangerous to our health (Johnson 1987). As Mark Turner (1997) has aptly remarked, when we use the metaphor of a snake to describe a person, we will likely start to imagine the person turning into a snake in our imagination, experiencing the metamorphosis psychosomatically. It was this power of metaphor that Franz Kafka exploited in his 1915 novella *Die Verwandlung* ("The Metamorphosis"), which starts with a salesman waking one morning to find himself transformed into a monstrous *Ungeziefer*, which has been translated into English with an array of metaphors, including "gigantic insect," "monstrous cockroach," 'monstrous vermin," and "gargantuan pest," all of which produce similar kinds of synesthetic reactions, indicating that the translators understood the embodied power of Kafka's metaphor.

It is in decoding and exposing such underlying rhetorical mechanisms that semiotics can be enlisted to help neutralize these very mechanisms, by attempting to extract them from the perceived unity of the semiotic network in which they exist. By decoding Putin's denazification trope as an index of falsely enlisting the historical memory of the Second World War, it shows how he plays on fears that there would be an intrusion into Russia by foreigners—defining Ukraine as part of historical Russia. It is an indexical metaphor that works on various levels of belief, instilling a semiotic system of connected meaning that once introduced into the mind is difficult to eradicate. Significantly, in a speech Putin gave just before the one-year anniversary of his invasion (on February 21, 2023), he rhetorically reinforced the meaning system he had constructed over the preceding year, editing his original denazification stance by injecting into it what he clearly saw as necessary unscrupulous detail, claiming that the Neo-Nazi regime set up in Ukraine actually came about after 2014, when Putin had annexed Crimea as part of the Russian Federation. This kind of "adjustment" to the constructed meaning system helps sustain it under changing conditions and situational contextual shifts. Adding to his metaphorical concoction was his claim that the so-called Azov regiment of the Ukrainian military was concrete evidence of the presence of Nazi ideology in Ukraine. What Putin did not say was that the regiment was actually formed to resist Russian-backed separatists, who had seized areas of eastern Ukraine in 2014. Only subsequently was it absorbed as a unit within the Ukrainian military. In true Machiavellian fashion, Putin drew a comparison between the Azov unit and the Nazis' First Mountain Division, which committed war crimes in the Second World War, using the strategy of false equivalency in order to reinforce the semantics of his denazification metaphor. By no coincidence, Putin assigned the title of Edelweiss to the regiment, so as to reference indexically the wearing of this flower symbol on the cap and sleeve of First Mountain Division soldiers. But Putin failed to mention (intentionally, no doubt) that the Edelweiss flower has been used as a symbol by other European mountain military divisions, including a Russian unit called Edelweiss formerly, which was changed, strategically, to Avanguard in 2016. Putin had clearly inserted the symbol into his network as an S-node, to further support his *rationale* for a denazification operation, further enhancing his ploy of distracting from his own record of atrocities. Putin grabs from history what is opportune and discards everything else as false or irrelevant.

Significantly, hate and conspiratorial groups that are born directly online show a similar utilization of Putin-like rhetorical strategies to ensconce their false messages into global consciousness. It is no coincidence that far-right groups support Putin against Ukraine, sharing a common enemy—the liberal values espoused by Western democracies which are believed to be ideological weapons used by a cabal of élites who control the economy and the media. Ukraine is seen as the latest victim of the cabal, having come under the direct control of the cabal. One such group is QAnon, which exists mainly on social media, but which motivates real-world violence and aberrant behaviors. Followers believe that an anonymous government insider, known as "Q," provides key clues on his own social media platform that, when collated, will expose the cabal or "deep state" apparatus working behind the scenes against America and Americans, made up of prominent Jews operating behind the scenes to gain control over the world. QAnon believes that a single leader, Donald Trump, is the one who can expose the members of the deep state, put them in prison, and restore America to its glorious past. The echoes of Nazism are unmistakable. The difference is that the cabal in this case is populated not only by Jews, but by satanists, pedophiles, sex traffickers, Democratic politicians, and liberal intellectuals. In one of his first posts (October 29, 2017), Q warned that it was time to "clean out the bad actors who worship Satan," recalling the purging efforts of the Nazis.

Like the Nazis, QAnon has developed its own dangerous rhetorical language with indexical functions, including reference to pseudo-religious themes, such as the belief that an epic apocalyptic battle with the deep state, called "the Storm," is coming—an event that QAnon adherents call "the Great Awakening." The storm metaphor reverberates with ancient meanings of mythic floods sent to earth by the divinities to purify people of their evil ways. The trope also alludes to a religious revival movement in the English colonies in America during the 1730s, which was intended to restore religious values, at a time when, purportedly, secular rationalism was spreading, and passion for religion was diminishing. Like the zealots of that era, QAnon conspirators have developed a three-musketeers rallying cry, "where we go one, we go all," abbreviated to "WWG1WGA." QAnon rhetoric is a dangerous discourse, because it has not been limited to online communications, but has spread to some radical conservative political groups in the United States Congress. QAnon members were part of the attempted coup of the American government on January 6, 2022.

QAnon instills its illusory truth system among followers via constant repetitions of its rhetoric based on the cabal code, which it reinforces with symbolic and imagistic nodes throughout its network (to be discussed subsequently). As discussed in Chapter 1, this type of strategy was employed in ancient Greece, when crafty populist politicians such as Cleon used "rhetorical strategies to generate alternate realities for their followers, as a way to deceive people and thus be able to lead them in any self-serving direction the politicians desired, especially those who wanted to be deceived," as Jennifer Mercieca (2018) has perceptively pointed out. It is essentially a gaslighting ploy that was seen by Machiavelli (1513), who was well-versed in ancient history, as a crucial verbal weapon for the ruthless ruler:

> It is necessary to know how to conceal this characteristic well, and to be a great pretender and dissembler. Men are so simple, and so subject to be won over by necessities, that a deceiver will always find someone who is willing to be deceived.

The aim of rhetorically based gaslighting is to create doubts and confusion through selective metaphors that disrupt the normal neural processing of information. Once a malicious metaphor is absorbed, the truth no longer matters. Labels such as "pigs" or "monkeys" trigger sentiments of aversion in people's minds, activating the emotional and sensory-motor brain centers, as discussed above (Lai, Howerton, and Desai 2019). The result is a diminishment in the normal reasoning filters used in processing lexical input. Orwell (1949: 44–5) saw the state of doubt and confusion generated by such rhetoric as a way to hypnotize people:

> To know and not to know, to be conscious of complete truthfulness while telling carefully constructed lies, to hold simultaneously two opinions which cancelled out, knowing them to be contradictory and believing in both of them, to use logic against logic, to repudiate morality while laying claim to it, to believe that democracy was impossible and that the Party was the guardian of democracy, to forget whatever it was necessary to forget, then to draw it back into memory again at the moment when it was needed, and then promptly to forget it again: and above all, to apply the same process to the process itself. That was the ultimate subtlety: consciously to induce unconsciousness, and then, once again, to become unconscious of the act of hypnosis you had just performed.

Orwell ascribed the hypnotic effect to the ploy of "doublethink," whereby the meanings of words are designed to be intentionally ambiguous. He called the language that generated doublethink, "Newspeak," rephrased subsequently as doublespeak. As media analyst Edward S. Herman has cogently argued, the principal feature of doublespeak is its skillful utilization of lying (Herman 1992: 3):

> What is really important in the world of doublespeak is the ability to lie, whether knowingly or unconsciously, and to get away with it; and the ability to use lies and choose and shape facts selectively, blocking out those that don't fit an agenda or program.

Orwell explains that doublespeak expressions may appear absurd at first; but by constant usage they gain a form of cogency, which is exploited by totalitarian states to exact conformity among the populace, as doublethink becomes habitual. As Benjamin Lee Whorf (1941: 81) claimed, words manufacture a "thought world" that is carried in the brain, by which an individual "measures and understands what he can of the macrocosm." The work of George Lakoff in particular has shown how metaphors affect the mind and influence behaviors and bodily states. As he stated in 1979: "metaphors can be made real in less obvious ways as well, in physical symptoms, social institutions, social practices, laws, and even foreign policy and forms of discourse and of history" (Lakoff 1979). The reason why this is so is explained by the fact that metaphor encodes experience and feelings in a proxy way within the brain, via the blending of information in different neural regions involved in processing experience (Fauconnier and Turner 2002).

Throughout history, orators and philosophers have been intuitively aware of the power of rhetoric to change minds. Machiavelli gave the example of Pope Alexander the Sixth as the master mind changer, because he knew skillfully how to employ rhetoric to his advantage throughout his papacy, showing that people are easily deceived by such language (Machiavelli 1513):

> Alexander the Sixth did nothing else but deceive men, nor ever thought of doing otherwise, and he always found victims; for there never was a man who had greater power in asserting, or who with greater oaths would affirm a thing, yet would observe it less; nevertheless his deceits always succeeded according to his wishes, because he well understood this side of mankind.

As Lakoff and Johnson suggested in their ground-breaking work, *Metaphors We Live By* (1980), metaphor is not the only rhetorical form that has the capacity to shape thought. They claimed that metonymy also affects cognition, albeit in a different way, namely as a part-whole mode of thinking whereby the part becomes indistinguishable from the whole. Metonymy works by the contiguity that is perceived to exist between two concepts, unlike metaphor which maps qualities from one referent to another, amalgamating the two into a new thought form. A distinction between the two is often difficult to make. The Edelweiss symbol evoked by Putin is, at one level, a metaphor mapping Nazism conceptually onto a Ukrainian military unit; but it is also a metonym that involves a part-whole thinking process, with a symbol standing not only for a specific group, but, by extension for an entire nation. Both figurative processes, however, show that neural blending occurs, but in different ways, namely through mapping one semantic domain onto another (metaphor) versus using one domain to stand for another (metonymy).

A third major trope, according to Lakoff and Johnson, is irony, which involves using one domain contrastively for another, or else invoking a range of meanings by contrast or supposition. Significantly, irony as such is rarely found in dangerous discourses of any kind, arguably because it deconstructs false beliefs. Leaving aside technical linguistic matters relating to irony, there is a "rhetorical relative of irony," as *apophasis* is called, whereby the speaker evokes a subject by either denying it, or denying that it should be brought up, which is a common speech pattern in rhetorically contrived locutions, such as those used by Hitler, Putin, and other dictators, past and present. Apophasis is explained by so-called ironic process theory, which was encapsulated originally by Fyodor Dostoyevsky in his work, *Winter Notes on Summer Impressions* (1863), with the following thought experiment: "Try to pose for yourself this task: not to think of a polar bear, and you will see that the cursed thing will come to mind every minute." As this shows, deliberate attempts to suppress certain thoughts make them more likely to surface (Wegner 1989). This strategy was used cynically by Putin during his state-of-the-nation address in February of 2023, where he claimed how Russia had been weakened and humiliated by the collapse of the Soviet Union. He then bragged about how Russia's current military stockpile of weaponry is bigger and better than that of NATO or the United States, showing to his audience a video of multiple nuclear warheads, fired into space on a new ballistic missile, falling down over Florida. He then implored his audience not to think that this was in any way a threat or sign of aggression, which was a direct use of apophasis. As he cleverly declared: "I would like to emphasize specifically that this military power is not to threaten anybody. We have no plans nor have we ever had plans to be an aggressor and attack anybody. We are not going to take anything away from anybody. We have everything we need." In this way, Putin called attention to exactly what he was negating.

In an interesting relevant article, Nyyssönen, and Humphreys (2016) ascribe the Munich Agreement to the operation of metonymy. The agreement, concluded at Munich in September of 1938, was between Germany, the UK, France, and Italy, providing cession to Germany of the Sudeten German territory of Czechoslovakia, despite the existence of a 1924 alliance agreement and 1925 military pact between France and the Czechoslovak Republic. Most of Europe celebrated the Munich agreement, since it was presented as a way to prevent a major war on the continent. However, as Nyyssönen and Humphreys (2016: 173) observe:

> The appeasement of Hitler and the Munich Agreement is a rhetorical comparison used commonly in international relations to defend politico-military action ... our hypothesis is that "Munich" has proved very instrumental politically; it has been a key element in the final push to use force on numerous occasions, and we conclude that it is a very dangerous form of anti-diplomacy.

In sum, the point to be emphasized here is that the R-nodes in a semiotic network embed the desired meanings of a code in rhetorically effective ways. These delineate the derived meanings in powerful conceptual ways. For these to be effective, however, language must come under the control of the state, as Orwell certainly knew, and the contrived semantics spread throughout the state by all kinds of communicative media and channels. The Nazis gained control over minds by controlling the German language, both in its everyday and official uses. Putin adopted a similar rhetorical strategy and control of word meaning, whereby "denazification" meant that Ukraine was corrupt, while it actually obscured his real intention, based on a Lebensraum code, envisioning Ukraine as a Russian territory.

It should be noted at this point that a general pattern has emerged from researching and compiling the speeches of dictators and the discourses of conspiratorial groups such as QAnon—namely the existence of a handful of codes that undergird many, if not most, of such discourses, among which is the cabal, Lebensraum, replacement, and a few other codes, which also are connected to each other conceptually and historically. This may be the most useful insight that has come from using semiotic network theory in this domain of human behavior and action. QAnon followers even use the term "The Cabal" overtly to refer to what they perceive is a secret worldwide organization aiming to undermine freedom and implement a globalist agenda. As masters of conspiracism, QAnon members have spawned derivative narratives based on this code as a means to support autocrats such as Trump and Putin, producing gaslighting effects. For instance, some followers claim that the Russian invasion of Ukraine is a false flag operation, perpetrated by the media controlled by the cabal; others believe that Putin is conducting a secret war to root out the global cabal; others still believe that it is a covert operation to attack American biolabs in Ukraine. Significantly, Putin himself is a master conspiracist, taking advantage of effects such as the illusory truth one that are generated by the use of powerful deceptive semiotic networks. As Ilya Yablokov has aptly noted, Putin has instrumentalized conspiracism to justify his regime and the invasion of Ukraine to ordinary Russian citizens, who are blocked from information that is outside of Putin's control:

> [Putin's] conspiracy theories have become a way to reject mounting evidence of Russian atrocities–which are recast instead as foreign skullduggery. The crimes at Bucha, for example, were immediately blamed on the Ukrainians, who apparently either staged the photos or killed innocent people to set up the Russian Army. Hollywood, meanwhile, is believed to be working hard to produce scenes of mass poisoning to further discredit Russia. The C.I.A. is spinning its web. From battles of words on talk shows and online, conspiracy theories have effectively turned into a weapon that kills real people.

Threatening Symbolism

The Ku Klux Klan, an extremist right-wing secret society in the United States, founded after the Civil War to oppose social change and the emancipation of African Americans, continues to exist to this day, constituting a threat to unity in America, even though it is made up of a relatively small group of members. Although it no longer attracts members itself as a distinct group as in the past, the danger lies in the fact that its core ideology and methods have been adopted by, or incorporated into, a diverse and large assortment of white supremacist groups. In fact, it can be suggested that the KKK, Neo-Nazism, and white supremacy are implicit synonyms. Kat Chow (2018) has perceptively described this evolution from the KKK to current white supremacy hate groups, guided by the Internet, as follows:

> Then the last wave [of the KKK] is where we are now, which is where the Internet appears. The movement has been in every other era as the movement of people in physical space like in meetings, rallies, protests and demonstrations and so forth. It becomes primarily a virtual world, and has its own consequences—many consequences. It's much harder to track. And then there are these blurred lines between all these various groups that get jumbled together as the alt-right and people who come from the more traditional neo-Nazi world. We're in a very different world now.

So, although an autonomous KKK group may be evanescing as such, its rhetoric and symbolism have migrated to the many white supremacist and

Neo-Nazi groups that organize themselves online. In the historical Klan, members wore white robes with conical hoods covering the face, using a burning cross as a pseudo-religious symbol standing at the same time for the purging of racialized groups in America and the purification process that would result. Without such symbolism, one could argue that the appeal of the KKK and its offspring would diminish and might even evanesce completely. Symbolism covers a wide circuity range in the hate code network that white supremacy groups espouse, which stipulates that there is only one true (master) race, and that all other races must be eradicated or exiled from America.

The main S-nodes in this meaning system are the following ones:

- *Robes and hoods.* Most Klan groups wore (and continue to wear) white robes, with colored stripes that distinguish the officers from the rank and file. Leaders (Grand Dragons) sometimes wear green robes or even black to distinguish themselves from the other members. Robes bespeak of solemnity and secret knowledge, creating a distinct pseudo-religious dress code to draw people into the ranks and to terrorize victims. As Elaine Parsons (2005) has written, the reason for the choice of white, according to Klan mythology, is its reference to Confederate ghosts, who died in the Civil War purportedly defending the racial integrity of America. Another possibility is that white connotes purification and racial whiteness. The hood with eye holes helps prevent identification of the member, but it also generates an aura of fear and mystery at the same time.
- *Blood Drop Cross.* This is a primary symbol of the traditional Klan—it is a white cross on a red disk with a blood drop in the middle. Although its origins are not clear, it alludes to Nazi symbolism, recalling the shedding of the blood of enemies so that world order can be restored. The cross also indicates that the Klan espouses Christianity as its religion, albeit a warped form of the religion. The drop of blood suggests an array of meanings, including the tears shed over the loss of white hegemonic America after the Civil War or the blood that enemies of the real America will be shedding. The circle in which the symbol is encased and the square in which the drop is placed are highly suggestive of geometrical symmetry, evoking a form of sacred geometry (See Figure 2.1 below).
- The triangular symbol used by the Klan is made up of triangles within the outer triangle with the three Ks of the KKK inserted in the three upright internal triangles (facing upward), while the one facing downward is left empty. As another geometrical figure, it complements the circle and square

Figure 2.1 The Blood Drop Cross.

Source: Wikimedia Commons, https://commons.wikimedia.org/wiki/File:Emblem_of_the_Ku_Klux_Klan.svg; this file is licensed under the Creative Commons Attribution-Share Alike 3.0 Unported, GNU Free Documentation License, Version 1.2.

of the previous symbol to complete the sacred geometry connotations built into the semiotic network, whereby the KKK envisions itself as a religious entity. (See Figure 2.2 below).

Such symbolism constitutes a powerful emotional system, intended to both link the Klan to its belief that it is a religiously sanctioned organization and to evoke fear in those who are different racially and ethnically, much like the robed figures of Inquisitors or even of the Grim Reaper, a skeletal figure shrouded in a hooded robe, carrying a scythe to reap human souls. This symbolism is reinforced by R-node slogans within the semiotic network, including "One hundred percent white," "Preserve Racial Purity," "The Invisible Empire," "America first," and others. It comes as little surprise to find that the "America first" slogan was used during the Second World War by isolationist political organizations in the United States and by Donald Trump during his presidency and electoral campaigns

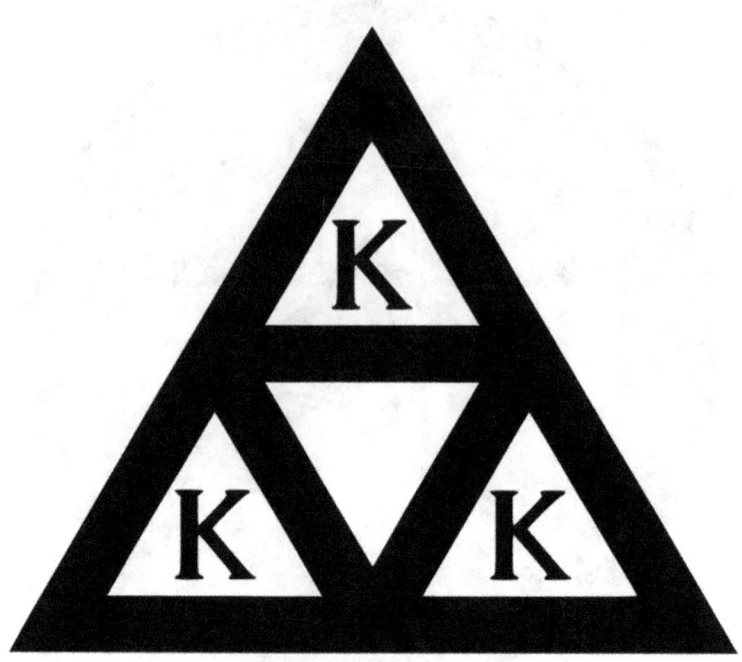

Figure 2.2 KKK Triangle Symbol.

Source: Wikimedia Commons, https://en.wikipedia.org/wiki/File:3_Triangles_KKK.svg. This file is licensed under the Creative Commons Attribution-Share Alike 4.0 International.

(Emery 2018). The correlation between rhetoric and visual symbolism is what makes a dangerous discourse threatening and intimidating, ascribing a sense of purpose and unity to it. Clifford Geertz (1973: 5) used the analogous term, "webs of significance," to explain why groups like the KKK gain such emotional power in a society, claiming that people need symbolic "sources of illumination" to espouse a cause or adopt a belief system. Even a simple hand gesture can accrue coded meanings within the semiotic network that defines a group. For example, the "OK" hand gesture, which appears innocent, is used by white supremacist groups as an iconic symbol, with the looped and extended fingers made to resemble the letters W and P, standing for "white power."

Nazi symbolism has also been adopted and recycled by white supremacy groups, including the Nazi swastika, worn often as a tattoo on the upper arms—implying threat and strength, and the Viking Othala Rune, which was a node in the Nazi Germany Lebensraum code—a symbol of the Aryan homeland (Figure 2.3 below).

Figure 2.3 Othala Rune.
Source: Wikimedia, public domain, https://commons.wikimedia.org/wiki/File:Odal.svg.

Other Nazi-indexing symbols include an iron cross, the number 1488, where the 14 refers to the "14 Words" of a popular white supremacist slogan and "88" to "Heil Hitler" (H is the eighth letter in the alphabet), and the Heil salute gesture used to greet leaders of a group. When considered together, the symbols constitute a clear network of intimidatory meaning, intended to create an aura of brazen power as well as to establish a linkage to Nazism and its pseudo-religious ideology.

The swastika has been adopted by most white supremacy groups as a symbol of racial superiority. It originated as a spiritual symbol in various Eurasian religions, and the word meant originally in Sanskrit "conducive to well-being." It was adopted by the Nazis to symbolize their claim of pseudo-divine origins and thus as a key S-node in their semiotic network based on their Aryan code. The term Aryan (*Arier*) was used specifically to refer to a "master race" of tall, blond, and light-eyed people. Some digressions from this ideal anatomical-physiological "model" were allowed as examples of normal statistical variation within a race—Adolf Hitler himself had dark hair and was of medium height. The Nazi belief that the swastika originated with the master Aryan race was shaped by several events in the nineteenth century. One of these was German linguist Friedrich Max Müller's claim that a group of priestly Brahmins, which he called the "Arya," had invaded India, bringing their advanced culture with them. He came to this conclusion after translating the sacred *Rig Veda* in the 1840s (Müller 1859). In later work, however, Müller (1866, 1883) revised this view, maintaining that "Aryan" alluded to a linguistic rather than racial category. As Esleben, Kraenzke, and Kulkarni (2008: 62) note, reviewing Müller's later work, he was "deeply saddened by the fact that these classifications later came to be expressed in racist terms." For Müller, his discovery of common Indian and European ancestry was, actually, a powerful argument against racism, maintaining that "an ethnologist who speaks of Aryan race, Aryan blood, Aryan eyes and hair, is as great a sinner as a linguist who speaks of a dolichocephalic dictionary or a brachycephalic grammar" (Müller 1888: 120).

But it was Müller's initial theory that became the basis of Aryanism shortly thereafter—a view bolstered by German archaeologist Heinrich Schliemann's discovery of a swastika-looking hooked cross on the site of ancient Troy (Schliemann 1875). Schliemann connected it to similar shapes found on ancient pottery in Germany, claiming that it was a "significant religious symbol of our remote ancestors" (Schliemann 1875: 34). While contrasting evidence emerged to challenge Schliemann's findings and Aryanism generally, the Nazis incorporated this whole line of false archeology to support their view of a master race, adopting the swastika as the symbol of "Aryan identity." In *Mein Kampf*, Hitler wrote the following (1925):

> I myself, meanwhile, after innumerable attempts, had laid down a final form; a flag with a red background, a white disk, and a black swastika in the middle. After long trials I also found a definite proportion between the size of the flag and the size of the white disk, as well as the shape and thickness of the swastika.

Even though Müller had withdrawn his notion of an Aryan race, claiming instead that he was describing a dialect of Sanskrit, not an actual race of people, the damage was done. As Baijayanti (2016: 217) observes, Müller's theory was the start of identity politics in the world:

> Müller's intellectual legacy [left] a scholarly influence on the formation of homogenous and potentially majoritarian community identities from the end of the nineteenth century up until the middle of the twentieth century in India

and Germany. Müller's contribution to the politicization of the Aryan discourse was the trope common to the emergence of group identities among the Hindus in India and Germans in Germany who regarded themselves as 'Aryan'. These groups, formed on the basis of identity politics, used the Aryan question as part of their aspirations for political power.

The key role assigned to the swastika symbol in the semiotic network of Aryanism made it an emblem used throughout German society, becoming a central feature of the Nazi flag, which featured a black swastika in a white circle placed in the center on a red-colored background—a configuration that collated a set of related meanings in this one artifact (Figure 2.4 below).

As discussed, the red color symbolizes the *Blut und Boden* theme in a visual-iconic way, while the white circle is highly suggestive of the perfection of racial whiteness. Hitler (1925) described the juxtaposition of the swastika and the color red as follows: "In red we see the social idea of the movement, in white the nationalistic idea, in the swastika the mission of the struggle for the victory of the Aryan man, and, by the same token, the victory of the idea of creative work, which as such always has been and always will be anti-Semitic."

The swastika is, in sum, an ideological visual symbol in the S-region of the network that delivers the core Nazi code of racial superiority, conveying the complex sets of beliefs and ideas that the Nazis espoused, in a compact way.

Figure 2.4 Nazi Flag.

Source: Wikimedia Commons, https://commons.wikimedia.org/wiki/File:Flag_of_Germany_%281935–1945%29.svg. Public domain.

As such, it summarizes the political ideas and practices for which it stands. An isomorphic use of this type of symbolism can be seen in the letter "Z," used by Putin to emblemize his invasion of Ukraine, arguably intended at an iconic level to refer to the letter "Z" in the word "Nazi" (as hypothesized in Chapter 1). Significantly, it is a Latin-script letter, not a Cyrillic one. At a denotative level, the "Z" is intended presumably to help Russian forces distinguish themselves from Ukrainian forces. But at a connotative (coded) level it constitutes an ideological symbol that stands for the denazification code, and, as some have suggested, for the Russian word *zapad*, which means "western" in that language. When looked at in a certain way, it even appears to suggest a "half" swastika form—a detail that has not escaped attention—indeed, it has been called a *zwaztika* and a *ziga* in reference to *Sieg Heil* by Ukrainian officials, who have also satirically referred to Russia as *RuZZia* in online posts.

The war in Ukraine also gave rise to a host of rhetorical and symbolic structures among the Ukrainians, such as the defiant words of the Ukrainian defenders of Snake Island, "Russian warship, go ... yourself!," which became a symbolic motto used on an official Ukrainian postage stamp. On the other side, alt-right social media is replete with Neo-Nazi symbols supporting the Russian invasion, which is seen by white supremacists as part of an ongoing Aryan war against effete liberal democracies. Military conflicts are not just physical ones; they are also symbolic ones. Aware of the power of letter symbols to evoke strong feelings, it is relevant to note that the neutralization of the meanings of alphabetic characters was behind the World Health Organization's decision to use Greek letters to designate COVID variants. Prior to this, the variants were named according to their place of origin, which stigmatized the location, evoking racialized stereotypes. Even so, certain letters were omitted in case they accidentally led to unwanted associations—the Greek letter X, for instance, was discarded because it was an iconic sign resembling the name of the president of China, Xi Jinping.

In sum, symbolism is a key strategy in the construction, build-up, and perpetration of the semiotic network sustaining a dangerous discourse; it constitutes an ideological meaning-making tool, twisted by hate groups to embed a constant array of hateful thoughts in the minds of followers. Sometimes, a single symbol can stand for a group. This is the case of QAnon, which revolves around the falsehoods spread by an unknown individual called "Q." Its low frequency in writing words implies (connotatively) exceptionality, which is transferred to the character of the secret Q individual, who leaves "Q drops" in his social media messages—namely, clues alluding to the supposedly nefarious events that are occurring behind the scenes, orchestrated by the deep state. The followers are supposed to connect these "symbolic dots" to unravel the message that Q is conveying to them in a puzzle-solving way. This is designed to activate apophanies (Chapter 1) in followers, who see the drops as nodes in the pseudo-network of unrelated sign forms, assigning "abnormal meaningfulness" to them, to cite Conrad (1958: 12) again. By joining the Q drops together in the framework of the cabal code perpetrated by QAnon, followers are impelled to believe their apophanies as revealing the machinations of the deep state cabal. The whole approach by QAnon is based on embedding the Q symbolism into a network of false meanings that are uncovered apophenically.

The QAnon apparatus is an apophenic system of falsehoods that has various precedents, even in the pre-Internet era. One of these is the conspiracy perpetrated by Erich Ludendorff, the German general and political theorist, who proclaimed publicly that the Jewish people had been responsible for Germany's First World War defeat. In 1922, he wrote (cited in Cohn 1967: 149): "The supreme government of the Jewish people was working hand in hand with France and England. Perhaps it was leading them both." As proof, he put forth a document, the *Protocols of the Elders of Zion*, which supposedly contained the notes taken at a secret meeting of Jewish leaders to allegedly take over the world. As it turned out, the *Protocols* was a forgery, written by the Russian secret police in the early 1900s to incite hatred against the Jews. Nonetheless, many believed (or wanted to believe) that the *Protocols* clarified seemingly "inexplicable" events, such as the war, the economic crises that followed the war, the revolutions in Russia, and even the Spanish flu. That conspiracy is still believed to this day, indicating how difficult it is to eradicate a belief that is a result of apophenic reasoning—the *Protocols* allowed hate groups to connect the dots between the war, the economy, social upheavals, and the Jews. Interestingly, the fake document was analyzed critically by the late semiotician Umberto Eco in his novel *Foucault's Pendulum* (1989):

> The great importance of *The Protocols* lies in its permitting antisemites to reach beyond their traditional circles and find a large international audience, a process that continues to this day. The forgery poisoned public life wherever it appeared; it was self-generating; a blueprint that migrated from one conspiracy to another.

Eco also dealt with the *Protocols* in his 1994 *Six Walks in the Fictional Woods* and 2010 novel *The Cemetery of Prague*. Numerous parts in the *Protocols* were plagiarized from Maurice Joly's 1864 political satire, *Dialogue in Hell Between Machiavelli and Montesquieu*, which was a veiled attack on the political ambitions of Napoleon who plotted to rule the world. The *Protocols* appeared in Russia in 1903, used from the start as a propaganda tool for scapegoating Jews, blaming them for the defeat suffered by Russia in the Russo-Japanese War. As the Russian Revolution unfolded, the text became an instrument used against the Bolsheviks who were depicted as Jewish, allegedly executing the "plan" described in the *Protocols*. Shortly thereafter, the Nazis adopted the *Protocols* as proof of the Jewish world-domination plan, making its study compulsory in schools.

QAnon introduced a *"Protocols*-in-the making" textual node in their semiotic system, assigning leadership of the deep state in large part to the Jews. As Gregory Stanton (2020) has cogently argued and illustrated in detail, central to the mythology imprinted into the *Protocols* was that of the so-called "blood libel," which claimed that Jews kidnapped and slaughtered Christian children, draining their blood to mix in with food consumed on Jewish holidays. The same mythology is central to QAnon (Stanton 2020):

> QAnon purveys the fantasy that a secret Satan-worshiping cabal is taking over the world. Its members kidnap white children, keep them in secret prisons run by pedophiles, slaughter, and eat them to gain power from the essence in their blood. The cabal held that the American Presidency under the Clintons and Obama, nearly took power again in 2016, and lurks in a "Deep State" financed by Jews, including George Soros, and in Jews who control the media. They want to disarm citizens and defund the police. They promote abortion, transgender rights, and homosexuality. They want open borders so brown illegal aliens can invade America and mongrelize the white race.

It is hardly surprising to find that QAnon has attracted Neo-Nazis and radical right political nationalists. In July of 2022, the Texas Republican Party even unveiled a new QAnon slogan, "We Are the Storm." Trump welcomed QAnon supporters to his rallies. When asked about this on national television, he replied: "I understand that they like me very much, which I appreciate." While the origins of QAnon are unclear, one possibility is that it was inspired by popular culture. Believers claim, in fact, to have been "red-pilled," a metaphor describing the process of enlightenment in *The Matrix* (1999). Q constantly urges believers to "follow the White Rabbit," a line from *The Matrix*, which indexes Lewis Carroll's *Alice's Adventures in Wonderland* (1865). The trailer for *White Squall* (1996) warned of "the calm before the storm," which is the likely source for the phrase as appropriated in a twisted fashion by QAnon.

As a symbol, the red pill shows how dangerous discourses appropriate symbolism to distort meaning. In the *Matrix*, there are two pills, a red and blue pill, representing a willingness to learn the real truth behind everyday reality and a tendency to accept ordinary reality respectively. As the character Morpheus says to Neo, the main protagonist: "You take the blue pill, the story ends, you wake up in your bed and believe whatever you want to believe. You take the red pill, you stay in Wonderland, and I show you how deep the rabbit hole goes." Morpheus then goes on to reveal the true nature of the Matrix to Neo—a sophisticated computer simulation of Earth created to keep humans docile while their bodies are stored in massive power plants, consumed as fuel by the machines that have enslaved them. The appropriation and distortion of the symbolism by radical conspiratorial groups led one of the directors, Lana Wachowski (2012), to make the following comment: "What we were trying to achieve with the story overall was a shift, the same kind of shift that happens for Neo, that Neo goes from being in this sort of cocooned and programmed world, to having to participate in the construction of meaning to his life."

The warped symbolism was spread primarily through social media, where the cabal code crystallized shortly after the release of the movie among conservative and libertarian pundits, claiming that it stood perfectly for the need to open one's eyes to the nefarious dealings of those in control of the world's finances and governments. It quickly became a battle cry for some groups that the "truth" is that white men are under attack, eventually leading to the formation of QAnon around the time of the electoral campaign, helping Trump gain the presidency. As David Neiwart (2020) has written, based on his investigations into conspiracism, symbols such as the red pill one have handed to alt-right leaders a sign system that allows them to gain a firm hold on the imagination of their followers. Recruitment to alt-right ideologies has been called "getting red-pilled" because believers become convinced that their alternate reality is the real one. It is significant to note that the makers of *The Matrix* asserted that they were inspired, in part, by Baudrillard's (1981) notion of hyperreality—a make-believe world that is perceived as more real and believable than the real world, and which, as Baudrillard maintained, contemporary western civilization actually prefers.

Fearsome Images

QAnon's belief that Donald Trump was chosen to save the world has become a core theme in the group's coded conspiracy theory. To support the claim, QAnon has used images designed to highlight Trump's role as a godly figure. One of these, posted on social media platforms by QAnon adherents, shows

Trump wearing a Q lapel, looking angrily askew, as he awaits the "storm" that will finally catapult him to the seat of power permanently, allowing him to guide the world correctly. Such images are designed to portray Trump as a fearsome Messianic figure, who is fulfilling a divine mission—a conspiracy theory that he has opportunistically promoted himself (cited in Thornbury 2020):

> If I can help save the world from problems, I'm willing to do it, I'm willing to put myself out there and we are, actually. We're saving the world from a radical left philosophy that will destroy this country and, when this country is gone, the rest of the world will follow.

Images are powerful I-nodes in semiotic networks. In the QAnon image mentioned above, Trump is depicted as an anointed spiritual leader by God, and the only one with the capacity to rid America of God's deep state enemies. Significantly, the same type of image was used to show Hitler and Mussolini as angry warriors who would save the world from ugliness and malice. Like these dictators, Trump fashioned his own image into that of an ersatz stern military leader, overseeing a cultural-spiritual war that aimed to retrieve America's past glory, recalling Mussolini's cry for a recovery of Italy's great imperial Roman past. Trump eerily employed a similar type of body posture at his rallies that was used by Mussolini and Hitler at their own rallies, raising his head imperiously after reciting a falsehood.

In both Nazi Germany and Fascist Italy, images of handsome young men, looking fearsome and strong, were everywhere—on posters, in movies, in newspapers and periodicals, in pamphlets, and the like. The respective propaganda machines employed all media channels to spread these images, contrasting them with images of dreadful-looking people, with the implication that they defiled society by their very presence. Nazi films went even further, portraying male Jews as predators, who abused young women, at the same time that they featured young attractive Germans, producing a jarring contrastive picture. The Nazi-organized youth movement, called Hitler Youth (*Hitlerjugend*), made these images the core of their public relations, creating posters in which German youth wore the same uniforms, and films in which they sung the same Nazi songs and participated in Nazi activities gleefully and triumphantly. An example of such a poster is the one below (Figure 2.5).

The poster shows a smiling young man with blond hair and a handsome appearance—a veritable portrait of the ideal Aryan youth. He is wearing the standard Nazi uniform and is holding the Nazi flag cheerfully and proudly. The caption provides the interpretive key—*Kämpf für Führer und Volk* ("Fight for the

Figure 2.5 Poster of a Nazi Youth.
Source: Created by Ludwig Hohlwein, 1936.

Führer and our folk"). In effect, the image is a visual metaphor for Aryan power. Such images constitute a visual iconic subsystem within a meaning network. Among the first to describe their semiotic power was Roland Barthes, in his pivotal 1964 article, "The Rhetoric of the Image," where he showed how images are emotively powerful because they encode all kinds of connotations in a largely unconscious way and, thus, are effective shapers of ideological worldviews—as can certainly be seen in the Nazi poster above. In *Camera Lucida*, Barthes defined an image as a sign that falls outside the space-time constraints imposed on consciousness by verbal language, producing a unique form of awareness (Barthes 1977: 44):

> The type of consciousness the photograph involves is indeed truly unprecedented, since it establishes not a consciousness of the being-there of the thing, but an awareness of its having-been-there. What we have is a new space-time

category: spatial immediacy and temporal anteriority, the photograph being an illogical conjunction of the here-now and the there-then.

At around the same time, the psychological and social importance of images was further emphasized by Rudolf Arnheim in his book *Visual Thinking* (1969), and Jonathan Berger, in *Ways of Seeing* (1972). Evidence of the power of images comes today from research on social media which shows that a post accompanied by images is much more likely to prompt engagement and to spread virally than one without images (Li and Xie 2019).

An image such as the Hitler youth one above captures attention directly, encoding a vast array of meanings that are spread throughout a semiotic network in a contextualized way (i.e., in terms of familiarity with the origin and meaning of the underlying code). Trump's Messianic image would have no meaning for anyone who has not had exposure to the QAnon code; analogously, the poster of the Hitler youth today would hardly resonate in the same way as it did in Nazi Germany, given the lack of the historical-social context of Nazism. It is a virtual law of semiotics that the meaning and interpretation of signs will vary broadly along contextual lines (Lotman 1991, Uspenskij 2001). Even mental (imagined) images are subject to this law. When asked to visualize a triangle, for example, people living in western culture will tend to call to mind an equilateral triangle, because in this culture, traditions dictate that it is the prototypical (representative) form of triangularity. Obtuse-angled, right-angled, and acute-angled triangles are perceived, instead, to be subtypes. The reason for this reaches back into the meanings of triangles as both geometrical and aesthetic constructs in ancient Greece—meanings carried over into Renaissance geometry and art, where symmetry and perfection of form were praised. The equilateral triangle as a cultural prototype is the result of this tradition, working its way into groupthink through representational practices.

An early methodological framework for examining visual images as powerful meaning-bearing structures, constituting a form of "visual rhetoric," was the one put forth by Group μ (1970)—a group of scholars interested in the rhetorical structure of all signs, not just verbal ones. The core notion developed by the group is that visual texts are interpreted in the same ways that rhetorical texts are. As Watson (1990: 42–3) has remarked, images and metaphors are two sides of the same mental system:

> They are slices of truth, evidence of the human ability to visualize the universe as a coherent organism. Proof of our capacity, not just to see one thing in another—as Blake saw the world in a grain of sand—but to change the very nature of

things. When a metaphor is accepted as fact, it enters mythology, but it can also take on an existence in the real world.

The reason why images evoke powerful emotional reactions may lie in how the brain processes images. A review of the relevant neuroscientific research by Kosslyn, Ganis, and Thomson (2001) revealed that mental imagery makes use of the same neural substrates as perception, namely the ventral and dorsal regions. Images of emotional events or themes (such as the Trump and Hitler youth ones) activate the autonomic nervous system and amygdala, leading to physiological changes, including an increase in heart rate, skin conductance, and breathing rate. Neuroscientific research has also come forth to explain why we are attracted to certain articles or posts, even if they contain fake information. Im, Varma and Varma (2017), for instance, discovered that people are more likely to believe articles and posts accompanied by images.

Ideological images such as those discussed here can be said to freeze a political moment in time, providing a basis for cultural memory to crystallize in interpretively differentiated ways. Consider the Messianic Trump image once again. Some might see in it the meaning of the QAnon storm; others may see it as the image of a con artist acting out the role that QAnon has proscribed for him; others still may see it is a political statement of strength. Barthes used the term *punctum* to explain how meaning varies, defining it as an incidental but personally meaningful detail in a photograph with respect to an image which produces an intensely subjective effect on the viewer; opposing it to the *studium*, which are the historical, social, or cultural meanings ascribed to the image (Barthes 1980). As Sonja Foss (2005: 150) has stated, it is the hidden symbolism of images that assigns the punctum or studium to them: "The image must be symbolic, [involving] human intervention," and as such will communicate different things to different audiences.

Epilogue

On May 19, 1933, the Nazi government enacted a law prohibiting the use of "symbols of German history, of the German state, and of the national revolution from being publicly used in a way that was likely to damage the feeling of dignity of these symbols." The legislation aimed to prevent companies, individuals, and groups from using the swastika and other Nazi symbols to promote themselves or their commercial goods and services without the approval of the regime. The swastika had become ubiquitous, put on products such as coffee and cigarettes, and postered on walls everywhere. The Nazis feared that its symbolic power would become diluted and even trivialized through such commercial and frivolous public uses (Swett 2014). Paul Tillich (1964: 59) noted that the Nazis were deeply aware of the power of a symbol such as the swastika to "point beyond itself" to something that they wanted to remain unspecifiable. When a symbol loses its emotional-connotative meaning its power to control ideology also becomes diminished—and this is what the Nazis clearly feared. Two years later, in September of 1935, at their annual rally in Nuremberg, the Nazis announced new legislation aimed at further disenfranchising Germany's Jews, declaring that the swastika flag would constitute the official flag of the German Reich and that Jews were banned from using or displaying the flag.

Decoding the interconnections among words, symbols, and images is the crux of semiotic network method, identifying the emotive source undergirding dangerous discursivity. As Peirce argued in *Illustrations of the Logic of Science* (1877), it is in the linkage of semiotic forms that beliefs are embedded and become habitualized. Without meaning to support beliefs there are no beliefs; and meaning is achieved semiotically via an interlinkage of rhetorical, symbolic, imagistic, and textual forms and artifacts. As discussed here, connecting the imagistic dots apophenically, guided by a conspiracy code, is what generates many false beliefs, which are sustained and reinforced by the distorted semiotic network of meaning related to the code. Apophanies can only arise within such networks, otherwise the "connect-the-dots" process would end up having no sense, just a random pattern, which Michael Shermer (2008) calls "patternicity," defining it as "patterns in meaningless noise."

This linkage is what leads eventually to the illusion of truth, which can be brought about by the connection of a rhetorically charged word, as evidenced by Putin's "denazification" ploy, combined with symbolism (the "Z" sign), and other semiotic strategies. Rhetoric lays out the key points in a cognitive map of hate (Korzybski 1933), while symbols and images become "legends" on that map. To extend the notion, a phrase such as "deep state" on that map can be seen as constituting a locus or punctum in Trump's attempts to establish a studium of mind control—to loosely paraphrase Barthes. The phrase takes on powerful meaning when it is connected to cabalistic codes and theories that have existed long before Trump. In that one phrase, allusions to a supposed sinister plot against Trump are given a concrete point on the conspiratorial map, conjuring up a secretive cabal of bureaucrats determined to sabotage the Trump agenda and Trump himself. So, to block the cabal from success, it was necessary to "drain the swamp" of the cabalists. It is the same code that was perniciously elicited by the "elders of Zion" phrase used against Jews since at least the turn of the twentieth century; and of Putin's denazification stratagem, which alluded to a cabal of Nazi leadership within Ukraine that was, as he put it, "running the country." As Geoffrey Nunberg (2018) has perceptively remarked, the deep state metaphor is an "elastic label" that "conforms to the intricate grammar of those conspiracy narratives" embedded in a particular ideology. It is this elasticity that makes the conflictual strategies discussed in this chapter elusive and thus hard to pin down and extinguish.

An interesting 1943 short film, titled *Don't Be a Sucker*, was produced by the US War Department and the Warner film studio as a way to warn people of the danger of the rise of Nazi sympathizers within the United States, cautioning audiences to beware of the language used to entice them into their fold. A young man is shown being duped by the persuasive rhetoric of a Nazi sympathizer who claims that all the "good jobs" in America were being taken by minorities, domestic and foreign. The young man then initiates a discussion with a refugee professor standing with him, who warns the youth that the same pattern of talk brought Hitler to power in Germany, splitting the country into groups, each one hating the other. As a cautionary tale, this film pinpoints the source of hate—rhetoric and its coded meanings.

Figure 2.6 Tweet from the Ukrainian Government, February 24, 2022.

It is relevant to note that a counter-strategy that might work psychologically and semiotically is meaning reversal, as was done by Ukraine the instant that Putin announced his special operation, as can be seen in Ukraine's official Twitter account, which showed a caricature of Putin being groomed by Hitler, implying that the Russian leader had similar dreams of domination (see Figure 2.6 above).

The tweet aimed to expose the ruse, showing who Putin really was, portraying him as a gnome-like personage caressed by his ideological mentor. This is clearly an attempt to reverse the denazification meaning, ascribing to Putin the real nazification of his own country.

The following line from *On Truth and Lies in a Nonmoral Sense* (1873), by Friedrich Nietzsche, summarizes the gist of the argument put forward in this chapter: "some people use language as a mask and create designed language that appears to reveal them but does not." Masking is the strategy behind words and phrases such as "denazification" and "deep state." They are coded verbal ruses, intended to create emotional dissonance. The power to either oppress or to liberate starts with words, reinforced by symbolic and imagistic counterparts.

3

Denial Discourses

Prologue

Michael Crichton's novel, *State of Fear* (2004), is about a conspiracy regarding global warming manufactured by scientists and intellectual liberal elitists to create public panic for self-serving reasons—namely, to promote a particular type of science agenda for funding reasons or to promote a liberal ideology as mainstream. To make the novel realistic, Crichton included footnotes, which he claimed provided a factual basis for his plot. They were actual scientific facts that he had collected, but which he had adapted in an opportunistic way to suggest the reverse of what they actually meant. The work was fiction, but it nonetheless led to the spread of climate change denial discourses and politics. In a congressional speech in 2005, Republican Senator James Inhofe erroneously (or falsely) described Crichton as a "scientist" and the book as a depiction of truth. What made the novel particularly attractive to far-right conservative ideology was that it fit in with political discourses that were coalescing in America about truth—a situation described several decades earlier by Hannah Arendt (1972: 4) as follows:

> The deliberate falsehood deals with contingent facts; that is, with matters that carry no inherent truth within themselves, no necessity to be as they are. Factual truths are never compellingly true. The historian knows how vulnerable is the whole texture of facts in which we spend our daily life; it is always in danger of being perforated by single lies or torn to shreds by the organized lying of groups, nations, or classes, or denied and distorted, often carefully covered up by reams of falsehoods or simply allowed to fall into oblivion. There always comes the point beyond which lying becomes counterproductive. This point is reached when the audience to which the lies are addressed is forced to disregard altogether the distinguishing line between truth and falsehood in order to be able to survive. Truth or falsehood—it does not matter which anymore, if your

life depends on your acting as though you trusted; truth that can be relied on disappears entirely from public life, and with it the chief stabilizing factor in the ever-changing affairs of men.

Although climate change denial existed before Crichton's novel, there is little doubt that his enormously popular and widely read book provided traction to the denial discursivity, pushing it more broadly throughout the Internet. The novel exemplifies how denial discourses work semiotically—it twists the meanings of scientific notions, using coded terms such as "hoax" and "cabal" to create an aura of sinister conspiracies behind the scenes. It also reverses the meanings of the words and symbols that climate scientists and environmentalists use to convey their warning messages, suggesting that the science behind global warming is fallacious, speculative, or incomplete. His insinuation of a scientific cabal promoting climate change as a fact can be seen in the following excerpt from the novel (Crichton 2004):

> Right now, scientists are in exactly the same position as Renaissance painters, commissioned to make the portrait the patron wants done, and if they are smart, they'll make sure their work subtly flatters the patron. Not overtly. Subtly. This is not a good system for research into those areas of science that affect policy. Even worse, the system works against problem solving. Because if you solve a problem, your funding ends. All that's got to change.

As far as can be told, this is one of the first insinuations that a cabal of scientists involved in researching global warming were part of a deep state conspiracy along with intellectuals, liberal politicians, and others. It became a key source of pseudo-justification used by Trump, who denied climate change throughout his presidency (and beyond). The cabal code introduced by Crichton did not stop at scientists, but included members of the Hollywood élite, the news media, the intelligentsia, and liberal politicians generally as conspiring together to maintain global power via fabrications such as climate change science. He suggests that global warming hysteria became a media "fad" because the reins of communication were in the hands of the members of the cabal, who have constantly used mainstream media to persuade the general public that climate change is real. In effect, Crichton suggests that climate change science is political discourse. The gist of the book's intent is summarized perceptively by Rick Piltz (2018) as follows:

> Every aspect of the novel seems designed to make up a sustained, scurrilous misrepresentation of the climate science community and the environmental movement. His environmentalists are either eco-terrorists planning to cause

a murderous disaster to further their sinister, authoritarian political aims, or they are ignorant fools and hypocrites. The leading climate scientists don't know what they're talking about, misrepresent their data, and trade their intellectual integrity for continued funding by bureaucrats with whom they are in collusion to mislead the world into believing that anthropogenic global warming and its impacts are real.

The focus in this chapter is on applying semiotic network theory to decoding denial discourses, which, as Crichton's novel shows, emerge through the manipulation of facts by using semiotic strategies, grounding these on a central code, such as the purported cabal whose agenda is to create global warming hysteria for self-serving ends. The danger is that such discourses are spreading more broadly today given the social media universe in which we now communicate, attracting larger and larger groups of people, who might believe that there is consensus on issues such as global warning, vaccinations, and other kinds of fact-based science and politics. Humans have an instinctive tendency to think and act like the majority in their group. As social beings, we are inclined to follow and accept the beliefs of others in order to fit in. This tendency, called social proof by psychologist Robert Cialdini in his 1984 book titled *Influence: The Psychology of Persuasion*, is seen in the propensity of people to copy others, or follow along with what others consider to be important. Social proof theory suggests that we often assume that other people are more informed or knowledgeable about something than we ourselves are. This belief is reinforced today by the number of followers, likes, shares, and views on websites and platforms, which lowers resistance to the effects of conspiratorial language. As Bertrand Russell (1950) insightfully remarked long before the Internet era: "Collective fear stimulates herd instinct, and tends to produce ferocity toward those who are not regarded as members of the herd."

The rejection of scientific or historical facts that are either undisputed or well-supported in favor of ideas that are controversial or fabricated is typically supported by political ideologues and demagogues whose ultimate aim is to grab power on the shoulders of believers in the denialism, as was the case in Trump's ascendancy to the presidency. Denialism allows such populist politicians to tap into fears and to activate defense mechanisms meant to protect the psyche of people against disturbing facts and ideas. Overstressing the dangers of denying science itself can further ensconce the denialism (Dodds 2021), whereby, as Arendt put it, "truth that can be relied on disappears entirely from public life."

The cases-in-point examined in this chapter are Holocaust, climate change, and pandemic denial. Denial discourses create confusion and generate social dissonance by producing a "perversion of reality," to use Baudrillard's (1981) apt phrase—namely the vague feeling that something is amiss and needs to be rectified. The discord, disharmony, confusion, and conflict that the discourses bring about erect a barrier to truth which divides people into an "us-versus-them" social dynamic, which is ultimately the most destructive outcome of denialism.

Holocaust Denial

There is little doubt that perhaps the most heinous scheme of the Nazis was their ethnic cleansing policy called the Holocaust, whereby some six million Jews were systematically murdered between 1941 and 1945, mainly in gas chambers located in extermination camps, although shootings were committed as well within Germany, throughout occupied Europe, and within territories controlled by Germany's allies. The word *Holocaust* comes from the Greek *holokauston*, a translation of the Hebrew word *'olah*, meaning a burnt sacrifice offered to God. This word was chosen, and gained wide usage, because in the extermination camps the bodies of the victims were consumed in crematoria or open fires. For the Nazis it was the "final solution" to the Jewish question. As a result of the Holocaust, genocide was made a crime punishable under international law by the United Nations in 1946.

Holocaust denial is any endeavor to negate the established facts of the Nazi genocide of Jews. Its psychological motivation is either based on a defense mechanism or, more likely, as the continued promotion of hatred against the Jews. In typical reverse-logic fashion, Holocaust deniers claim that the Holocaust was invented or exaggerated by the Jews themselves as part of a plot to advance their self-interests. Among other themes around which Holocaust denial discourses revolve is the false belief or mendacious claim that there were no extermination camps or gas chambers; yet another falsehood is that the number of Jews murdered is significantly lower than the accepted figures, which is more of a revisionist than a strictly denialist discourse.

The anti-Holocaust discourses started right after the Nuremberg Trials in 1946, spreading broadly today, given the global reach of social media, becoming a dangerous form of discourse worldwide. An abiding peril of Holocaust denialism is that it can also penetrate intellectual sectors where it is sometimes revised or downplayed. One example is found in academician David Hoggan's 1961 book, *Der erzwungene Krieg* ("The Forced War"), in which he claimed that

Germany had been the victim of an Anglo-Polish conspiracy in 1939, justifying Nazi anti-Semitic measures as reasonable responses, including fines imposed on the Jewish community to prevent what he called "Jewish profiteering." In his subsequent 1969 book, *The Myth of the Six Million*, Hoggan denied the Holocaust outright—a book that immediately caught on broadly with anti-Semitic sympathizers and cited to this day on alt-right and white supremacist social media platforms. Also influential in promoting Holocaust revisionism-denialism was Paul Rassinier, whose 1964 book, *The Drama of the European Jews*, continues to be highly popular among Holocaust deniers, especially since, ironically, Rassinier was himself a concentration camp survivor; and yet he was one of the first post-war intellectuals to promote Holocaust revisionism. It is difficult to explain why Rassinier took this stance, which seemingly denied his own Holocaust experience. Perhaps it is one of the most salient of all instances of a defense mechanism aiming to bury difficult memories. On the other hand, Rassinier may have calculated that he could gain legitimacy among certain academicians and intellectuals, since he asserted that he wanted to "bring people back to a sense of objectivity and, at the same time, to a better conception of intellectual honesty."

In terms of semiotic network theory, anti-Holocaust discourse can only gain its emotional power via the construction of a chain of meanings, made up of different kinds of signs that reference a cabal code in a connective way. For instance, the metaphorical framing of Jews as "parasites," organisms that live in other species, deriving nutrients from them, is found throughout Holocaust denial discourses. As Andreas Musolff (2010) has amply demonstrated, such biological metaphors have always influenced public perception of otherness, shaping racist ideologies. He argues that the Nazi metaphor of the German nation as a body that required rescuing from a deadly "poison" (another hate metaphor) constituted the "conceptual basis rather than a mere propagandist by-product of Nazi genocidal policies" (Musolff 2010: 34). The strategic goal of such language is to represent a political entity as an organic body that is subject to sickness because of parasites and poisons. Metaphor is powerful, clearly because it shapes perceptions of reality at an unconscious, unreflective level, which in turn has the ability to ignite passions against a group such as the Jews.

The parasite metaphor can be traced to Hitler's *Mein Kampf* (1925), in which he states:

> Never was a State founded by peaceful economy, but always only by the instincts of preserving the species, no matter whether they are found in the field of heroic virtues or sly cunning; the one results then in Aryan States of work and culture,

the other in Jewish colonies of parasites … With the Jew, however, this attitude is non-existent; therefore he never was a nomad, but always only a parasite in the body of other peoples.

To strengthen the metaphor, the Nazis spread images on posters portraying Jews iconically as parasitic vermin. In one caricature, from a September 1944 issue of *Der Stürmer*, we see a parasite crawling over the Earth—a clear allusion to the Jewish cabal code. The caption alludes to a passage from the Old Testament, "Thou shalt eat the nations of the Earth" (Roos 2014: 419). The parasite trope is based on the idea that the Jews were incapable of forming their own states and would therefore parasitically attack and exploit legitimate states, which was a major subtext in the denialism discourses of Rassinier and others in their attempts to blame Zionism for the Holocaust. This prejudicial idea finds its historical source in the medieval notion of the "usurious Jew" who sucked the blood out of people. Voltaire (1764) explicitly denied the Jews the capacity to establish their own culture and to achieve statehood. Herder (1791) reinforced this stereotypical portrait as follows, using the parasite metaphor (arguably for the first time):

> The people of God, to whom heaven itself once gave its fatherland, has been a parasitic plant on the tribes of other nations for millennia, almost since its creation; a race of clever negotiators almost all over the world who, despite all oppression, long nowhere for their own honour and home, nowhere for a fatherland.

The parasite strategy allowed the Nazis to justify their isolation of the Jews, forcing them to remain in ghettos, along with actual parasites. German authorities even posted quarantine signs at the entrance of these ghettos, warning people of the danger of contagious diseases. Given inadequate sanitation coupled with starvation rations, the warnings became a self-fulfilling prophecy, as the health of the Jews deteriorated in the ghettos, with typhus and other infectious diseases spreading throughout them. Nazi propaganda utilized these manufactured epidemics to justify isolating the "filthy" Jews from the larger population (Bein 1964). This combination of hateful dehumanizing rhetoric and imagery has a reifying effect on people's minds, especially when it is repeated constantly and spread ubiquitously, by which the relevant sign forms are felt to enfold more information than the surrogate sensory reactions they are designed to bring about, similar to Kafka's metamorphosis metaphor. The Nazis even produced a training booklet in 1944, *Der Jude als Weltparasit* ("The Jew as a World Parasite"), for their *Wehrmacht*, the unified armed forces of Nazi Germany from

1935 to 1945, projecting a sense of politicized legitimacy to their degrading representations, making them appear to the public to be right and proper, thus instilling a form of consent and mutual understanding, not coercion.

The Holocaust was thus rendered a politically legitimate strategy because it was conveyed as a huge parasitic extermination campaign. As Musolff (2010: 55) perceptively remarks, the rhetorical-imagistic strategy was "not just a propaganda ornament but was at the core of his [Hitler's] racist ideology … [an] integral part of the ideology that was necessary to make the Holocaust happen." As Bein (1964) has also argued, the demeaning, humiliating language illustrates how the Nazis fought a social-political war through a war of words. To ensure that they controlled meaning, the Nazis enacted changes to the German lexicon, so as to shape public opinion, including artificially created terms such as *Einvolkung* ("assimilation") and *Entjudung* ("de-Judaization") (Esh 1963).

As Wasniewska (2017: 48) has also emphasized, the Nazi use of the parasite metaphor was a powerful one, bolstering support for the Holocaust and, later, for its denial, spreading subsequently as one of the most used words in racist political discourses:

> The general people are parasites metaphor is aimed not only at degrading, demeaning, and dehumanizing an individual or group; it also serves as an argument justifying banishment and, in extreme cases, total annihilation of whoever happens to be the target. The categorisation of an outgroup as parasites is a prototypical example of semantic mapping between the source domain of biology and the social target domain, where the parasite is presented as a menace for two reasons: first, it feeds off the life force of the host, and second, it simultaneously infects the body with a deadly disease. The metaphor implies the urgent need to get rid of the parasite in order to save the host body, which makes it the weapon of choice in propaganda discourse advocating the total extermination of the enemy.

By spreading parasitic imagery throughout newspapers, magazines, and other print sources, the Nazis aimed to embed it deeply into groupthink, coupled with stereotypical images of male Jews with large aquiline noses, beady eyes, and large eyebrows, traced back initially to the Middle Ages (Marger 2008: 324). Some forms of Holocaust denialism are guided to this day by such imagery, having become an intrinsic part of anti-Semitic discourses (Hübscher and Mering 2020). In the social media universe in particular the stereotypes show up as memes, such as the so-called "Happy Merchant" meme that has circulated virally among anti-Semitic online groups, which originated in 2015 when a racist cartoonist uploaded the image on his social media platform, from where it spread globally. It depicts a Jewish man with heavily stereotyped facial features (such as those described above), greedily rubbing his hands together. It is often accompanied, in its iterations, with images of a rat or a cockroach, emphasizing the fact that the parasitic metaphorization strategy of the Nazis has become an embedded one.

The perception of Jews as parasitic beings is an unconscious subtext in the genre of Holocaust denial discourses that blame the Jews for perpetrating the Holocaust as a hoax. The Holocaust was legitimized as a way to eliminate those parasites which threatened the health of a nation. Politically inspired violence may have various sources, including economic ones, but it can also be motivated through the manipulation of minds via language, images, and false narratives, which make up the circuitry of hate-based semiotic networks, building upon a rescue fantasy from parasitic otherness. The manipulation, as the Nazis understood, echoing Machiavelli, had to have its foothold in historical memory, which is why they adopted the same stereotypical metaphors of Jews that were perpetrated in the medieval period—it is the same collective memory that continues to undergird the diffusion of the ancient stereotypes. As Stephen Smith (2014) has aptly observed:

> Historical memory is dangerous. In times of crisis, its demons emerge, ugly, toxic, and potentially lethal. When historical memory strikes, it is particularly insidious because it draws on precedents that have resonance—and therefore ring true—for the local population, and have chilling recall for the Jews themselves. All Jews and their descendants stand accused ... But who did what and why is not the point. Whatever the crisis, and whatever the cause, historical memory is always at hand to manipulate the truth ... myths of the Jews as a source of treachery prevail, even for those who neither know the past nor associate with the Jewish community. Their very existence represents a threat, even if no one quite knows why. As soon as the extremists in the balaclavas appear on the streets and recall the past and the untrustworthiness of the Jews, then they once again become the untrusted. No one asks about the veracity of the statements–past or present—and by not denouncing the perpetrators, the threat of the Jews becomes a present threat.

Machiavelli advocated an intensive study of the past, which he felt was a key to understanding the present, leading him to deny the classical opinion that virtuous politics always leads to the happiness of the populace. He viewed misery as "one of the vices that enables a prince to rule" (1513), understanding what the Nazis certainly did as well centuries later, namely that the ruler must adopt unsavory manipulative practices for the sake of the continuance of his regime.

Climate Change Denial

Michael Crichton, whose controversial book, *State of Fear*, was arguably the narrative stimulus that propelled climate change denialism throughout the Internet (above), made the following revelatory statement during a speech he gave in San Francisco in 2003, one year before the publication of the novel, which, taken out of context, appears to contradict its conspiracist theme (Crichton 2003):

> In the end, science offers us the only way out of politics. And if we allow science to become politicized, then we are lost. We will enter the Internet version of the dark ages, an era of shifting fears and wild prejudices, transmitted to people who don't know any better.

However, in the context of the whole speech, the actual meaning of the statement becomes clear. Crichton attacks environmentalists as fanatical zealots who refuse to listen to any contrasting "scientific" view. He goes on to describe environmentalism as a form of religion, not science: "Today, one of the most powerful religions in the Western World is environmentalism ... the religion of choice for urban atheists." The speech and the novel exemplify what a climate change denial discourse is about—blaming the climate scientists as producing false science for self-serving ideological purposes—it is they who have "politicized" science. One of the most prominent deniers of climate change was Donald Trump, who echoed Crichton's sentiments almost to perfection—taking advantage of the ever-spreading climate change denialist discourses among his followers. He thus presented himself as a true leader who fought against the "urban atheists" and their "religion of environmentalism." His frequent denials were coded attacks on the deep state and its liberal denizens, again mirroring Crichton, who are purportedly lying to people for their self-serving political objectives. Below is a typical example—the fact that hundreds of thousands "liked" the tweet was a sure sign that his denialism strategy was an effective one among his followers and supporters:

> In the East, it could be the COLDEST New Year's Eve on record. Perhaps we could use a little bit of that good old Global Warming that our Country, but not other countries, was going to pay TRILLIONS OF DOLLARS to protect against. Bundle up! (Tweet, December 28, 2017, 4:01 PM)

During his presidency, Trump became the self-appointed leader of the climate change denialists in the United States, transforming the anti-scientific discourse into political opportunism, taking charge of what Collomb (2014) describes as "the strong ideological commitment of small-government conservatives and libertarians to laisser-faire and their strong opposition to regulation." Online anti-science groups came out in full support of Trump's denialism, spreading conspiratorial theories related to climate change science broadly, including Crichton's accusation that there is no scientific consensus on global warming and that nefarious actors in the deep state are manufacturing and manipulating data to suppress dissent against them. This came to constitute the core semiotic code in climate change denial discourses, as a survey of various social media posts, blogs, and journalist articles conducted for the present purposes has revealed. Among the strategies discovered to convey the coded meaning, the following are typical ones:

- *Use of rhetorical questions.* This strategy is designed to raise doubts and thus to block true dialogue. For example, a Republican candidate for Congress stated in 2014 (in Bobic 2014): "I don't necessarily think the climate's changing, no?" Given the interaction with reporters that followed, where the candidate attempted to attenuate the implications of her statement, she answered her own rhetorical question in a way that typifies a large portion of climate change denialist discourse: "Is the climate changing? Yes it's changing, it changes all the time, we heard it raining out there." "I'm sure humans are contributing to it."
- *Use of pseudo-scientific jargon.* Pseudo-scientific jargon is common in the denial discourse; it is designed to make alternative scientific explanations (to the mainstream ones) plausible, echoing Crichton's overall approach. In a 2009 op-ed published in a conservative Danish newspaper, the claim was made that "the sun had entered a cooling cycle, and therefore the Earth would begin to cool as well" (Svensmark 2009). On a 2022 TikTok post, uploaded by a climate change denial group, the melting of glaciers was explained in a bizarre way as being caused by "cosmic pulses of galactic interactions" (in Silva and Thomas 2022).
- *Denialiasm buzzwords.* In speeches and posts, various anti-environmentalist buzzwords have emerged as R-nodes in the denialist semiotic network, including "resiliency," whereby it is claimed that the earth responds with resiliency to all kinds of catastrophic changes, including global warming. This is, in effect, a metaphor aimed at countering the arguments used by climate scientists to allow people to imagine how global warming is affecting the entire atmosphere.
- *Irony.* The use or irony to ridicule climate science is a common discursive practice, used often by Trump before and during his presidency. An example is a tweet he published on October 19, 2015: "It's really cold outside, they

are calling it a major freeze, weeks ahead of normal. Man, we could use a big fat dose of global warming!" In another tweet (January 29, 2014), Trump referred sarcastically to cold trends in areas of the United States that are normally warmer, suggesting that climate science is a hoax: "Snowing in Texas and Louisiana, record setting freezing temperatures throughout the country and beyond. Global warming is an expensive hoax!"

- *Claims of faked scientific data.* In 2002, the so-called Cooler Heads Coalition published an article claiming that hundreds of scientists had tampered data to support climate change theory in order to protect their research funding. In 2007, John Coleman recycled this conspiracy theory as follows (Coleman 2007): "Our universities have become somewhat isolated from the rest of us … So when these researchers did climate change studies in the late 90's they were eager to produce findings that would be important and be widely noticed and trigger more research funding." This is a primary discursive tactic used in climate change denial aiming to manufacture political and public controversy by disputing scientific consensus (Diethelm and McKee 2009).
- *Corrupted peer-review process.* Related to the previous strategy is the false claim that the peer-review process behind the publication of climate science studies has become corrupted by scientists seeking to suppress dissent. One of the first to suggest this was Frederick Seitz, in a 1996 article, in which he claimed that: "A comparison between the report approved by the contributing scientists and the published version reveals that key changes were made after the scientists had met and accepted what they thought was the final peer-reviewed version … Nothing in the [rules] permits anyone to change a scientific report after it has been accepted by the panel of scientific contributors."
- *Liberal extremism.* Many denialists claim that global warming is a hoax perpetrated by leftist radicals to promote their socialist ideology. In 2017, the denialist Senator, James Inhofe, made the following statement during a speech to the International Conference on Climate Change: "The liberal extremists are not going to give up. Obama has built a culture of radical alarmists, and they'll be back" (cited in Davenport 2017).
- *Personalization.* This strategy aims to attack key figures in the environmentalist movement directly, as political operatives. The one most attacked is Al Gore, the ex-Democratic Vice President, who became the central target of the denialists early on. During the 2000 presidential campaign, the Republican Party created ads falsely contending that Gore was profiting from pollution on his own property by allowing mining companies to mine zinc from land owned by him in his home state of Tennessee.

The linkage between verbal and nonverbal nodes in the network is what strengthens the belief in climate change as a hoax perpetrated by a cabal of scientists and liberal politicians, despite the fact that evidence for global warming due to human influence has been recognized by the national science academies of all the major industrialized countries. The false argument in climate change denialism is based, clearly, on the same type of cabal code used in Holocaust denialism, whereby a group behind the scenes aims to control the world, be they scientists or Jews. The discursive instantiations of the code continue in political and conspiratorial arenas. In a speech given to the US Senate in 2003 Inhofe (mentioned above) encapsulated the denialist view with the following rhetorical question: "With all of the hysteria, all of the fear, all of the phony science, could it be that man-made global warming is the greatest hoax ever perpetrated on the American people?" The 2007 television documentary, *The Great Global Warming Swindle*, put forth the very same point, claiming that global warming was a multi-billion-dollar worldwide industry, created by anti-industrial environmentalists.

What makes such conspiracism spread surreptitiously is that it comes at people constantly through all kinds of media, and especially via social media memes, with one meme alluding to another meme through iterations, which reinforce the denialism through a combination of apophenic and illusory truth symptomatologies. As Ryan Milner (2016) has argued, memes gain credibility because of the fact that they are collectively created and transformed by users across vast digital networks, generating a *sui generis* participatory hyperreal culture, which assigns plausibility to the denialism, especially since algorithms create feedback loops of similar content, reinforcing the credibility level of discourses perpetrated massively in this way. The memes are gradually woven together into larger and larger discourses, as evidenced by the millions of views and comments on different platforms with hashtags such as #climatehoax and #globalwarmingisfake. Hashtags constitute a means for deniers to affiliate with the ideas expressed in the content. This has led to what some linguists call "searchable talk," whose subtext is "Search for me and affiliate with my values" (Zappavigna 2018). As a result of the Internet, clearly, climate change denialism is no longer locatable within specific groups; it has become itself a form of identity politics. As Weddig (2022) has aptly put it: "Climate change denial has become woven into certain cultural, political, racial, and religious identities. It further traces the tactics for spreading climate change denial, like social media targeting and conspiracy theories designed to cast doubt on scientific findings." Trump understood all this during his presidency, using fear-mongering to instill both dread over the loss of jobs that would ensue from laws designed to protect the environment and suspicion of the aims of those who claim that climate change is real. It was during his presidency that climate change denialism became associated with the Trump-based MAGA (Make America Great Again) movement, allowing it to spread even more broadly.

On the surface, the movement seems simply to want the recovery of an idyllic past, free from the moral relativism of political liberalism associated especially with the presidency of Barack Obama, even though the idea behind it predates Trump. But below this surface, it enfolds a rejection of otherness—that is, of anyone who is not racially white, like the original American colonists. Trump realized from the outset of his 2016 election campaign that he could tap opportunistically into this fear of otherness destroying the "real America," starting with his "birther" claim that Obama was in reality a Muslim and was not born in the United States. His perpetration of this self-serving conspiracy theory had a powerful impact on those who were dissatisfied with the style of liberal government that Obama and his followers had espoused. The birther falsehood thus stoked an inner sense of resentment in a large group of people, making it virtually immune to counter-argumentation. Attempts to dispel the birther fabrication, in fact, have often gone awry among MAGA supporters, even after Trump had to begrudgingly admit that it was not true. The MAGA movement recalls Mussolini's cry for a recovery and revival of a country's great past—in his case, Italy's imperial Roman past. Mussolini even used the Roman hand salute at his rallies to evoke the symbolic importance of this past. Followers see Trump as a similar warrior-leader who has raised the MAGA flag, symbolizing a return to the real America. It is little wonder that Trump used the handle "@realDonaldTrump" for his Twitter communications.

It is relevant to note that Ronald Reagan used the expression "Make America Great Again" in 1980. But it was Trump who had an attorney register it as his trademark in July of 2015, using it as a rhetorical stratagem throughout his 2016 presidential campaign, from where it spread across the country as a battle cry for the recovery of a hegemonic white America.

Pandemic Denial

The cabal code used in denial discourses is operative as well in the last case-in-point discussed here—pandemic denialism, which takes on various rhetorical-symbolic forms. In its most common form, the discourse warns that "global élites" manufactured the Covid-19 pandemic to advance their "world order" aspirations, destroying American sovereignty and prosperity. References to this conspiracy (known as the "Great Reset") are found throughout alt-right social media platforms, coordinated thematically and communicatively via the #greatreset hashtag. Significantly, the denialism emerged as a semiotic distortion of the "Great Reset" initiative of the World Economic Forum, which introduced the term at its 2020 international conference to represent the need to reduce global inequality and advance environmental initiatives in the wake of the devastation of climate change and the coronavirus. The denialists saw this as "proof" that global élites were using the coronavirus and climate change science as a means to reorganize global societies and economies in order to control world order. In an October 2020 open letter addressed to President Trump that has since become a cornerstone for the Great Reset conspiracy, the Catholic Archbishop Carlo Maria Viganò wrote the following (in Viganò 2022):

> A global plan called the Great Reset is underway. Its architect is a global élite that wants to subdue all of humanity, imposing coercive measures with which to drastically limit individual freedoms and those of entire populations. In several nations this plan has already been approved and financed; in others it is still in an early stage. Behind the world leaders who are the accomplices and executors of this infernal project, there are unscrupulous characters who finance the World Economic Forum and Event 201, promoting their agenda.

The letter gave impetus to QAnon and other conspiracy groups to perpetrate the false claim that the coronavirus was a pretense to enforce lockdown measures, destroying businesses and weakening the economy, as well as stripping away freedoms, increasing mass surveillance practices in totalitarian-regime fashion, as well as forcing vaccines on Americans. Great Reset believers cast Trump as the only leader able to combat and defeat the cabal behind it. As Henry Giroux (2016) has so insightfully observed, cabalistic discourses are cognitively destructive because they deeply alter people's understanding of facts and reality, controlling their perceptual filters to the point where the believers of the falsehood will see nothing but what they are told to see by the congeners of the falsehood, leading to the acceptance of an alternative reality. The momentum that the Great Reset conspiracy achieved during Trump's presidency is proof of Giroux's assertion. Spurred on by Viganò's letter, pandemic denialists resisted public health measures, perceiving them as part of the Great Reset plot, delaying the resolution of the pandemic via the usual public health measures of the past, including prophylaxis (mask wearing, disinfection, hand washing) and vaccination.

The perpetration of cabalistic codes has always had the goal of derailing the ethical foundations of truth and facts in order to construct false realities and alternative political universes. These block critical thinking about crucial issues, encouraging emotional reactions to them instead, which lead to the acceptance of, and belief in, factually impossible things as equally valid. In Lewis Carroll's *Through the Looking-Glass* (1871), the White Queen encapsulates this type of thinking as follows: "Why, sometimes I've believed as many as six impossible things before breakfast."

In their book, *I Know Who Caused Covid-19: Pandemics and Xenophobia* (2021), Zhou Xun and Sander Gilman insightfully remark that "in times of stress such as during pandemics, ancient prejudices and primeval fear, always beneath the surface, can be brought to life to haunt us" (2021: x). In medieval Europe, the scapegoats for the bubonic plague were Jewish citizens, who were attacked by mobs as a result. In the early twentieth century, as cholera spread across Europe, the scapegoats were the lower classes, who were seen as unhygienic. Riots followed, as even the police and medical practitioners were assaulted and killed. Before the Great Reset code, the spread of pandemic conspiracy theories led to the coinage of the term *infodemic* to describe the crisis of misinformation that besets the politicization and racialization of pandemics. An infodemic—a blend of *information* and *epidemic*—refers to the rapid and far-reaching spread of misinformation about a disease, whereby facts, rumors, and fears are mixed together, making it difficult to separate the facts from the falsehoods (Mooney and Juhász 2020). The term was coined by David Rothkopf in a 2003 *Washington Post* article, in the context of the SARS outbreak. He characterized it as follows:

> [It] was not the rapid spread of simple news via the media, nor is it simply the rumor mill on steroids. Rather, as with SARS, it is a complex phenomenon caused by the interaction of mainstream media, specialist media and internet sites, and "informal" media, which is to say wireless phones, text messaging, pagers, faxes, and e-mail, all transmitting some combination of fact, rumor, interpretation, and propaganda ... [setting] off a chain reaction of economic and social consequences.

Today, the cabal code that undergirds denial discourses is difficult to eradicate because, as Sauter (2017) has remarked, social media and the Internet are an "apophenic machine," whereby "one thing leads to another, always another link leading you deeper into nothing and no place, floating through self-dividing and transmogrifying sites until you are awash in the sheer evidence that the internet exists." This machine is a conspiracy-in-the-making one, impelling believers to think that they came up with the "conspiracy insight" themselves, after connecting the semiotic dots (rhetorical, symbolic, imagistic). As a result, they tend to interpret any contrary evidence as actually confirming their belief, since they assume that the cabal is behind the "false evidence." The belief is bolstered by social-media algorithms—when someone clicks on a conspiracy-oriented post, the algorithm offers up similar posts, sites, and platforms, which contain more false information, perpetuating the cycle of falsity that becomes larger and larger. The infodemic thus spreads through minds, like the pandemic spreads through bodies—both are invisible and thus unavailable to perception.

Resistance to contrary facts is an attempt to counteract cognitive dissonance—coined and described initially by psychologist Leon Festinger in 1957, which he characterized as any attempt to attenuate or eliminate any cognitive discord between one's beliefs and contrary facts. To resolve the dissonance, people will seek out information that confirms their false beliefs, rather than reject them, avoiding information that is likely to be in conflict with them. Festinger found that people with strong beliefs and convictions will rarely change their minds. Festinger, Riecken, and Schacter (1956: 3) put it as follows:

> A man with a conviction is a hard man to change. Tell him you disagree and he turns away. Show him the facts or figures and he questions your sources. Appeal to logic and he fails to see your point … The individual will frequently emerge, not only unshaken, but even more convinced of the truth of his beliefs than ever before. Indeed, he may even show a new fervor for convincing and converting other people to his view.

So, counteracting a conspiracy such as the Great Reset one through facts and logic is rarely successful because of cognitive dissonance, especially since the Internet allows for the supporting misinformation to strengthen the conspiracy by its sheer massiveness. QAnon memes claiming that the World Economic Council is controlled by Jews who are using the Great Reset to set up a "One World Government" have spread to all kinds of online venues, making the conspiracy evermore difficult to eradicate, especially since the conspiracy links the historical Jewish cabal code to the one pertaining to climate scientists. This type of code linkage can be called inter-codability (discussed in Chapter 6). This is the tendency of semiotic codes to coalesce into larger codes, which can be called, for lack of a better word, meta-codes. The racial purity code of the Nazis, the conspiratorial code of climate scientists collaborating with liberal politicians, and the Great Reset theme in pandemic denialism all converge around the same cabal-based meta-code.

It is relevant to note that the English word *cabal* is derived from *Kabbalah*, the Jewish mystical interpretation of scripture. In European culture it became associated with occult doctrines and secretive cliques, starting with medieval French *cabale* and assuming, by the seventeenth century, its current meaning. The relevant event is traced to 1668, when a group of British King Charles II's ministers formed a "Cabal Ministry," which was an acronym of the names of the group members—Sir Thomas Clifford, Lord Arlington, the Duke of Buckingham, Lord Ashley, and Lord Lauderdale. They were the signatories of the Treaty of Dover that allied England to France in a prospective war against the Netherlands, and served as a cover for the Secret Treaty of Dover. The orthographic coincidence of the acronym to the word *cabale* established the notion of a clique of powerful people working behind the scenes to dominate the world.

QAnon followers overtly use the expression, "The Cabal," to refer to what they perceive as a secret worldwide élite organization of sinister political actors who espouse liberal views. On their official "Q News" online site, they have frequently linked the Cabal to the Great Reset, claiming that vaccines were not designed to save lives and to bring the pandemic toward its eventual end, but rather, as bioweapons concocted by the Cabal of corrupt government officials and drug companies, whose goal is to mutate the very genetic structure of the species. Uploaded on the site are videos with captions such as "Murder By Vaccine" and "Doctors and Nurses Giving the Coronavirus Vaccine Will Be Tried as War Criminals." The link between violence against health practitioners and these messages cannot be discarded, given that at the start of the pandemic these very same people were praised and lauded across the world. As Timberg and Dwoskin (2021) have remarked:

> QAnon, with its false claims about shadowy political forces and rampant pedophilia among Democratic leaders, is older than the pandemic, tracing its roots to anonymous postings in 2017. But the arrival of the pandemic last year supercharged QAnon's growth, as did former president Donald Trump's baseless allegations of widespread voter fraud.

One QAnon video claimed that tens of millions of people who had been vaccinated became "superspreaders" of Covid-19, which ironically the video calls a "hoax," contradicting itself. As Hay (2022) has observed, as the coronavirus started to recede, because of vaccinations, the QAnon denialist discourse simply evolved into a different version of the falsehood—a common trait of all forms of dangerous denialism; so, "rather than accept that the pandemic didn't precipitate the dystopia they predicted, several prominent conspiracy theorist channels argue that covid was actually just the first major attempt at—or phase in—the Great Reset."

The seemingly ingrained psychic archetype of cabals may have an evolutionary source, explained by evolutionary psychologists in terms of early tribes fearing what other tribes were plotting against them (Godfrey-Smith 2009). Studies of the epigenome—a dynamic layer of information associated with DNA that differs between individuals and can be altered through various experiences and environments—have revealed that genes are influenced by experiences and thus that the environment may shape the DNA in various ways (Carey 2013), suggesting that the biosphere and the semiosphere may have always been interactive agents in human evolution (Lotman 1991). One way to envision the process, from biological mechanisms to semiotic ones, is provided by Terrence Deacon (2021: 537), who suggests that the structural features of DNA molecules "have provided semiotic affordances that the interpretive dynamics … are not the source of biological information but are instead semiotic artifacts onto which dynamical functional constraints have been progressively offloaded during the course of evolution."

So, whether or not the cabal is an archetype traceable to our evolution, it is the intentional manipulation of the cabal code that is of relevance here. While the dictators of history have blamed secret cabals for bringing about dystopia in the world, using a reversal strategy, blaming their victim, though they themselves were the ones who made up the real cabals, allowing them to take control of the reins of power via historical happenstance and the manipulation of meaning via distorted semiotic networks of signs. Stalin, Hitler, Mussolini, Trump, and Putin are just a small selection of historical personages who have deployed the reverse cabalism strategy—as a means to attack those whom they wanted to reject or eliminate. As the research for this book has revealed, to some extent, the cabal meta-code is to be found everywhere, motivating events in history. The meta-code theme is also found commonly in literature, including in modern times, such as in Dan Brown's *The Da Vinci Code* (2003) and other conspiratorial novels. Pseudo-scientific works also peddle cabalism, from the Illuminati myth, a purported secret sixteenth-century Bavarian cabal, alleged to be an all-powerful secret society that controls the world to this day, to the Priory of Sion, a hoax created as an esoteric puzzle, for people to connect the historical dots via false information. At times fiction and pseudo-science merge to produce conspiratorial discourses. An example concerns a late eighteenth-century American writer, named Charles Brockden Brown. When a yellow fever epidemic hit New York, Brown caught the disease, surviving it. Upon discovering that a medical doctor (whom he knew) had died from it he took out his grief by writing dark tales about secret societies, published in *Wieland* (1798), spreading fears of an Illuminati cult throughout America, which became the basis of conspiratorial books about the cabal, such as William Cobbett's *Detection of a Conspiracy* (1798). These helped spread the baseless rumor that the Illuminati's members were part of a global élite which aimed to harm America, as evidenced by the yellow fever outbreak.

As Frederick Kaufman (2020) has aptly remarked in reference to the yellow fever pandemic:

> When medical systems fail, so do logic and reason, clearing a path for contagions of fear and blame. The Illuminati panic, exploding in a country battered by a covert enemy, which experts could neither explain nor contain, brought to the fore a theme that historians would later call the "paranoid style" of American politics ... [which] flourishes amid the chaos brought on by covid-19.

In *Proofs of a Conspiracy* (1798), John Robison, a Scottish professor, was likely the first to spread the story of the Bavarian Illuminati, founded in 1776 by Adam Weishaupt, a professor at Ingolstadt, as an underground cabal that used Masonic lodges or set up their own lodge as a cover for their activities. Robison laid the groundwork for current conspiracy discourses by implicating the Illuminati as responsible for the French Revolution. The Bavarian Illuminati were an actual group of intellectuals, who held radical atheist, anti-monarchist views. Thanks to Robison, and more recently to the novels of Dan Brown, today, the Illuminati have today become a byword for a secret society that runs America, and other nations, behind the scenes. It is significant to note that such cabalism is not restricted to the discourses of radical right-wing groups. Conspiracy theories are blind to politics. QAnon is hardly a traditional alt-right ideological group; it has members who associate with left and right political ideas. Distrust in government and big business comes from all parts of the political spectrum, but, ever since Trump's reign, has become mainly a right-wing discursive phenomenon.

Epilogue

Denial discourses are hardly matters of differences of opinion, as Crichton suggested cleverly in his novel *State of Fear*. They affect people's minds profoundly, motivating distrust and promoting false beliefs that there are cabals behind the scenes that are running the world. They have spread falsehoods about such dire events as the Holocaust, global warming, and pandemics in order to shape politics and people through fear. The semiotic view espoused here is that false beliefs could only have arisen from the promulgation of an archetypal cabalistic code, which, once accepted as true, filters how reality is construed, putting up cognitive-emotive barriers to counter-arguments. As Crichton argued throughout his novel, scientific counter-arguments are nothing more than attempts by the cabalists, or those who are duped by them, to obfuscate the supposed truth. Significantly, critiques of the novel have not been effective, as it continues to be popular among conspiracists to this day. The antidote to denial conspiracism is, clearly, not to attack believers directly. As history has repeatedly shown, this has never been successful; it just exacerbates the division between people. The view taken here is that by exposing how denial discourses twist the meanings of signs, a more objective two-way dialogue can hopefully emerge.

Interestingly, semiotic approaches, although not identified as such, seem to have been used intuitively in the past to warn people of the dangers associated with global warming. As far back as the early twentieth century, images were used as visual metaphors to show the deleterious environmental effects of burning coal, as the following image from a 1912 issue of *Popular Mechanics* bears out (Figure 3.1 below).

Visual-iconic signs may well be the most effective ones to be used in emphasizing dangers, rather than dialogical interactions, which might end up exacerbating conflicts, not resolving them (Ranta 2016). Key to the semiotic approach is exposing the cabalistic code on which most (if not all) forms of denialism are grounded, and how the sign forms that are used in the construction

Figure 3.1 Image from *Popular Mechanics*, 1912.

of the semiotic networks supporting denial discourses are based on the code. For instance, one way to expose the danger of the blood libel code used against the Jews is to focus on the meaning of blood, and how it has been distorted by the code, which is an anti-Semitic trope, emerging largely in the medieval period, that falsely and perniciously accused Jews of murdering Christian children in order to use the blood for their religious rituals. This accusation has resulted in the persecution of Jews throughout history. QAnon has clearly adopted the blood libel trope, extending it to a larger cabal, including a perverse sect of Democratic politicians and Hollywood élites who, the conspiratorial group claims, are harvesting adrenochrome from children through satanic ritual abuse in order to achieve immortality.

In the *Meaning of Folklore* (2007), Bronner and Dundes showed how blood symbolism can insidiously penetrate minds through its suggestive power, as well as, on the other hand, how it can be used as a counter strategy to vanquish anti-Semitism. Their analysis of the historical meanings of blood is, in itself, a penetrating semiotic one (Bronner and Dundes 2007: 383):

> As a legend, the narrative drew attention to itself because of its bizarre content, frequently thought to be true when it was circulated orally in song and story, in print and image, and even in courts of law. Or else its legendary context raised questions, if not doubts, about a central belief in blood sacrifice, conveyed in the actions of the text. Structurally, its ending invited commentary on the unusual feature of murder-lust, resulting from inhuman or un-Christian ritual uses of blood. The blood libel legend drew listeners from members of the dominant group and possessed symbolic characteristics because Jews, as a marginalized group, often conveyed a degree of mystery. It was as if a secret was revealed about their true nature, encapsulated in key actions and objects within a narrative.

Never before has the semiotic approach been as critical as it is today, given the omnipresence of conspiratorial groups like QAnon, who have adopted codes, such as the blood libel one, twisting them for their own self-serving purposes. In one of the first posts by Q, in 2017, the anti-Semitic worldview of the group became saliently obvious: "Trump is gonna night of long knives the jews!" clearly referencing Hitler's bloody purge of rival power centers inside and outside the Nazi Party. While QAnon has already started to recede to the margins (at the time of writing this book), and will dissipate in the ether of cyberspace, its toxic impact on national politics might be an indelible one. Dangerous discourses always leave traces in the transmission of sign structures from one generation to the next—hence the continued perpetuation of Holocaust denial. Whoever controls meaning controls the mind—as Orwell put it.

It is clearly imperative to deconstruct dangerous denial discourses if it is ever going to be possible to ensconce an ethical system of governance and human interaction in societies across the world. As Tharoor (2015) aptly remarks, "There was a time, though, when 'Mein Kampf' was not just the repugnant treatise of the twentieth century's greatest villain … More than seven decades ago, Hitler and the message of Nazism had great traction, and it required clear-eyed thinkers to cut through its seductions." Significantly, Orwell wrote a review of *Mein Kampf* in 1940, which revolves around a central idea discussed in this chapter—namely that of reverse projection, whereby the victimizer portrays himself as the victim:

> It is a pathetic, dog-like face, the face of a man suffering under intolerable wrongs. In a rather more manly way it reproduces the expression of innumerable pictures of Christ crucified, and there is little doubt that that is how Hitler sees himself. The initial, personal cause of his grievance against the universe can only be guessed at; but at any rate the grievance is here. He is the martyr, the victim, Prometheus chained to the rock, the self-sacrificing hero who fights single-handed against impossible odds. If he were killing a mouse he would know how to make it seem like a dragon. One feels, as with Napoleon, that he is fighting against destiny, that he can't win, and yet that he somehow deserves to.

If the hidden meanings of nefarious discourses are not tackled head on, then the real danger is that historical amnesia will emerge, leading to an inability to recognize the recycling of hate-based codes. Without this ability to "see" through them, not only will they continue to proliferate, but will arguably become even more dangerous. In her 2015 book, *Mind Change*, Susan Greenfield warned of the danger of developing a habitual amnesia in the age of the Internet, referring not so much to the loss of memory as to the loss of how and when a memory was created. Those who have never known a world without the Internet may be losing interest in factual, truth-based historical memory, she claims, because of the unprecedented bombardments of audiovisual stimuli on the mind on a daily basis, which can shape the chemistry of the brain, placing a premium on information *du moment*, rather than on deep knowledge and understanding of historical issues. This may explain why QAnon-type conspiracy groups gain so much traction—they spread misinformation broadly by making it seem relevant in the moment, as it quickly recedes to the social margins. In this constantly mutable universe of meaning, a code such as the blood libel one is seen as "new information," suggesting something sinister behind the scenes—hence the perpetuation of the myth over and over. That is the real danger we face today.

4

Decoding Big Lies

Prologue

Interest in lies and especially in powerful figures renowned for their lying has intrigued philosophers, artists, and writers since antiquity. One of the most famous personages of ancient literature, who was renowned for his clever lies, cunning, and resourcefulness, was Odysseus, the central figure of the Homeric epic, *The Odyssey*. As O'Connor (1975) has aptly pointed out, Odysseus used lies effectively as a protective strategy, not only to keep his identity a secret, but also, and more pertinently, to invoke specific feelings and opinions in the people to whom he lied, manipulating language to make them question reality and thus to think along the lines his lies had laid out. When Odysseus returned to his own kingdom after ten years of wandering, he continued to lie habitually, as if driven to do so by some inner compulsion, manipulating anyone who came into his sphere, including his wife, Penelope.

As this ancient story implies, lying to control others and take advantage of a situation requires the ability to manipulate or distort the meanings of words and other types of signs, so as to make something that is not true, believable (Walcott 1977). Odysseus is described in the story as "many-sided," "resourceful," "devious," and "subtle" by his very nature. His counterpart in the Realpolitik of Athens was Cleon, as discussed previously, who presented himself as a populist, despite the fact that he was an aristocrat himself, using mendacity and deception to endear himself to the *hoi poloi* of the city. Cleon was elected in 424 BCE, using oratory that resonated with people, crafting it to reflect their irate feelings against the state, instilling a mistrust of intellectuals and even aristocrats opportunistically in their minds, suggesting that they were the liars, responsible for all the ills that were endemic to society. Cleon's strategy was essentially that of projection, in the sense of attributing to others mendaciously what he himself said and did.

The same manipulative strategy has been used throughout time, destroying ethics and often altering the course of history, of which the most lethal example was Hitler's projective tactic of blaming the Jews as consummate liars. As far as can be told, he was the one who introduced the term "big lie" (*große Lüge*) as a lie so colossal that people cannot help but believe it, since he saw common people as basically malevolent, simplistic, and credulous, and thus easily duped into accepting big lies as factual (from *Mein Kampf* 1925):

> People in the very bottom of their hearts tend to be corrupted rather than consciously and purposely evil, and that, therefore, in view of the primitive simplicity of their minds, they more easily fall a victim to a big lie than to a little one, since they themselves lie in little things, but would be ashamed of lies that were too big. Such a falsehood will never enter their heads, and they will not be able to believe in the possibility of such monstrous effrontery and infamous misrepresentation in others; yes, even when enlightened on the subject, they will long doubt and waver, and continue to accept at least one of these causes as true. Therefore, something of even the most insolent lie will always remain and stick—a fact which all the great lie-virtuosi and lying-clubs in this world know only too well and also make the most treacherous use of.

As a gross distortion of the truth, Hitler claimed that the big lie technique had been used by the Jews throughout their history. His goal was to turn sentiment against the Jews as manipulators and tricksters. In 1941, Joseph Goebbels used this very same form of propaganda against Winston Churchill, writing: "The English follow the principle that when one lies, one should lie big, and stick to it. They keep up their lies, even at the risk of looking ridiculous." Hitler and Goebbels had clearly understood that lying is a powerful political tool, recalling Machiavelli's assertion in *The Prince* that a successful ruler "must be a great liar [because] a deceitful man will always find plenty who are ready to be deceived."

Early in life, as we develop the ability to use language for social interaction, we realize instinctively that lying can help us avoid negative consequences, evade trouble, circumvent hurtful truths, and so on. No one teaches a child to lie; it emerges spontaneously during infancy as an early act of manipulation of language to shape social interactions. As Richard Wright observes in *The Moral Animal* (1995), lying involves the ability to understand what is in someone else's mind in order to be able to deceive that person through some clever verbal tactic so as to gain some personal advantage. Whatever the evolutionary-developmental truth of the matter, it is clear that some lies are more destructive than others, especially the big lies of political manipulators. Hitler's notion of "big lie" refers, in fact, to something that transcends the simple functions of ordinary lies, indicating a political strategy unto itself. This chapter will discuss big lies from the perspective of semiotic network theory, which can expose how the big lie is constructed on the basis of a hidden code and the circuitry of sign forms that are associated with it.

Lying has marked key points in human history, suggesting that it may indeed be an evolutionary trait. The fall from Paradise, as recounted in the Book of Genesis, ultimately comes from a temptation induced by the first liar of the heavens, Lucifer, who is described in John 8:44 as follows: "He was a murderer from the beginning, and abode not in the truth, because there is no truth in him; he is a liar, and the father of it." The biblical story makes two major points about human nature: (1) since their origins, humans have been vulnerable to lies, which weaken their ability to grasp reality; and (2) the human species has used lying to help it separate itself evolutionarily from other species. In an interesting article, Daniel Dor (2017: 44) offers the following relevant observation in this regard:

> Without the lie, language would not be as complex as it is, linguistic communication would be much simpler, the cognitive requirement of language would not be so heavy, and its role in society would be radically different ... Lying and language came to be entangled in a never-ending co-evolutionary spiral, which changed the map of communicative relationships within communities, and participated in shaping our languages, societies, cognitions and emotions. We evolved for lying, and because of lying, just as much as we evolved for and because of honest communication.

Whatever the truth, it can be argued that the emergence of ethical systems across the world may have been motivated by the need to counteract the deleterious effects of lying. Aristotle held that the destructive effects of lies and deceit constituted humanity's greatest weakness, seeing virtues such as justice, charity, and generosity as necessary antidotes to these effects (in Aristotle 2009). Immanuel Kant (1781) even saw duty to society as based on rejecting deceitfulness and embracing honesty and integrity as central to the maintenance of functional societies. To cite Carson (2010: 67), "Kant claims that lying is always wrong, no matter what. He is probably the most well-known defender of an absolute prohibition against lying in the history of Western philosophy." Throughout history, ethical behavior has been hailed as the only protection against lying—the only way to counteract our apparent instinct to lie and our vulnerability to lying.

It is disconcerting to note that the same reverse projection strategy used by Hitler and Goebbels is used commonly today in radicalized politics. A well-known recent example is Dinesh D'Souza's book, *The Big Lie: Exposing the Nazi Roots of the America Left* (2017), in which he claims that left-wing ideologies in American politics have a Nazi origin—a claim he has used constantly to support Donald Trump, the prototypical big liar, as a way to distract people from Trump's own mendacious behavior and to implant the myth of a cabalistic deep state further into American groupthink. As in all dangerous discursive strategies, such reversals inject unethical meaning in people's minds via the deceptive use of semiotic linkages. These allow the big liar to "make sense" (literally), and thus to control people's minds by a kind of semiotic "remote control." As Zachary Jacobson (2018) has aptly observed, the reversal strategy threatens the stability of a polity—a strategy that has been effective throughout history, as the case of Nazism and Hitler's big lie in particular has made saliently obvious—indeed, the takeover of German society by the Nazis would not have occurred without this strategy:

> Adolf Hitler first defined the Big Lie as a deviant tool wielded by Viennese Jews to discredit the Germans' deportment in World War I. Yet, in tragically ironic fashion, it was Hitler and his Nazi regime that actually employed the mendacious strategy. In an effort to rewrite history and blame European Jews for Germany's defeat in World War I, Hitler and his propaganda minister accused them of profiting from the war … The Nazis built an ideology on a fiction, the notion that Germany's defeat in World War I could be avenged (and reversed) by purging the German population of those purportedly responsible: the Jews.

Hitler even referred to Schopenhauer as an attempt to ground his own mendacity about the Jews on an authoritative pseudo-philosophical basis (from *Mein Kampf* 1925):

> From time immemorial, however, the Jews have known better than any others how falsehood and calumny can be exploited. Is not their very existence founded on one great lie, namely, that they are a religious community, whereas in reality they are a race? And what a race! One of the greatest thinkers that mankind has produced has branded the Jews for all time with a statement which is profoundly and exactly true. Schopenhauer called the Jew "The Great Master of Lies." Those who do not realize the truth of that statement, or do not wish to believe it, will never be able to lend a hand in helping Truth to prevail.

Signs of Deception

Lying is a twisting of the referential codes of signs and sign systems, away from their usual range of meaning. Umberto Eco (1976: 7) once famously defined semiotics as the discipline which, in principle, should study "everything that can be used in order to lie." As Polish semiotician Jerzy Pelc (1992: 249) also put it:

> Those who lie, always use signs. There is no lying without the use of signs. Lying is a semiotic activity, with a sender and a receiver. It is thus an activity taking place in society.

Interestingly, Augustine of Hippo, a proto-founder of sign theory, wrote two books on lying—*De mandacio* and *Contra mendacio* (Deferrari 1952). Augustine divided lying into eight categories according to the effects that it brings about, including positive ones, such as downplaying mistakes someone else might make for kindness or charitable reasons (Gramigna 2020). He concludes, however, that most lies are unethical signs "to which no real state of things corresponds" (Eco 1976: 58). The constant deformation and distortion of the referential systems associated with signs lead to the crystallization of alternative meaning systems associated with the same signs, which bring about a collapse of the mind's ability to assess information as real or false, recalibrating the mind's filters according to the contents of the lie. As Rodríguez-Ferrándiz (2019) puts it, an effective lie is a strategy that "serves the purpose of extortion, manipulation, and war." Evolutionary psychologists see lying as a particular form of intelligence, called rather aptly, "Machiavellian intelligence," defined as the ability to decipher other people's thoughts and influence them through deceptive language (Waal 1982). Big lies are particularly effective in breaking down the normal referentiality of signs and sign structures for self-serving purposes. This form of intelligence is explained by Byrne (1995: 195) as follows:

> The essence of the Machiavellian intelligence hypothesis is that intelligence evolved in social circumstances. The individuals who are favoured are the ones who are able to use and exploit others in their social group, without causing disruption and potential group fission liable to result in naked aggression. Their manipulations might as easily involve co-operation as conflict, sharing as hoarding–but in each case the end is exploitative and selfish. Consistent with the Machiavellian intelligence hypothesis, social species of primate display both complexity of social manipulation and considerable knowledge of social information. This social complexity needs to be fully appreciated in order to understand the strength of the case for Machiavellian intelligence.

To reiterate, a big lie can be defined as a sign that denies the established referential range of signs, altering the semiotic network in which it occurs normally, so as to allow for a control of its meaning. The big liar keenly understands, in other words, how to distort the normal referential linkages between signs and meaning (Nuessel 2013). A lie can be characterized as a semiotic illusion, created by a derailment of meaning ranges and their redirection to the deceptive range that the liar is constructing. The master liar is thus a master illusionist, who performs tricks with semiotic systems deflecting their referential linkages onto his self-made system. Like a magic act on stage (Macknik, King, Randi, and Robbins 2008), the trickery involves tapping into the ingrained habit of mind of equating reality with the semiotic maps used to represent it, essentially redrawing the map to alter the perception of reality. In effect, the effectiveness of lying indicates that perceiving reality is not a simple matter. The brain does not see the whole picture, so it constructs a picture of reality standing for what things are supposed to look like. Liars, like stage magicians, capitalize on this process. Lies work only because the master liar knows intuitively how we look at the world, and even though we might know that we are being lied to, we still cannot see through the lie, suggesting that the liar has the ability to reach deeply into the mind.

The skillful use of mendacity and deceit in politics to persuade or dissuade others has many dangerous aims, among which is the goal of duping people who have detected the deception into silence or compliance. The liar knows that if his lie is big enough, and is believed by many, it can also instill fear in those who see through the liar, because they know intuitively that the liar can utilize lying and deceit against them strategically, destroying their reputations in the process. Another primary aim is that big political lies enhance the chances of the liar to rise to leadership by forging followers, allies, and alliances. Machiavelli saw this as a powerful form of political psychology—a way to use words to circumvent reason. He put it as follows (Machiavelli 1513):

> Everyone admits how praiseworthy it is in a prince to keep his word, and to behave with integrity and not with craft. Nevertheless our experience has been that those princes who have done great things have held good faith of little account, and have known how to circumvent the intellect of men by craft, and in the end have overcome those who have relied on their word.

Interestingly, prefiguring Hitler's biological metaphors (Chapter 2), Machiavelli portrayed the state as an "organism" with the prince as the "head" of the body. A "healthy" state was orderly and in balance, allowing its denizens to experience happiness and security. An "unhealthy" state was disorderly and unbalanced, requiring strong measures to restore its health. The prince must know how to dupe people into believing that only he, and he alone, can restore the state to health. To do this, he cannot be bound by traditional ethical norms. He should be concerned only with strategies and actions that will lead to his successful overtake of the state. It is ironic to note that Machiavelli may not have taken his own advice. He had himself organized a political takeover of Medici-controlled Florence in 1512; but his coup ultimately collapsed. The Medici family was restored to power, and as a consequence Machiavelli was arrested, tortured, and imprisoned on suspicion of plotting against the family.

A key condition for a big lie to work, emphasized by Machiavelli, is that it must be directed at specific groups seen as undesirable, calling them "liars," whereby the victim is portrayed as the victimizer. As discussed several times, this projection stratagem was used by Hitler in *Mein Kampf*, where he described the Jews and Marxists as skilled in the art of falsehood:

> But it remained for the Jews, with their unqualified capacity for falsehood, and their fighting comrades, the Marxists, to impute responsibility for the downfall precisely to the man who alone had shown a superhuman will and energy in his effort to prevent the catastrophe which he had foreseen and to save the nation from that hour of complete overthrow and shame. By placing responsibility for the loss of the world war on the shoulders of Ludendorff they took away the weapon of moral right from the only adversary dangerous enough to be likely to succeed in bringing the betrayers of the Fatherland to Justice.

The same projection strategy was used by Donald Trump in his attempt to cling on to power after having lost re-election in 2020, claiming that the deep state "liars" had "stolen the election" from him, using subterfuge, iniquity, and outright fraud, whereas the actual big liar was Trump himself, who used all kinds of deceptive strategies and even outright immoral activities to hold on to power. There is little doubt that his big lie resulted in the incentivization of his supporters to attack the US Capitol on January 6, 2022. What is disconcerting is that even after the attempted coup, which was highlighted abundantly across the mainstream media, Trump's fervent supporters either see the attempted coup as a legitimate part of cultural warfare, denying that it ever occurred as reported, or else that it was a false flag operation of the deep state.

The psychological power of big lies to control people's beliefs and cognitive processes is a primary reason why totalitarian states have been successful, for a time, to hold on to power; which is why they invariably establish Ministries of Truth to control the meaning system which big lies generate. As Andrew Weiss (2022) has argued, when a big liar perpetrates lies constantly, they mutate into a discourse that is perceived as legitimate and truthful. This is why, Weiss suggests, lying is so intrinsic to Putin's construction of a political culture of acquiescence and subservience to official discourses, since it allows him to control meaning and to ensure that, even though people might know he is lying, they will ignore it because they too are immersed in that culture—which is called *vranya* in Russian, loosely defined as knowledge that lies are part of political culture and accepted as such. For example, Putin's lie that NATO's enlargement is what forced Russia to invade Ukraine is seen as part of presenting a situation in terms of *vranya*, and a means to intimidate both his own citizens and outsiders, as Bort (2022) points out:

> The Kremlin uses transparent lies to project brazenness at home and abroad. The lies enhance its powers of intimidation and demonstrate that Moscow sets its own rules. ... transparent lying is a way for the Kremlin to troll Western elites and turn the tables on them for supposed hypocrisy, policy mistakes, and attempts to impose their values on others. On such occasions, the Kremlin appears to be inviting its domestic supporters and foreign sympathizers to join in on the joke.

In such a political culture, there emerges a feeling of futility with regard to the expression of dissent. Charged terms such as "denazification" are semiotic reins that allow Putin to restrain and even repress contrasting opinions, being also keenly cognizant of the repetition principle in lying (repeating the same lie over and over in all types of media) and performing the lie publicly in a consistent manner—especially via rallies and other large public gatherings.

Neuroscientific research strongly suggests that, when people are exposed to such systemic lies, the brain's ability to discern between truth and falsity is diminished considerably. In 1991, psychologist Daniel Gilbert presented evidence to show that lies change neural processing in three phases: (1) the lie is held temporarily in storage as truth, as (2) the brain avoids the "mental certification process" because it takes time and energy to decipher a lie, and so, (3) the brain involuntarily accepts the lie as truth. As the lie gets repeated, this process becomes habitual, turning the lie into a form of alternative truth (Ofen et al. 2017). Over time, this has the ability to generate an alternate reality in the mind, where signs and their linkages are perceived as mapping this illusory world, as their conventional referential systems collapse under the weight of lies.

Alternative Truth

The goal of the strategy of big lies is to inject into believers a semiotic system that generates alternative truths, whereby the lies not only disrupt the conventional relations between signs and their meanings, but redirect them in a way that is controlled by the liar. The term alternative truth is used here to indicate the effect that systemic lying might produce, whereby people come to perceive the redirected and even fabricated range of meanings that lies are intended to generate as revealing hidden truths, as if the lies were the red pills of *The Matrix* that flesh them out. This creates a sense of alternative truth to conventional truth—hence the term—which is the only truth that will eventually be accepted. By making lies appear to be red pills, the consummate liar is the one who, like Morpheus (which in Greek mythology was the god of dreams), presents himself as the one who will open up people's eyes. The result is that different or alternative truths become inserted into cognitive states as plausible, destroying the normal assumption that communication is ethical in the norm. Big lies can thus be said to trap true believers, and those who want to believe for self-serving reasons, in the clutches of the big liar, who then exerts enormous emotional power over people and, by extension, targeted segments of society. This creates the conditions for a political takeover by the liar, whose true plans remain intentionally obscure.

The notion dovetails considerably with Baudrillard's (1981) concept of hyperreality, the inability to distinguish between reality from its semiotic representation. This produces a cultural system based on fragmentations of meaning, whereby signs and sign structures are viewed as having multiple, alternative meanings. The creation of alternative truth systems has occurred since the beginning of history. It has always been a part of organizations that depend on it to survive, including organized criminal ones who create alternative truth to justify their illicit activities, portraying them as correct. The word "Mafia" appeared in an 1868 dictionary, where it is defined as "the actions, deeds, and words of someone who tries to act like a wise guy." As sociologist Diego Gambetta (1993: 4) points out, the term was a largely fictitious word, "loosely inspired by the real thing," that "can be said to have created the phenomenon." It was, in other words, a classic case of the fabrication of a reality, which becomes believable after the fact, gaining credibility over time. People at the time knew that criminal gangs existed, but they were perceived essentially as groups of street thugs. The Sicilian name *mafiusu* was probably being bandied about to provide a name for these gangs. When it became a veritable label, it literally culled the Mafia into social existence, catapulting it into a semiotic category in the minds of people and, thus, influencing its evolution into a major criminal organization. The case of the Mafia reveals an intrinsic principle of semiotics—there is no reality without a name (sign) for it. It is worthwhile repeating here what the linguist Edward Sapir (1921: 75) wrote about this, since the link between language and reality is a relevant one in any discussion of lies:

Human beings do not live in the object world alone, nor alone in the world of social activity as ordinarily understood, but are very much at the mercy of the particular language system which has become the medium of expression for their society. It is quite an illusion to imagine that one adjusts to reality essentially without the use of language and that language is merely an incidental means of solving specific problems of communication or reflection. The fact of the matter is that the "real world" is to a large extent unconsciously built up on the language habits of the group.

A big lie fabricates an "alternative" to the "real world." The Mafia is thus born of a lie. Criminal groups existed in Sicily long before the coinage of the word "Mafia." But a collective label for them did not exist. When it was coined, it gave the groups a real-world status. However, the results were disastrous for Sicily. As Paul Lunde (2004: 54) aptly remarks, the "lie of the Mafia as a historically based society has been a disastrous one for Sicily." Already in 1900, Antonino Cutrera (1900: 2), an early anti-Mafia activist and an officer of public security, wrote the following words: "For historical and ethnographic reasons, Sicily has for many years suffered a social vice perpetrated on it by the Mafia. This vice has hindered its social development and has compromised the thrust of its civilization."

Big lies have great power to affect the course of history, by creating false alternative realities that spread throughout a collectivity unsuspectingly, via a calculating manipulation of words and phrases. One of the main slogans that Trump used throughout his electoral campaign and his presidency was "drain the swamp." Its emotive power lay in the fact that it was perceived as referring to a hidden truth by his followers, alluding to Democratic politicians and the Washington establishment, who had to be drained from the "swamp" that they had created. The swamp metaphor is a constant leitmotif in the alternative-truth strategy that Trump and his followers used to promote the MAGA movement, as an attempt to thwart the takeover of America by liberal élites who have undermined the nation's traditional values. The metaphor is an obvious R-node in the cabalistic code, in which the élites are portrayed and perceived as the "enemies" and the mainstream media as their accomplice, ignoring the values of "real" Americans, looking down on them as antiquated or outdated. Whatever critiques the "liberal media" would articulate about Trump, this strategy allowed him to dismiss them as "fake news," and thus as the lies that the swamp would level at him maliciously—in line with the projection strategy of all big liars. R-nodes such as "élites," "swamp," and "fake news," among others, repeated over and over create a semiotically altered mind-world of alternative truth. This might explain why Trump's most ardent followers are prepared to stay with him, no matter what the consequences are, including the risk of losing everything to the MAGA cause. To quote Sun Tzu (2002: 74), the clever subterfuges of the liar-prince cause "the people to be in complete accord with their ruler, so that they will follow him regardless of their lives, undismayed by any danger."

Oscar Wilde (2007: 94) wrote famously that "Life imitates Art far more than Art imitates Life." He was challenging the long-standing Aristotelian notion of mimesis that art is an imitation of life. Wilde turned mimesis on its head because, as he put it, "the self-conscious aim of Life is to find expression." Creating false realities through lies indirectly corroborates Wilde's notion that we have difficulty differentiating between reality and our representations of it. Wilde used the example of the London fog to make his case. Although fog has always existed in London, one notices the qualities and effects of the fog because "poets and painters have taught the loveliness of such effects. They did not exist till Art had invented them." The big liar is a deceitful poet in a sense, able to create a similar mental "fog," but hardly with the normal poetic intent—rather with a malevolent one.

The creation of alternative truths via lying is at the core of unethical systems of politics and society (Ben-Ghiat 2016). Mussolini, for example, confounded everyone when he came onto the political scene, setting himself apart from the intelligentsia of his era, tapping into people's fears and concerns that the intellectuals were destroying Italy's historical values, as well as looking down on everyone who did not think and talk like them. He founded Fascism as an "anti-party" to the existing party of élites just after the First World War. He was seen as an outsider who came forward to drain Italy's political and social swamp—the same metaphor adopted by Trump later. He was perceived as a disrupter of the system of self-serving unctuous liberal politics, and as a political fighter aiming to restore Italy to its great past. His followers took up his cause enthusiastically, supporting him with their own incendiary rhetoric and violent protests. Mussolini's rise to prominence was thus paved by the big lie that portrayed liberal thinkers, or more precisely his opponents, as part of a cabal of élitists who had thrust the nation into social chaos as a result of their espousal of cultural relativity, which he claimed was at the source of the rampant criminality that was strangling Italian society. In a similar vein, Trump promised that if he was elected, "The crime and violence that today afflicts our nation will soon come to an end" (speech, July 2016, at the Republican National Convention). Both Mussolini and Trump warped the idea of relativism, turning it into a pejorative political ideology, so as to isolate their opponents from the rest of society.

Many big lies are designed to stoke xenophobia. This was clearly an objective of Hitler's big lie—the depiction of Germany as a besieged land. To make it believable, the Nazis utilized four main techniques to produce the alternative reality required to make the lie believable: (1) blame others (the Jews) for lying, and thus claim that they had victimized German culture and society; (2) repeat it constantly until it becomes embedded as a habit of mind; (3) reinforce it with rhetoric, images, and symbolic artifacts (such as the swastika and phrases like *Blut und Boden*); and (4) deny all facts that contradict it. Nazi propaganda repeatedly claimed that Jews held power behind the scenes, based on this four-part strategy, which they built into their 1940 anti-Semitic film *Der Ewige Jude* ("The Eternal Jew"). The film consists of documentary footage combined with materials filmed after the Nazi occupation of Poland, depicting the Jews as an unclean and disease-ridden people. Significantly, the movie ended with footage of Hitler's January 1939 Reichstag speech in which he made the following false allegation:

> If international Jewish financiers in and outside Europe should succeed in plunging the nations once more into a world war, the result will not be Bolshevization of the earth and thus the victory of Jewry, but the annihilation of the Jewish race in Europe.

The film's documentary-style narrative revolved around several main themes. The first one was that of Jews as a parasitic people, emphasized by actual photographs of Jewish ghettoes in Poland, showing unhygienic living conditions, infested by vermin and rats, with close-ups of people who were deliberately chosen to be badly dressed, dirty, with toothless grins. The locations shown are filthy and infested by vermin. The opening line of the film encapsulated the imagery in words as follows: "This film shows genuine shots of the Polish ghettos. It shows the Jews as they really are, before they conceal themselves behind the mask of the civilized European." At this point, the narrator comments that Jews have the ability to change their appearance becoming part of their "human hosts," as the camera shifts to bearded men in traditional religious Jewish garb and then to shaved Jews in modern business suits. This represents a second theme of the film—namely the view of Jews as manipulative people, able to change outward appearances opportunistically. This implies, further, that Aryan culture had been corrupted by Jews.

Hitler and Goebbels believed that this type of film was a vital propaganda instrument for molding public opinion, given that it presents their big lie narratively, enhancing credulity in it (discussed further in the next chapter). The

Nazis established a film department in 1930 to promote the Nazi worldview and political agenda. The department created anti-Semitic filmography throughout the regime, alongside other media-based propagandistic attacks against the Jews and other races. The Nazis perceived human history as a struggle among people of different races, with the Aryan race threatened by "inferior races," which had to be marginalized (and worse).

Disparaging rhetoric against otherness was used by Trump, starting with the 2016 presidential campaign. In his case the strategy was outright populist political opportunism. When he spoke to states bordering Mexico and whose citizens were affected by immigration he proclaimed that "we will kick em' the hell out" and "we will build a great, big, beautiful wall across our border with Mexico" (August 19, 2016, speech at Tucson, Arizona Rally). When he spoke to communities whose citizens had grown weary of the purported interference into their local cultural affairs by government, to promote multiculturalism, he would decree, "We will restart Washington" (November 4, 2016, speech at Harrisburg, Pennsylvania Rally). He knew shrewdly what type of discourse worked with a specific audience, using polling research that allowed him to grasp what concerns an audience in a specific area had so as to shape his discourse to promise a convenient alternative reality to each audience. In each speech, moreover, Trump feigned victimization at the expense of the deep state. Rich Lowry (2017) delineated the strategy insightfully as follows:

> Trump has created a dynamic for his supporters where the more seemingly victimized he is, the better. He's a victim because he's strong and has stirred the hornet's nest in a way no one else would dare. He's a victim because the system is rigged against him and anyone who challenges it. He's a victim because he's so closely identified with his supporters, who have been, likewise, allegedly treated unfairly by large-scale economic and social forces. "We will be attacked," he told his fans at his announcement. "We will be slandered. We will be persecuted just as I have been." ... If he constantly maintains that he isn't getting his due, it increases the odds that he'll get his due, or—better still—more than his due.

A big lie is perpetrated above all else to suggest that the despot is the "savior leader" who is ready to free the people from the captivity of the cabalists. This is why a big liar develops an appropriate name moniker for himself. The name Mussolini adopted for himself, *Il Duce* ("The Leader"), conveyed self-grandeur; similarly, Hitler was the *Führer,* Stalin the *Man of Steel,* and Putin a self-anointed modern-day *czar*. The earliest recorded political usage of *Führer* was by the Austrian Georg von Schönerer, who was a major exponent of German nationalism in Austria at the turn of the twentieth century; Hitler also used the Roman salute, as did Mussolini a little later, with the right arm and hand held rigidly in an outstretched fashion—a gesture that some claim may be the origin of the term "far-right." Hitler took the title as head of the Nazi Party in 1921. Significantly, the title became a morpheme in the denomination of the Nazi Party's military titles, as, for instance, *Sturmbannführer* ("assault unit leader") and *Oberführer* ("senior leader"), thus connecting them to the leader via linguistic suggestion. *Man of Steel* was the actual meaning of the word "Stalin," which the dictator adopted as his legal name—his birth name was Ioseb Besarionis dze Jughashvili. He started using the name "Stalin" after signing an article he wrote on Marxism in 1913 with the pseudonym "K. Stalin," meaning "man of steel." Putin openly declared himself to be a czar in the mold of Peter the Great, in a speech he delivered on June 10, 2022, equating his invasion of Ukraine with Peter's nationalist wars centuries before.

As noted by Madeleine Albright in her 2018 book, *Fascism: A Warning*, dictators such as Mussolini are masters of metaphor, which they know can easily create alternative truths in the mind. Interestingly, as John Kelly (2016) observes, the phrase "drain the swamp" appeared in a Wisconsin newspaper in 1903: "Socialists are not satisfied with killing a few of the mosquitoes which come from the capitalist swamp; they want to drain the swamp," which were the words uttered by a Social Democratic Party organizer. Ronald Reagan used it as well in 1993 as part of a verbal attack on the same Washington bureaucracy that Trump has assailed in a more verbally aggressive manner. For the sake of historical accuracy, it should be noted that this phrase has been used in politics since at least the nineteenth century. Even Democratic politician Nancy Pelosi used it in 2006 while announcing a plan meant to counteract Republican politics.

Mind Control

To reiterate, for a big lie to work cognitively it must be so outrageous that people will be inclined to accept it as necessarily true. As Hitler put it in *Mein Kampf* (1925):

> Even though the facts which prove this to be [false] may be brought clearly to their minds, they will still doubt and waver and will continue to think that there may be some other explanation. For the grossly impudent lie always leaves traces behind it, even after it has been nailed down, a fact which is known to all expert liars in this world and to all who conspire together in the art of lying.

In effect, Hitler was suggesting that the best way to control people's minds is through the creation of big lies as indirect, and thus surreptitiously powerful, forms of brainwashing, able to diminish people's ability to think critically, introducing thoughts and ideas into their minds via the alternative truth strategies, which may lead to people changing their values and beliefs.

Research exists that largely confirms big lies as effective mind control schemes (Kurlansky 2022, Hart and Curtis 2023). Three key regions of the brain are stimulated by lies: (1) the frontal lobe (of the neocortex), which has the ability to suppress truth, due to its role in intellection; (2) the limbic system (and especially the amygdala), which generates anxiety during deception; and (3) the temporal lobe which is responsible for retrieving memories and reinterpreting them. When these three areas are activated in tandem by a big lie they generate a kind of self-prophesying "logic" that the truth is buried within the lie. The claim made here is that it is the organicity of the semiotic linkages (rhetorical, symbolic, and imagistic) that accrues in the mind to generate the neural mechanisms involved in accepting the big lie. Take, for instance, QAnon's adrenochrome conspiracy, which claims that liberal politicians and Hollywood élites are harvesting the blood of children to extract adrenochrome for its life-extending benefits—adrenochrome is a chemical compound produced by the oxidation of adrenaline. As ridiculous as it sounds, blood-based conspiracies have always existed, as discussed (recall the *Blut und Boden* one here). To bolster this big lie, QAnon resorts to the use of images, such as one showing Hillary Clinton, a major target of QAnon, with bloodshot eyes, a slightly open mouth suggesting hunger, and wearing a hood connoting secretive cabalism. QAnon creates such images as a way to expose the plans of the cabal to murder children for their blood. Now, while this may seem preposterous, once the cabalistic code has penetrated the mind, even such fabrications gain cogency, especially in those who perceive liberal politicians as evil.

People are willing to believe anything, and to even act violently, in order to gain a sense of control over their own lives. A classic example is the French Revolution, the overthrow of the Bourbon monarchy in France in the period between 1789 and 1799. It started with a meeting of the legislative assembly in May of 1789 when French society was undergoing a serious economic crisis. The Bastille was stormed later in July of that same year. The revolution became increasingly violent under the Jacobins and lawyer Maximilien de Robespierre. The execution of Louis XVI in January of 1793 was followed by Robespierre's so-called Reign of Terror, which failed to produce a stable form of republican government, and was eventually overthrown by Napoleon in 1799. The people who rose up against the monarchy had become disenchanted, feeling dispossessed and disparaged by the political élite—a sentiment that came to be symbolized by Marie Antoinette's infamous "Let them eat cake," which she purportedly uttered upon learning that the peasants did not even have bread to eat.

The term alienation was coined by Karl Marx (1844) to describe the sense of estrangement that working-class people supposedly feel in a capitalist system, leading to a sense of purposelessness. Sociologist Émile Durkheim (1912) suggested instead that alienation stemmed not from social conditions tied to a political system, but rather from a loss of moral traditions in a secularized and materialistic world. He coined the term *anomie* to refer to the sense of irrational purposelessness experienced as a result of living in this kind of world. Anomie is arguably a reason why big lies seem to work best in certain periods of time, providing the scheming liar with an opportunity to claim that he will restore the moral basis of a society. As Harriet Sherwood (2018) has written, this is the likely reason why the religious right came to see Trump as a "savior sinner," who was sent by God to America to set things right, recalling episodes in biblical history where sinners became religious leaders. Trump cleverly took their side on moral issues, assuring legislation against abortion, among other issues of great resonance to this community. Before Trump's rise to power, the mass media hardly paid attention to the religious right, generating a perception among its members of media bias toward a liberal secular agenda and worldview. The sense of anomie and exclusion that the religious right felt before Trump's leadership allowed him to become their "spiritual leader," no matter his philandering past. This was one of Trump's earliest and most effective big lies—claiming that moral values were undermined by the deep state and that he would restore them.

As a quintessential strategy of mind control used in the creation and sustenance of totalitarian states, big lies weaken resolve through contradiction and the denial of objective truth which, together, allow the dictator to exact conformity to his own way of seeing things. Contradiction is at the core of the warped semiotic system on which big lies are based, since it can go both ways, as Hitler maintained. The following excerpt from a speech given by Stalin to the 16th Congress of the Russian Communist Party in 1930 encapsulates this political strategy perfectly (cited in Evans 1993: 39):

> We are for the withering away of the state, and at the same time we stand for the strengthening of the dictatorship, which represents the most powerful and mighty of all forms of the state which have existed up to the present day. The highest development of the power of the state, with the object of preparing the conditions of the withering away of the state: that is the Marxist formula. Is it "contradictory?" Yes, it is "contradictory." But this contradiction is a living thing and wholly reflects the Marxist dialectic.

In his insightful book, *Beyond Hypocrisy* (1992), Edward Herman argues that our minds are extremely vulnerable to this type of verbal tactic, more so than they are to outright intimidation and confrontation, because vagueness of meaning obscures and may even obliterate our basic assumptions about reality, leading to a sense that any combination of words and their distortions produce logical sense. If such manipulation spreads broadly within a certain group, it can lead to the communal acceptance of contradiction as a "living thing," as Stalin so aptly put it. In Orwell's novel (1949), Newspeak was the primary means for spreading contradiction as a semiotic strategy at different levels of meaning, allowing for a social order that could be controlled by Big Brother, who made sure that the articulation of opposing ideas was blocked through a control of meanings. Mind control is thus reinforced by catchwords and slogans used over and over. This might explain why dictators used the exact same stock phrases, such as "State ownership," "Anarchist," and "Relativism," in their own form of Newspeak, reinforcing the notion of a dangerous cabal of élites attempting to take over a country so as to strip it of its traditional moral values. Below are some examples from Mussolini's speeches and statements (Mussolini 2018):

- State Ownership! It leads only to absurd and monstrous conclusions; state ownership means state monopoly, concentrated in the hands of one party and its adherents, and that state brings only ruin and bankruptcy to all.
- Every anarchist is a baffled dictator.
- If relativism signifies contempt for fixed categories and those who claim to be the bearers of objective immortal truth, then there is nothing more relativistic than Fascist attitudes and activity. From the fact that all ideologies are of equal value, we Fascists conclude that we have the right to create our own ideology and to enforce it with all the energy of which we are capable.

Those who frequented Mussolini's rallies were apparently mesmerized by his Newspeak, reacting in unison to his bluster by shouting consent and approval loudly. The master liar knows how to exude a charismatic magnetism, like a cult leader, inducing a kind of hypnotic trance in people that is hard to shake off (as Orwell emphasized in his novel). Sociologist Max Weber introduced the idea that cults were, in fact, compelling to many because of the "charisma" of the leader, who conditioned members to follow him through a "routinization of charisma." Below is his characterization (Weber 1922: 328):

Charisma is a certain quality of an individual personality by virtue of which he is set apart from ordinary men and treated as endowed with supernatural, superhuman, or at least specifically exceptional powers or qualities. These are such as are not accessible to the ordinary person, but are regarded as of divine origin or as exemplary, and on the basis of them the individual concerned is treated as a leader.

Big lies are, in the end, charisma-focused strategies, whose believability results over time through the routinization of charisma. Trump's "Stop the Steal" big lie, in which he claimed that the 2020 election was stolen from him by deep state operators, became increasingly believable to supporters, via speeches, social media posts, rallies, t-shirts, hats, and banners—all based on the same slogan and all emphasizing his charisma. Such coordinated communication makes it easier to process and accept falsity as truthfulness, indicating that familiarity can supersede rationality, because of the aforementioned illusory truth effect (Hasher, Goldstein, and Toppino 1977, Doland 1999). As Pierre (2020) puts it:

> But one of the most striking features of the illusory truth effect is that it can occur despite prior knowledge that a statement is false as well as in the presence of real "fake news" headlines that are entirely fabricated stories that, given some reflection, people probably know are untrue. It can even occur despite exposure to "fake news" headlines that run against one's party affiliation. For example, repeated exposure to a headline like "Obama Was Going to Castro's Funeral Until Trump Told Him This" increases perceptions of truth not only for Republicans but Democrats as well. And so, the illusory truth effect occurs even when we know, or want to know, better.

Because today massive numbers of false messages are communicated rapidly, repetitively, and continuously over multiple channels, truth becomes lost in an Orwellian mind fog. People are more likely to believe a story simply because it seems to have been reported by multiple sources. The same technique has been used not only by dictators, but by governments of all ideological stripes, and especially the intelligence services that are part of most governments. As Edward Hunter emphasized as far back as 1950, these forms of mind control are designed to make people cooperate with those in power (see Lovell 2019: 100–4).

Epilogue

"Divide and conquer" was an expression that Machiavelli interspersed throughout one of his lesser-known books, *The Art of War* (1521), to suggest that the most effective strategy for conquering people is to divide the forces of the enemy, by breaking up existing power structures, and stirring up rivalries within the populace, through a strategic use of deceptive oratory, because, he claimed, deceptive language crawls surreptitiously into the mind, below the filters of conscious reflection. In this way, the focus of atrocities is put on the enemy. As George Orwell (2017: 75) so insightfully put it: "Everyone believes in the atrocities of the enemy and disbelieve in those of his own side."

Machiavelli argued that, for the divide-and-conquer strategy to spread and become ever more effective as part of mind control, it was essential that the lies never be admitted or even attenuated. They must be perpetrated, perpetuated, and defended to the death (literally). The Nazis, Mussolini, Stalin, Putin, and other big liars clearly understood this, by assigning a special manipulative meaning to certain words, such as *Volk* ("the people") and *Fanatismus* ("fanaticism"), which reflected the official party line of the Nazis. Other terms were euphemisms designed to hide their acts of terror, including *Sonderbehandlung* ("special treatment") for execution, and *Endlösung* ("final solution") for the systematic extermination of the Jewish peoples (Hutton 1999). It is in exposing such aspects of the divide-and-conquer tactic, based on rhetoric, that semiotics can play a role in restoring some ethical sense of linguistic and communicative practices in a society that has been devastated by falsehoods and conspiratorial rhetoric. Aristotle (1952) also saw the need to unravel the hidden rhetorical structures in politics and other spheres of life because they are the main ones that provide the "means of persuasion." Ethical communication can be restored, he claimed, by examining what deceptive rhetoric does to the mind and using the same strategy to turn it on itself.

Charles Peirce had initially dismissed a semiotically based approach to ethics as impractical in his famous 1898 lectures, but he soon after changed his mind, conflating ethics with his theory of sign categories (Herdy 2014, Liszka 2022), suggesting that ethical behavior is imprinted in signs, which can be transferred to others during practical interactions. Ethics can be said, therefore, to be inscribed in an unconscious range of meanings on which truth-based semiotic networks are implanted, which, as suggested here, allow people to perceive semiotic elements as connected to each other and to larger frames of meaning. In the end, as Peirce suggested in his subsequent writings, for ethics to be achieved it must be associated with logic and aesthetics, as Nöth (2021: 60) has observed:

> For Peirce, aesthetics and ethics are only the first two of three philosophical sciences of values. The third is logic. The three constitute a triad of sciences that Peirce established within his general system of the sciences under the designation "normative sciences."

5

False Narratives

Prologue

Conspiracy theories have existed since time immemorial, even though they were not labeled as such. In 1307, French King Philip the Fair spread salacious rumors about the Knights Templar, aiming to destroy their honorable warrior image in the eyes of the public, fearing their financial power. Around the same time, made-up stories about Jews as blood suckers became widespread, laying the basis for the spread of an anti-Semitic trope that is still noticeable on radical social media platforms. Skipping forward to the nineteenth century, reporters in America started using the term "conspiracy theory" in reference to unfounded speculations as to why England purportedly supported the Confederacy during the Civil War. After the assassination of President James Garfield in 1881, the same term was used by newspapers broadly regarding the unproven theory that the assassin may have had accomplices (McKenzie-McHarg 2018).

But the term became widespread, assuming its current meaning, after the CIA used it in reference to the many speculations surrounding the assassination of President John F. Kennedy in 1963, which gave rise to endless conspiracy theories about diverse plots to assassinate the president, and which are still circulating to this day, traveling throughout the Internet, where they are now considered to be almost indisputably true. Why do made-up stories arise and why are they believed by so many? This chapter will deal with this topic, focusing on how false narratives are highly dangerous because they can bring about political and social instability. Historian Richard Hofstadter (1964) maintains that conspiracy theories emerge typically when those who feel that their interests are not represented socially or politically become alienated from the polity, developing the fear of being controlled by a cabal, thus making them vulnerable to charismatic rather than rational leadership—a state of affairs that has facilitated totalitarian rule (as understood today) since at least the start of the twentieth century. Although authoritarian and despotic political systems have certainly existed before that century, the specific type of rule known as totalitarian crystallizes in the early twentieth century with the establishment of the Soviet Union, considered to be the first true totalitarian state by political scientists. Totalitarian regimes are different from the authoritarian regimes of the past in founding their polity on the basis of an ideology, and establishing a system of control over all aspects of social life, from education and the arts, to the lifestyle norms that are imposed on citizens through standardization tactics. Such states also use a strategic form of confabulation to legitimize themselves as historically valid, creating false ideas about their own origins in the society's past. They do so by spinning myths about the past that they bend toward legitimizing the present.

The term "confabulation" is used here in reference to the construction of a historical *fabula*, a fictional story presented in the guise of historiography, so as to convey a specific interpretation of the world. It is an account of the past that is made up (duplicitously) by stitching together disparate bits of information narratively in such a way as to present the past according to a self-serving ideological scenario. This allows political actors to manipulate people's perceptions of the past and direct them toward their current goals. The classic example of a totalitarian state using confabulation to legitimize itself as the true documentarian of the past is Nazi Germany, which established its legitimacy on the basis of a myth of Aryanism, which Hitler cleverly juxtaposed against the age-old conspiracy theory of a Jewish cabal planning to take over the world, thus identifying the Jews as a threat to Germany. This false dual narrativity was embedded into groupthink via constant repetition and representation in films, posters, radio programs, and other media (as discussed in previous chapters). Joseph Goebbels even actively helped create the film scripts, shape the contents of radio programs, and influence the design of posters, so as to ensure that the same false myth was delivered constantly through different media forms and channels. The Nazis had clearly understood the power of narrativity to inject credibility into their racist messages—a phenomenon that Jerome Bruner (1991) called the "narrative construction of reality."

History itself is a narrative construct—an attempt to connect past events into a coherent story that is perceived as leading to the present state of affairs. As historian Hayden White (1973) has argued cogently, there is little difference between narrative fiction and historical narrative, since the historian uses the same kinds of literary techniques that the novelist employs to create verisimilitude and to make events of the past relevant to events of the present. Made-up histories, such as the Aryan one, are based on the power of narratives to explain the present in terms of the past, even if the past is completely made up. As Harmon and Holman (1999) point out, such stories work at an unconscious level because they present in a connected fashion those "episodes important to the history of a nation or race." Confabulation is a powerful form of mind manipulation, which can even lead to the justification of horrendous events such as the Holocaust. Once followers become entrapped into the narrative, through the false memories that it generates, they see themselves as valiant characters in the ongoing outcomes of the story. This makes it virtually impossible to cast doubt on the story's validity, given the high degree of emotional commitment made to it by individuals. Confabulation allows the Machiavellian liar to take hold of people's belief systems and twist them for his own objectives. The leader is thus not seen as a con artist or deceiver, but a possessor of the hidden truth that has been repressed by the very people that he singles out as the destroyers of history—that is, through the mythic storyline, he is perceived as fleshing out the truth and of identifying the villains in the story. In effect, false narratives such as the Aryan one are intentional distortions of world events created on purpose to recalibrate people's perceptions of current reality by activating mythic-narrative mechanisms in the unconscious.

In the semiotic model espoused here, false narratives provide the core meaning codes sustained and delivered by various signs and sign systems in the nodes within the semiotic network. Sometimes, a single image (an I-sign) within the network can deliver the entire narrative code in compressed form. Consider the Nazi 1932 election poster below (Figure 5.1).

The caption reads, "We workers have awakened," implying that common people have finally understood the "truth" of Aryanism. The central figure in the scene is a tall, blond, muscular man who, clearly, represents the idealized Aryan worker. He towers over everyone else—petty little men attempting to show him their useless petitions. The whole scene conveys the supremacy of Aryan individuals over everyone else, depicted as miniscule people who will have to yield to the will of the Aryan—a message bolstered by the swastika in the background, made of solid steel against a red sky, suggesting the blood symbolism of the Nazi movement. As Hitler wrote: "In red we see the social idea of the movement, in white the nationalistic idea, in the swastika the mission of the struggle for the victory of the Aryan man and, by the same token, the victory of the idea of creative work, which as such always has been and always will be anti-Semitic" (*Mein Kampf* 1925).

Figure 5.1 Nazi Election Poster, 1932.

Source: Library of Congress, https://www.loc.gov/item/2016651625/. "No known restrictions on publication in the U.S." Reproduction Number: LC-DIG-ds-09833. Artist: Felix Albrecht, 1932.

Léon Polikov (1974) has perceptively noted that the Nazi Aryan myth became widely accepted because it was mapped against the social conditions of Germany at the time, becoming a story of survival in an expanding context of nationalist sentiments. Aryanism emerged as a concrete idea in the nineteenth century (as mentioned previously), promoted by racist theorists, such as Vacher de Lapouge in his book *L'Aryen*, who claimed that the Aryans were a superior race of long-headed, blond Northern Europeans destined to rule over more short-headed peoples (which is rendered semiotically by the I-sign above). Similar pseudo-claims were bandied about in the same era (Yenne 2010), forming the ideological basis for the Nazis' Aryan myth which they exploited to justify their pursuit of *Lebensraum* and their anti-Semitic racial policies.

It should be noted that after Hitler and Mussolini signed a treaty of friendship on October 25, 1936, pledging to pursue a common foreign policy (the Rome-Berlin Axis), the friendship became an awkward one from the outset, given that the Nazis viewed the downfall of the Roman Empire as resulting from the contamination of blood from racial intermixing. The Italians were thus seen as a hybrid race, who did not fit perfectly into the pseudo-classificatory paradigm of Aryanism (Gillette 2012). In a 1921 speech, Mussolini had stated that Fascism was born of both Aryan and Mediterranean historical experiences, bound together by their common cultural foundations. The speech thus made it clear that Mussolini actually rejected the notion of a biologically pure race, promoting a version of cultural superiority instead, which was contrary to strict Aryanism. The dilemma between the two dictators was never totally resolved, leading to the suspicion on the part of the Nazis that the Italians were not committed to their cause, and that they were harboring and hiding Jews from being captured. To ensure that the Holocaust in Italy was carried out, between 1943 and 1945 Italy was occupied by the Nazis after the Italian surrender on September 8, 1943.

The Aryan myth thus clashed with Mussolini's own mythology of a great cultural and political Roman past that he wanted to retrieve with Fascism. The competing mythologies created a society-wide cognitive dissonance across Italy, generating conflicts among the populace. Despite the Axis treaty, Mussolini generally refused to permit deportations of Jews from Italy to extermination camps. Under pressure from Germany, the Fascist regime did pass anti-Semitic legislation in 1938, removing Jews from government jobs, banning marriages between Jews and non-Jews, prohibiting Jews from joining the armed forces, and removing Jews from positions in the mass media. But the Italian authorities rarely enforced the legislation. Nevertheless, the psychological insult and real economic consequences from the legislation eroded the quality of life for many Jews, who consequently emigrated primarily to North America. It can be suggested here that the main problem between the Nazis and Fascists was embedded in a clash of narratives, with the latter narrative actually attempting to attenuate the notion of racial superiority, preferring cultural hegemony instead.

False Mythic Narratives

Roland Barthes (1957) characterized myth as a "second-order semiological system," which is latent in shaping the semantic categories of everyday speech and cultural texts, thus continuing to guide unconscious patterns of thought and understanding. In terms of the semiotic method adopted here, myth can be seen to undergird various meaning circuits related to specific nodes in the network. So, a gesture such as the Fascist Roman salute, executed by extending the right arm and raising it with the palm of the hand facing down and the fingers stretched out and touching each other, is a mythic S-sign, which was used by the Fascists to reference the glory of Italy's Roman past, a symbol suggesting images of ancient sculptures commemorating military victories with the salute (Winkler 2009). As such, it is designed to evoke the Fascist mythology of Roman Imperialism in a compact allusive fashion. As Barthes (1957: 34) put it, "myth is a system of communication, a mode of signification, a form."

Dictators and autocrats employ mythic sign forms and narratives to stoke unconscious memory mechanisms of past glory. The Aryan myth is a perfect example of how this latent semiotic-psychological system was stoked by a confabulated origin story that rendered it viable through its coherent narrative structure revolving around the theme of national identity and nationalism. As historian-linguist Ernest Renan (1882) wrote: "A heroic past, great men, glory, this is the social capital upon which one bases a national idea." Mythic stories involve legitimizing present reality on the basis of a narrative system that taps into sentiments and beliefs that accrue over time in a society. As a result, the myth of Aryanism, adapted to nationalist sentiments, was used to justify any action that the Nazis claimed to be in the "national interest."

As discussed several times, the mythology of a past superior race was based on pseudo-scientific claims that surfaced in the latter part of the nineteenth century, when the term "Aryan" was used to identify the Indo-Germanic peoples who settled throughout India, Persia, and Europe. This was not, however, based on any solid archeological evidence, but rather on phonetic correspondences that were found to occur in lexical cognates between languages such as Sanskrit and Persian. It was only later that French racial theorist Arthur Gobineau mapped the comparative linguistic forms onto racial categories. Aryanism became thus a biological theory of race that allowed the Nazis to claim genetically based superiority and to blame genetically inferior non-Aryans for Germany's (and the world's) social-political ills. The Nazis claimed, either fallaciously or delusionally, that their theory of Aryanism was based on strict scientific evidence of a hierarchy of the human race. In 1937 Hitler declared during a meeting of the Reichstag (in Gilman and Rabinbach 2013: 169): "I speak prophetically. Just as the discovery that the earth moved around the sun led to a complete transformation of the way people looked at the world, so too the blood and racial teachings of National Socialism will change our understanding of mankind's past and its future."

To circumvent the problem of distinguishing Aryans from non-Aryans on the basis of physical appearance and specific anatomical features, laws were passed, such as the Nuremberg Race Laws of 1935, to allow individuals of "related blood" and of European descent into the Aryan category. The fallacy of such biogenetic mythologies is that physical traits do not define race or character in any scientifically valid way. The Aryan myth constitutes, in effect, an example of biological racism, whereby physical and psychological categories are selected or even constructed to explain differences in actual human outcomes, including the nature of different social systems. As such, the myth distorted biology and archeology to subserve Hitler's plan of world domination, evoking a sense of divine destiny for Aryan peoples. This form of self-serving mythology has, needless to say, existed throughout history. In ancient Greece, for instance, the Trojan War was mythologized through literature, which, although based on actual events, shaped opinions about the war, representing the struggle of the Greeks against foreign powers in terms of a lost past glory when heroes were valiant and more honorable. The Nazis' mythic confabulation was designed, in sum, as a self-serving historiography to justify their imperialist ambitions.

The same form of confabulation was used by Trump with his MAGA mythology, which was not collated concretely in the form of written texts or purported archeological evidence (as was Aryanism), but implied through speeches and statements that alluded constantly to a "lost past" that should be retrieved to recreate the real America, allowing followers to collate his ideas narratively on their own into an implicit story of an America that had abandoned its founding values and which needed a rescuing hero—namely, Trump. To support his claim that he deserved to be president for life, Trump constantly portrayed himself as the only heroic warrior who would be able to restore true culture to America. Thus, MAGA was subtly suggestive of an "original white race" of colonists that made America great, which, because of deep state liberalism, was being gradually destroyed. Its central objective was to bind people of like mind together through a semiotic linkage of allusive narrative meanings, delivered through rhetorical devices, such as "the real America," and symbols, such as MAGA hats and banners.

Ironically, in a 2006 book titled *The Good Fight: Why Liberals—and Only Liberals—Can Win the War on Terror and Make America Great Again*, political commentator Peter Beinart used the same phrase to claim that only liberal politicians could truly create pride in America by branching out to embrace diversity, which has always been America's social strength (the melting pot metaphor). Using the strategy of twisting labels into self-serving symbolic artifacts, Trump turned MAGA into a political right-wing movement, aiming to restore the supposed greatness of colonial, pre-Civil War America. This allowed Trump to control meaning in an Orwellian way, characterizing those who opposed him as the villains who were destroying American values. This type of strategically coded mythic discourse was meant to tap into fears and resentments, which Trump manipulated through constant repetition, inducing a hypnotic effect on believers. The result was the peddling of an alternative view of history that was intended to shape the way some people envisioned themselves and their place in history. As J. L. Linstroth (2018) has insightfully observed, with his MAGA story Trump actually tapped into a long-standing mythology of nativism in America:

> Toward the end of the 19th-century and at the turn of the 20th-century, many in the US promoted "Nativism"—an all-white America where good jobs belonged to Whites, not foreigners. This was the historical period known as the "Second-Industrial Revolution," the "Gilded Age," and the "Progressive Era"—a time of enormous economic transformation for the country through industrialization and urbanization.

In Orwell's *Nineteen Eighty-Four*, historical narratives are controlled by the Ministry of Truth, which shapes them to fit the Party's worldview. They are preserved and written in doublespeak, which allows for a direct control of meaning. The protagonist of the novel, Winston Smith, works in the Records Department of the Ministry of Truth. His job is to maintain historical records in order to ensure that the past conforms to the party line, deleting any inconvenient facts used by "unpersons," so as to maintain a state of alternative reality, which allows the Big Brother totalitarian regime to shield people from the truth and to neutralize any opposition they may mount against the regime. As Chaim Sinar (2018) has perceptively observed, this very strategy was used first by Stalin to silence the opposition against him, keeping people in a state of fear and uncertainty; Vladimir Putin has used the very same tactic in order to maintain power, utilizing a skewed view of Russian history, which has always allowed him to keep his fabricated alternative reality operative in the minds of Russian citizens, which as Ernest Renan asserted as far back as 1882, is "essential in the creation of a nation." Literary scholars actually trace Orwell's source of inspiration for writing *Nineteen Eighty-Four* to Stalinism. Orwell himself asserted that his other iconic novel, *Animal Farm* (1945), was meant to reflect events that triggered the Russian Revolution of 1917, which led to the Stalinist era of the Soviet Union.

As mentioned, self-serving confabulated histories have been around since time immemorial. The Roman historian Tacitus even began his *Annals* (c. 68 CE) with the warning to his readers that some histories are falsified in order to "fester hatreds." The ancient historians realized that there was little difference between a work such as *The Iliad* and a non-mythic account of history. Even Thucydides, considered (along with Herodotus before him) to be one of the first historians to attempt writing about past events in fact-based ways, understood that history was bound to blend fiction with reality, like the Homeric poems. The Trojan War stirred the imagination of both writers and historians, but was celebrated mainly in literary form via the *Iliad* and the *Odyssey*. There is no single, authoritative text which recounts the actual events of the war. The story is assembled from oral stories, reports, and versions of the events as well as from visual representations (sculptures and etchings of various types). Mythologies always leave their traces through semiotic artifacts—from derived stories, artistic representations, and metaphors; it is not happenstance that we continue to use the term "Trojan Horse" as a metaphor of deceit. In a fundamental sense, all false mythic origin stories, such as the Aryan one, are Trojan Horses, spun to conquer minds through deception. As Orwell stated in 1942: "There are countless people who would think it scandalous to falsify a scientific textbook, but would see nothing wrong in falsifying an historical fact." The Soviet Union, as Cohen (2022) suggests, was born of Orwellian mind control, via the falsification of its history. Stalin even wrote his own "short course" on the history of the Soviet Communist Party. As Cohen (2022) notes:

> He was a master of what could be done with language; under him, the euphemism "extraordinary events" was used to cover any behavior he considered treasonable, a phrase that covered incompetence, cowardice, "anti-Soviet agitation," even drunkenness. The great Polish poet Zbigniew Herbert was to refer to Stalin ironically as "the Great Linguist" for his corruption of language.

Mythic stories cannot be demonstrated as being true or untrue in any objective way; they can only be believed on their own terms. This ambivalence is what makes false origin myths like the Aryan or MAGA ones impenetrable to rational counter-argumentation. As Orwell (1968: 7) so aptly put it, "Myths which are believed in tend to become real." Like big lies, false origin narratives are powerful tools which, as Michael Barkun (2003: 3–4) has noted, allow the political schemer to spin a mind fog wherein nothing happens by accident, nothing is as it seems, and everything is connected conspiratorially. Robert Paxton has aptly pointed out in his book, *The Anatomy of Fascism* (2004), that these undergird totalitarian systems which present and represent themselves as ensuring the historical purity of the state, and thus as mind shields against the supposed invasion of aliens who bring corruption and immorality to the nation—a view dramatized by Trump in his initial campaign speech, in which he referred to Mexican immigration as follows: "When Mexico sends its people, they're not sending their best. They're sending people that have a lot of problems, and they're bringing those problems with us. They're bringing drugs. They're bringing crime. They're rapists."

Morality is thus in the hands of the nationalist leader, who will restore it, no matter what the cost. Mussolini closed down wine shops and nightclubs, which were seen by religious people of the era as signs of degeneracy, perversion, and sinfulness, a situation that Mussolini implied was traceable to open immigration. He also made profane and obscene language in public a crime; and he pushed the view that women should stay at home and look after their families while their husbands worked—a model of family life endorsed officially by the Roman Church. He opposed the use of contraception and wanted to ban divorce in Italy. Mussolini was trying strategically to bring zealous believers into his camp. The parallels with Trump are remarkable, given the latter's stances on abortion, on women's role in the world, and similar Mussolini-type positions that are seen by white, right-wing religious groups as critical to the restoration of moral order to American society. As psychologist Frederik Lund (1925: 183) pointed out in the early era psychology, beliefs embedded in moral systems are the strongest ones, and they are the ones that are subject to manipulation and persuasion by ruthless leaders such as Mussolini and Trump, suggesting "the presence of a law of primacy in persuasion." As Brinkhof (2022) has cogently argued, all histories dovetail with shifting politics, aiming to remove all doubt about what a nation is about on the basis of how it originated. In America, there are always intense disagreements on whether or not history should focus on the darker episodes of the nation's past, from slavery to the Second World War internments. As a result, "the plot lines of history can be rather flexible," and can be manipulated for specific political objectives.

The ancient Greek philosophers divided belief into *pistis* and *doxa*. The former implies a sense of trust in something, and the latter the opinions that guide actions and behaviors, no matter what the truth of the matter. In all forms of belief, there are mainly binary choices—something is either true or false, right or wrong, moral or immoral. In his *Illustrations of the Logic of Science* (1877), Peirce described belief as something that impels us to act, not just a state of mind—a way to counteract doubt (the opposite of belief), from which we struggle to free ourselves. When belief is controlled via semiotic means, such as the deployment of unconscious codes of meaning, it becomes pliable and open to influence from the manipulator's stratagems. Sets of beliefs make up ideologies, a term coined by Enlightenment philosopher Antoine Destutt de Tracy (1817), which become psychologically powerful because they cannot be decomposed into individual beliefs as such, being perceived as inviolable and based on truth.

It is relevant to emphasize once again that a myth is not just a myth, so to speak; it gains its persuasive force by tapping into unconscious archetypal mechanisms where images of the past reside, imprinted in expressive forms such as language and visual texts representing previous eras. This then motivates a society to act in a specific way to preserve itself. After Hitler's appointment as Chancellor in 1933, the term "Aryan" became institutionalized semantically and socially, spreading to all areas of public life in Nazi Germany, including in legislation. The law revoking the rights of Jews, called the Law for the Restoration of the Professional Civil Service, included a clause referred to as the *Arienparagraph* ("Aryan Paragraph") which stipulated that only Aryans could be participants in public life, specifying that "Civil servants who are not of Aryan descent are to be retired." Because the word Aryan proved difficult to define precisely in racial terms (as discussed), Nazi officials stopped using the term in legislation after the Nuremberg Race Laws were passed, using instead the phrase "those of German or related blood." Officially, individuals of "related blood" were people of European descent. But the term Aryan continued to be used in unofficial ways. Recently, white supremacists across the globe have started using the word Aryan as a general label for white people, alluding to their support for the racist beliefs and genocidal practices of the Nazis.

Semiotic Infrastructure of Conspiracy Theories

The semiotic model of meaning-making utilized in this book involves positing a central code or codes of meaning on which a network of signs or sign structures—rhetorical, symbolic, imagistic, and textual—coalesce to deliver the meaning in different modes and media. This organic unity can be called, loosely, a semiotic infrastructure, defined as the coordinated structural interaction of the components of the network around a core meaning. It is meant to characterize the semiotic architecture of a discursive practice designed to convey a message via specific interlinked sign structures. In this model, a conspiracy theory can be seen to have a complex structure whereby signs are deployed to give it emotional power and believability through the unity and coherence of the infrastructure. Because they are based on interlinked structural forms, conspiracy theories constitute extremely dangerous forms of discourse, seeping into people's minds virtually indelibly, thus allowing the conspiracist to control belief systems psychologically, since they consist of many different and connected semiotic parts that are not easy to decompose and analyze.

An example of how a conspiratorial semiotic infrastructure is devised and used strategically is the one created by Republican Senator Joseph McCarthy's false story of America being taken over by communist ideologies espoused by liberals, Hollywood actors, and others—constituting a prefigurement of the deep state cabal code that Trump coopted subsequently. Starting in 1950, McCarthy's conspiracy theory fit politically into the era when Cold War tensions fueled fears of communist infiltrations into American society. McCarthy started by alleging that there were many communists, Soviet spies, and Marxist sympathizers who had infiltrated the US government, the academies, the film industry, and the mainstream media. His accusations were false and unfounded; but they set the stage for a deep state coding of events in America, designed to purify it of its ideologically radical elements. The political repression and persecution of so-called left-leaning individuals became widespread, as McCarthy's allies and sympathizers took up his cause. The conspiracy worked because of its complex semiotic infrastructure, which was based on a coded mythology of America as open to invasions, especially ideological ones. McCarthy claimed to have a "list" of Marxist ideologues working behind the scenes in the United States, including government employees, members of the entertainment industry, academics, left-wing politicians, media pundits, and labor union activists. This is, as just mentioned, the likely origin of the deep state code consisting of "un-American" individuals. A common belief stoked by McCarthy's deceitful meaning code was the view that liberalism was destroying America, given its promotion of internationalism, social welfare (established by the New Deal), and communist ideas. While the details were different, it is easy to see the same type of inter-codability in previous conspiratorial discourses, from Stalinism to Fascism—in all cases, the enemy is both within and without, and must be eradicated. The influential conservative pundit at the time, William F. Buckley Jr. (1954: 335), wrote a defense of McCarthyism, claiming that it was "a movement around which men of good will and stern morality can close ranks."

By the mid-1950s, McCarthyism started declining, after the US Supreme Court chastised the Senator on human rights grounds, which led to the overturn of several key laws and legislative directives that were enacted under McCarthy. Interestingly, the term McCarthyism is now used to characterize accusations of treason and extremism, along with demagogic personal attacks on the character and patriotism of political adversaries. A conspiratorial discourse such as the McCarthy one is a political-ideological demagogic fabrication; its targeted victims are the "enemies within" (the code) who must be eradicated to restore "purity" to the nation. A major element in the conspiratorial infrastructure of the conspiracy were "clues" of a communist takeover that McCarthy constantly presented as factual, allowing people to connect them into a conspiratorial narrative on their own, guided by McCarthy's own presentation of the clues, thus creating a context for political apophenia in America to crystallize. Most of the clues were the statements made by the purported members of the communist cabal, which would be interpreted otherwise as random assertions, but which, when united apophenically, seemed to point to the conspiratorial code.

In his novel, *Foucault's Pendulum* (1989), Umberto Eco laid out in fictional form what a conspiracy theory such as the McCarthy one is essentially about, showing how it congeals into verisimilitude via its semiotic infrastructure, thus constituting one of the first semiotic analyses of conspiracism in fictional form. The "pendulum" of the title refers at an uncoded level to the pendulum designed by French physicist Léon Foucault, but it could also be an indirect coded reference to Michel Foucault, who had developed a friendship with Eco.

The novel opens with a university student, named Casaubon, hiding in the Musée des Arts et Métiers after it had closed down for the day, believing that a secret society was after him. He had arranged a secret meeting with his friend Jacopo Belbo in the museum. As he waits, Casaubon starts reflecting on his life, which had been damaged by his belief in conspiracy theories. He was studying the story of the Knights Templar at university when he met Belbo, an editor, who then invited Casaubon to review a manuscript about the Templars submitted for publication by a certain Colonel Ardenti, in which Ardenti claims that he had uncovered a secret plan of the Templars to take over the world. A meeting between Ardenti, Casaubon, and Belbo is arranged, after which Ardenti mysteriously vanishes. After getting on with his life, Casaubon becomes involved with a publisher of occult books, becoming submerged in convoluted conspiracies based on flimsy connections between historical events. Seeing them as enticing intellectual games, Casaubon approaches Belbo to develop their own conspiracy in the form of a game, which they call "The Plan"—eerily foreshadowing (or perhaps inspiring) QAnon conspiracism. Even though the computer program they use for the game is a simple one that rearranges text at random, the Plan is reconstructed as an intricate web of conspiratorial clues about the Templars and their goal to reshape the world using "telluric currents." As it turns out, Causubon and Belbo become obsessed with the Plan and wonder if it could actually be true, even if it was sewn together textually from random bits of evidence. They even start to explain events in their own lives as controlled by the Plan. At the novel's end, Casaubon reflects on the tragedies that befell him as a consequence of his conspiratorial thinking, believing that the secret cabal that his game describes might actually bring about the end for him. The novel is a deconstruction of the persuasiveness of conspiratorial themes found in literature and occultist books. It shows how the connection of sign clues into a complex infrastructure binds people to the conspiracy, from which there is no easy escape.

The novel also highlights the presence of an intrinsic "meta-code" that has always motivated conspiracist thinking, no matter when or where it surfaces—namely, the notion that there is a secret society made up of a sinister and powerful cabal of élites and financial barons working behind the scenes, aiming to control the world—a meta-code that might have become inscribed archetypally into the brain as a kind of neural semiotic pattern that can be easily activated with fictional works, political narratives, and the like. The cabal may be communists (McCarthyism), Illuminati (Bavarian cabal), liberal élites (MAGA), or the Jews (Nazism)—but its semiotic infrastructure is always the same one, namely an array of sign clues that are united via apophenic reasoning. What is relevant here is that the meta-code generates derived ones (inter-codability) grounded on sign systems that are utilized intentionally to deliver its meaning. It does not matter what event or phenomenon is involved. During the coronavirus pandemic, for example, the theme of conspiratorial politics behind the scenes became a major theme of radical right-wing individuals, who pegged the culprit behind the pandemic as the deep state in the United States. The cabal had purportedly hired doctors and medical researchers to perpetrate the pandemic hoax. In the convoluted semiotic infrastructure of QAnon conspiracism, the hoax was portrayed as a strategy on the part of the deep state specifically to bring Trump down. As a result of such conspiratorial discourses, antivaccine protests and the belief that Covid-19 was even a form of biowarfare spread worldwide (Nie 2020). Because conspiracy theories resist falsification, one of the negative legacies of Covid-19 pandemic conspiracism has been to embed a widespread distrust of science and a spread of political cynicism.

Conspiracy theories are second-order mythologies, to use Roland Barthes's term (Barthes 1957). The major function of myth, Barthes claimed, was to "naturalize" a mode of thought or belief as being necessarily true, no matter the real truth of the matter. Modern myths are, however, to be differentiated from the original myths, which emerged as a means for people to understand real events, before the advent of science. They were *de facto* theories of why disasters such as floods and diseases were foisted upon the world. The false mythologies that are imprinted in conspiratorial theories today surface, instead, to provide explanations that fit in with biases, prejudices, fears, or belief systems. A false myth is a contrary-to-science narrative and even a contrary-to-logic story that is almost impossible to eradicate because it literally "makes sense" on its own once it is accepted. Barthes saw the spread of such semiotic infrastructure as emanating from the entertainment world, where, he claimed, mythologies are recycled for reasons of pacification of the masses and for financial gain on the part of their congeners. Orwell also equated entertainment with mind control in totalitarian states. This was one of the main tactics of the Ministry of Truth, "which concerned itself with news, entertainment, education, and the fine arts" (Orwell 1949: 7).

The entertainment value of conspiracism itself is evidenced by the popularity of conspiracy-based novels and movies, which, as Peter Knight (2021) has observed, are "often created under the guise of making sense of the world around us." Knight goes on to claim that some fictional works may even inspire real-world conspiracies, affecting the mental outlook of individuals and even entire societies:

> They repeatedly create scenarios in which the hero (nearly always a white man) feels that his liberty, identity and agency—and even his body—are in danger of being controlled by vast, shadowy forces. In order to understand What Is Really Going On, these fictions willfully embrace a form of what Pynchon has called "creative paranoia". They present conspiracy theory as a way of understanding impersonal systems in the age of state power, corporate capitalism and mass media. The conspiracy is no longer an easily detected foreign plot to infiltrate the nation, but a more ambiguous and pervasive threat from within. Given this situation, it is not surprising that much of this fiction focuses self-consciously on the question of how we know what we think we know.

As Priniski, McClay, and Holyoak (2021) found in their study of QAnon, fictional mythology plays a defining role in the formation of this conspiracy group. Particularly prominent in shaping the group's belief system are Lewis Carroll's Alice novels and the movie *The Matrix*. The researchers use the term "hypercoherence" to suggest that these works of fiction and QAnon beliefs are interlinked (Priniski, McClay, and Holyoak 2021):

> Conspiracies such as QAnon may be a natural consequence of a social media environment that: (1) prioritizes false information over verifiable information, and (2) allows for the easy and rapid formation of echo chambers, or pockets of

online communities that share and consume nearly identical, belief-confirming information. Once misinformation is introduced that coheres with the narrative of a particular echo chamber, it may foster the generation of additional content by simultaneously adding to the coherence of the community's narrative while reducing its standard of plausibility. Misinformation may therefore gradually reconfigure a person's belief network toward stronger degrees of coherence, making it more capable of binding disparate and implausible beliefs. The result is belief in conspiracies that cover a wide range of narrative clusters.

The ideational starting point for QAnon is traced by some media scholars and psychologists, in fact, to *The Matrix*. The closing monologue of the movie is a stark warning delivered by the hero Neo who has discovered that humanity was trapped in a simulated reality: "I don't know the future … I didn't come here to tell you how this is going to end, I came here to tell you how it's going to begin." It is relevant to note that the creators of the movie loosely based their dystopian vision on the book *Simulacra and Simulations* by Jean Baudrillard (1981), which they asked the actors to read so as to better prepare for their roles. In that book, the phrase "desert of the real" is used by Baudrillard in reference to what he called the illusions of capitalism. The film used this exact same phrase when Morpheus introduced Neo to the ruins of the outside world. Escape from the matrix involves escape from the simulated world created by technology to covertly enslave humanity.

The movie introduced several notions that QAnon has coopted, transforming them into core principles. One of these is *red-pilling*, which comes from a scene in which Morpheus offers Neo (then still a real-world hacker named Thomas Anderson) a choice between a blue or red pill. The former would allow Anderson to return to his normal life, unaware of the matrix (and thus the truth), whereas the red pill would lead him to enlightenment—awareness of the tyranny of machines. As Morpheus put it: "The Matrix is the world that has been pulled over your eyes to blind you from the truth." The red pill metaphor has been adopted, recycled, and reinterpreted constantly by conspiratorial online communities, thus removing it from its original context of meaning, such as opening one's eyes to reality, evoking Plato's cave analogy, rather than some inherent conspiratorial system in the hands of a hidden cabal. Red-pilling is a conspiratorial synonym for "freeing the mind"—a slogan for far-right populism that positions itself as anti-establishment. By "taking the red pill" believers will finally "wake up" to the truth, namely that something nefarious is harboring behind the scenes in America. It is little wonder that QAnon and other conspiratorial groups used the red pill metaphor as an intrinsic node with their mythological-narrative infrastructure, using it to galvanize support for Trump during the 2016 electoral campaign. As Madison (2021) has perceptively remarked:

> The red pill became synonymous with Trump supporters' message to establishment politics. Rather than referring to a choice, like the one Morpheus offered to Neo, the phrase was recast as a verb: to redpill. This is not an option you're given, but something done to you. The term became synonymous with the violent attitude of the alt-right movement—we're going to make you aware of our reality, whether you like it or not. After Trump's election, the term continued to evolve in curious ways … [as a result] the serious sense of "waking up to the truth" that alt-righters used redpilling to mean was weathered down with irony until it revealed what may be the true meaning of the term: to become a superfan of something, political or otherwise.

Narratives of conspiratorial groups working behind the scenes, as Eco's novel clearly suggested, have always existed becoming real when someone actually believes them. The red pill metaphor was appropriated by QAnon to reinforce the mendacious notion that cabalistic systems of government were hiding in plain sight. The consequences have been deleterious, as relevant research by Rajan et al. (2021) has brought out, which has shown that:

- conspiracy narratives radicalize susceptible audiences to condone, and even perform, acts of violence and terrorism;
- have profoundly harmful impacts on victims, affecting the mental health of many negatively;
- tend to radicalize segments of a society, which believe that élites are indeed controlling the world;
- help in recruiting radicalized individuals;
- raise the threat level for political violence.

As Cory Knudson (2018) perceptively remarks, Eco's novel emerges as crucial in "prefiguring an alarming and increasingly mainstream current of far-right conspiracy thinking that Eco could never have known would arise in the United States nearly a half-century after he started writing fiction." QAnon members, like the characters in *Foucault's Pendulum*, develop a fictionalized mind state, believing that the world they live in is dreadful because it is controlled by secretive puppet masters and their shadowy plots to manipulate people too blinded or comfortable to realize the truth. As Knudson goes on to note, the insight that Eco's novel introduced to semiotics at the time was that the source of conspiracism is apophenic thinking—the construction of an imaginary plot via the connection of random signs (clues)—which is the same source of belief in the mysterious character Q:

> This influence lies in the incredibly powerful story-construction model Q has put in motion. Dropping only hints, Q encourages self-styled investigators to trawl every nook of major and minor news media, every politician's slip of the tongue, every dubious paper trail, every stilted syllable out of the president's mouth until there is no event or word, however negligible, that does not fit neatly into a cosmology over which a nearly omniscient, four-dimensional-chess-playing Donald Trump calmly resides, waiting for his opportunity to vanquish evil for good and all.

The power of conspiracy thinking, as Eco had made obvious, is that, sooner or later, everyone is implicated in the story and we all become characters in its plot—a universal Plan (as he phrased it) that is unfolding before our eyes. As Causubon asserts upon seeing Foucault's Pendulum hanging from the nave of the Paris Conservatoire at the beginning of the novel (Eco 1989):

> The Pendulum told me that, as everything moved—earth, solar system, nebulae, and black holes, all the children of the great cosmic expansion—one single point stood still: a pivot, bolt, or hook around which the universe could move. And I was now taking part in that supreme experience. I too moved with the all, but I could see the One, the Rock, the Guarantee.

Eco's semiotic deconstruction of conspiracism comes at the end of the novel, when we are confronted with the fact that the Pendulum of conspiracism, from which Belbo is hanging by his neck, has had real-world consequences. In the end conspiracism is a search for meaning in the randomness of events that daily life presents to us. By projecting it against a semiotic infrastructure revolving around a code (the Pendulum), it gives the search a sense of meaningfulness. To cite Knudson (2018):

> Both Eco's and Q's stories are those of people desperate for meaning … Our willingness to submit to a story that makes it all make sense—the *complotto dei complotti* [our "meta-code"]—is as deep-seated and seemingly indelible in our psyche as difficult to resist as the momentum propelling the pendulum that swings from the nave of the Paris Observatoire. The point to which the pendulum is tied is void, but a void can fit a lot—even everything—given the right perspective or the right storyteller. "If you alter the Book, you alter the world; if you alter the world, you alter the body. This is what we didn't understand," says one of the editors shortly before the Game, in its way, kills him. The final, inevitable choice Eco leaves us with may be to either seize the momentum of Foucault's pendulum or hang from it.

Eco understood that conspiracism is based on confabulation. As Casaubon puts it in the novel, the goal is "not to discover the Templars' secret, but to construct it" (Eco 1989). A good conspiracy is like a web page, full of conceptual hyperlinks, which, when clicked on, impel us to notice increasingly complex connections, united through a complex infrastructure of sign forms, that we accept as true because our sense is that no one would bother to invent something so complicated just for the sake of it—hence the generation of belief in the verity of the infrastructure. As Causobon concludes: "Luck rewarded us, because, wanting connections, we found connections—always, everywhere, and between everything. The world exploded into a whirling network of kinships, where everything pointed to everything else, everything explained everything else."

Visualization

The Nazi Aryan election poster discussed above is a compact visual rendering of the Aryan myth, focusing on specific signifying elements within it that can be given a visual iconic form. It is, in other words, a self-contained visual narrative text that is suggestive of Aryanism. Such visual narrativity is a powerful node in the semiotic infrastructure that supports the Aryan mythology given the power of iconicity to shape interpretive processes, as discussed at length by Rudolf Arnheim (1969), who challenged the traditional differentiation between "thinking" (associated with language) and "perceiving" (associated with visual art), claiming that the two have been artificially separated, since they both co-occur in human understanding. This co-occurrence is the likely reason why visual representations that correspond to the discursive-narrative ones have been used in the construction of all kinds of dangerous conspiratorial discourses. As Aldous Huxley (1942) so perceptively remarked, visual communication affects how we see and thus how we come to know:

> Within your visual communication there will inevitably be some information or meaning beyond the image itself for the person seeing to find. This makes visual communication a very powerful tool, by influencing what people see, you influence what they know, and by influencing what they know you further influence what they see.

Matthew Hannah (2021) makes a strong case that a conspiratorial group, such as QAnon, is constantly relying on visual forms, such as diagrams, cartoons, photos, and even maps to instill its conspiratorial messages more deeply, given their iconic persuasiveness. Connecting the "visual dots" left by Q is guided, of course, by the underlying code (as discussed). The drops invariably incorporate images, showing individuals or locations relevant to a particular manifestation of the conspiratorial code, enhancing the suggestiveness factor. Q is purported to have insider knowledge, working undercover in the deep state apparatus—hence the belief in the truth that the images are assumed to embed. This extends even to maps, such as the so-called "Deep State Mapping" project, which purportedly identifies the exact geographical locations where the deep state conspiracies take place or where nefarious deep state actors operate. The illusion created by such strategies is that if something is "mappable" in the first place it must be true. In this case, the fabricated map *is* its own territory, providing intricate details of how the deep state has implanted itself into America, showing where 5G cell tower radiation, microchip implants in vaccines, and the like are presumably located. Such false maps work conceptually because they tie conspiracy threads together visually in real geographical space. As Hannah (2021) goes on to observe, the real power of QAnon conspiracism lies in such visuality as a means to construct its meaning system:

> Visualization is especially prominent among QAnon communities, and this adoption of information visualization has proven especially problematic when encountered by online users who may naïvely believe such visualizations are accurate representations of some data "out there" in the world without a framework to critique or deconstruct such data interpretations. Whereas the possibility of naïve readers being unduly influenced by the rhetoric of information visualization is nothing new, the scale of viral online development, spread, and recruitment using such visual data reflects an unsettling new trend in global communications. These visualizations do not accurately reflect actual data, but instead an informational framework already put into place by QAnon, and this slippage is used for full effect in advancing the movement.

The construction of maps for advancing a cause or movement is actually an age-old visualization tactic. A French map-poster from 1917, for instance, portrays Prussia as an octopus stretching out its tentacles to capture territory suggestively. Prussia was an independent state at the time with a powerful military. The Nazis engaged in similar cartographic propaganda, producing maps (Tyner 1974) based on three main deceits (Boria 2008): (1) maps showing Germany as a united Aryan nation, (2) strategic maps designed to keep the United States neutral in the war by changing the perception of threats, and (3) maps as blueprints of the post-war world.

Cartographic propaganda has been used by all ideologies and factions on the political spectrum. An archival example is traced to the early Cold War period, when in April of 1946 the liberal *Time* magazine published a map titled "Communist Contagion," emphasizing the strength of the Soviet Union at the time via a split-spherical presentation of Europe and Asia which made the Soviet Union seem larger, thus suggesting expansion through visual metaphor. The theme of communist expansion was reinforced by the use of the color red—associated both with communism and danger, suggesting that neighboring states were in danger of being invaded by the "red menace."

It is relevant to cite Peirce's anecdotal remark about the power of maps to influence thought, which is clearly relevant to the foregoing discussion (Peirce 1931–1958, volume 4: 530).

> But why do that [use maps] when the thought itself is present to us? Such, substantially, has been the interrogative objection raised by an eminent and glorious General. Recluse that I am, I was not ready with the counter-question, which should have run, "General, you make use of maps during a campaign, I believe. But why should you do so, when the country they represent is right there?" Thereupon, had he replied that he found details in the maps that were so far from being "right there," that they were within the enemy's lines, I ought to have pressed the question, "Am I right, then, in understanding that, if you were thoroughly and perfectly familiar with the country, no map of it would then be of the smallest use to you in laying out your detailed plans?" No, I do not say that, since I might probably desire the maps to stick pins into, so as to mark each anticipated day's change in the situations of the two armies." "Well, General, that precisely corresponds to the advantages of a diagram of the course of a discussion. Namely, if I may try to state the matter after you, one can make exact experiments upon uniform diagrams; and when one does so, one must keep a bright lookout for unintended and unexpected changes thereby brought about in the relations of different significant parts of the diagram to one another. Such operations upon diagrams, whether external or imaginary, take the place of the experiments upon real things that one performs in chemical and physical research.

The potency of visualization was also discussed insightfully by Susanne Langer (1946), who provided a plausible psychological reason why visual images have such a profound emotional effect on us. We do not experience a visual image, she emphasized, as a mere representation of people and things, etc., but as a total emotional experience of the referent. It is only when we attempt to understand why the visual text had such an effect on us that the holistic experience can be taken apart discursively. But, no matter how many times we try to understand the experience logically, by talking about it, the feeling we get from the picture remains larger than the sum of the words used to describe it.

In the end, visualizing something concrete (such as a map or a pendulum) as standing for something abstract is what seems likely to engender belief and shape worldview. As Causubon stated upon seeing Foucault's Pendulum: "The Pendulum told me that, as everything moved—earth, solar system, nebulae and black holes—one single point stood still. How could you fail to kneel down before this altar of certitude?"

Epilogue

Symbols such as the swastika are powerful sign forms when inserted into semiotic linkages that cohere into a unified meaning-referential infrastructure based on a core code (or set of codes). The swastika became associated, in fact, with the idea of a racially pure state because of its insertion into the infrastructure, emblemizing the false myth of Aryanism, constantly reminding anyone who saw it of the underlying code, used to construct the legitimacy of the Nazi totalitarian regime. Symbols and conspiracy theories are thematically interrelated, no matter what the code involved might be.

Consider the official emblem of a conspiratorial group called the Priory of Sion, which is a version of the fleur-de-lis, the symbol associated with the French monarchy, encircled by a knot, recalling a Gordian Knot symbolism that, if untangled, will show the truth according to the relevant mythology. The emblem and the conspiracy narrative on which it is based were fabricated in 1956 by a graphic designer named Pierre Plantard, as part of his strategy to become a major player in French monarchist circles. Plantard weaved together bits and pieces of what he claimed was evidence to support the historical existence of the Priory, including the so-called *Dossiers Secrets d'Henri Lobineau*, left opportunistically in various locations around France by Plantard and his accomplices. The dossiers were subsequently found to be forged; but despite this fact, many still persist to this day in believing the central false claim of the Priory that Jesus and Mary Magdalene were married and left a bloodline of which Plantard was a descendant. No doubt, the continuation and even proliferation of the false narrative are due in large part to the popularity of pseudo-historical books, websites, novels, and films inspired by the Priory of Sion hoax, which have imprinted the mythology into the popular imagination. All this shows the power of apophenic thinking to create an illusion of truth. In contrast to an epiphany, an apophany does not provide insight into the real nature of interconnectedness, but is the result of interpreting random clues, as if they did have an underlying meaning. When signs are linked in some systematic way they form semiotic networks almost automatically, which may or may not be referentially valid. As a result, conspiratorial thinking produces an illusory truth effect (Chapter 1), the proclivity to believe false information to be correct after repeated exposure and, as is claimed here, via the construction of semiotic connectivity among the elements in the information.

Conspiratorial thinking is everywhere because of the Internet today. As Julia Sonnevend (2020: 451) has emphasized, because of its broad diffusion it generates dangerous anti-science beliefs, such as those that emerged during the Covid-19 pandemic. It is the organicity of twisted aphophenic thinking that allows something like the Aryan myth to instill in people the hatred of others, allowing a charismatic individual (Hitler) and group (the Nazis) to gain mind control. Eradicating the others from society through any means possible became the rallying cry of the Nazis, leading to horrendous events such as the Holocaust. Once followers insert themselves into the apocryphal storyline, they see themselves as valiant characters in the outcomes of the story. The leader (the *Führer*) is perceived as the hero of the story, a possessor of hidden truth that has been repressed by the people that he singles out as the destroyers of history, and who will lead people to victory over the villains in the story.

It is chilling to consider that the same kind of mythic narrative infrastructure was projected (literally) onto the early cinema screen as a foundation story of America—namely, the silent 1915 film, directed by D. W. Griffith, *The Birth of a Nation*. The plot revolved around the supposed key role that the Ku Klux Klan played in the origins of the nation, implicitly suggesting that America was built on the cultural heritage of white settlers, even though other cultures had lived in America beforehand. The movie arouses controversy to this day. To be fair, there is no biographical evidence to suggest that Griffith himself was a racist. He claimed to have highlighted the role of the KKK in the birth of America in order to portray history realistically, rather than selectively or idealistically. His subsequent film, *Intolerance* (1916), was a lengthy epic covering four historical periods. It is seen as his apology for the horrible effects of racism on American history and culture. Whatever the truth, Griffith's movie laid down the narrative code for conspiratorial white supremacy groups to emerge centuries later. Its semiotic network structure can be described as follows:

- *Crusade symbolism:* The film portrays a crusade-type situation whereby the KKK is involved in removing the "heathens" from society.
- *Crosses symbolism:* The crosses used by the KKK further reinforce the crusade theme, symbolizing the quest to save and preserve the purported Christian origins of America.

- *Secret power:* The masks covering the identities of the Klansmen are suggestive of the power of secret organizations to work effectively behind the scenes, conveying fearsomeness.
- *Burning cross:* The image of burning crosses is one of the most powerful hate and terror symbols in the United States. Cross-burnings by KKK groups have been used to intimidate and terrorize victims.

Today, we get most of our conspiracy theories from social media, rather than from film or print texts. Modern-day historians point to conspiracism during the 2016 presidential election, orchestrated by Russian-based cyber-specialists, as a major factor in bringing about the completely unexpected election of a rich businessman, Donald Trump. The spread of disinformation by Russian operatives was designed to undermine the confidence of Americans in their electoral system and to denigrate Trump's opponent. Between January 2015 and August 2017, Facebook alone linked over 80,000 posts to the Russian Internet Research Agency and over 50,000 Twitter accounts to Russian bots, supporting Donald Trump through the hashtags #donaldtrump, #trump2016, #neverhillary, and #trumppence16. Most of the posts were aligned suggestively to long-standing mythologies of how America was born and how it has been destroyed by liberalism (Subramanian 2017). As this episode in American politics showed, the spread of falsehoods is now just an algorithm away. The algorithmic world has, in fact, greatly facilitated the spread and recycling of mythic narrativity, from versions of Nazi Aryanism to Priory of Sion conspiracies, turning the global village into one that appears to be increasingly based on falsity and pseudo-science. The following warning by Moskalenko and Bloom (2021) is worth repeating here:

> Why would outlandish conspiracy theories hold sway ... around the country? One way to comprehend the incomprehensible is to recognize the parallels between QAnon and addictive drugs like opioids—which are also manipulated by malicious actors to trap vulnerable people in increasingly unhealthy spirals that ultimately result in the destruction of families and even death. Recognizing these similarities is helpful in both accurately diagnosing the QAnon phenomenon and trying to treat it.

It is not coincidental that the term apophenia was introduced by Conrad (1958) as a syndrome consisting of "unmotivated seeing of connections [accompanied by] a specific feeling of abnormal meaningfulness." The question of how apophenia works semiotically was indirectly tackled by Eco with his novels, showing that it creates believability via its tacit narrative structure. This is in line with what Wendy Wheeler (2006) calls "tacit, semiotic knowledge," which, she suggests, is applied constantly to decode any system of signs that was "never encoded in the first place," but generated by the semiotic brain. It was such tacit semiotic knowledge that Eco was exploring in his novel, *Foucault's Pendulum*, which is what assigns credibility, or more precisely credulousness, to conspiracy theories. As the character Casaubon put it in the novel:

> Incredulity doesn't kill curiosity; it encourages it. Though distrustful of logical chains of ideas, I loved the polyphony of ideas. As long as you don't believe in them, the collision of two ideas—both false—can create a pleasing interval, a kind of *diabolus in musica*. I had no respect for some ideas people were willing to stake their lives on, but two or three ideas that I did not respect might still make a nice melody. Or have a good beat, and if it was jazz, all the better.

6

Semiotics with a Conscience

Prologue

In a historically famous letter, the French writer Émile Zola wrote the following words, which are worth repeating here, given that they encapsulate in microcosm one of the main goals of semiotics with a conscience, not only to expose the ways in which dangerous discourses produce twisted meanings, but also to provide a means to assail unethical forms of discourse. Zola designates such forms as crimes (in Zola 1996):

> It is a crime to mislead public opinion, to use this opinion which has been perverted to the point of delirium for a death task. It is a crime to poison the small and the humble, to exasperate the passions of reaction and intolerance, by sheltering behind the odious anti-Semitism, of which the great liberal France of human rights will die, if she is not cured of it. It is a crime to exploit patriotism for works of hate, and it is a crime, finally, to make the saber the modern god, when all human science is at work for the next work of truth and justice. This truth, this justice, which we so passionately wanted, what distress to see them thus puffed up, more unrecognized and more obscured!

The letter was written in response to the 1894 court-martialing of Jewish army captain, Alfred Dreyfus, by the French army on the basis of an intercepted message which the army claimed was written by Dreyfus, proving that he was carrying out espionage on behalf of Germany. The letter was a forgery, as it turned out, but the trials that ensued provoked anti-Semitic sentiments, splitting French society virtually down the middle—for or against Dreyfus. Zola's open letter was published on the front page of the newspaper *L'Aurore* on January 13, 1898, beginning with the accusatory phrase "*J'accuse.*" In the letter, addressed to the President of the Republic, Zola blamed the army for covering up its wrong conviction of Dreyfus, becoming instrumental in mobilizing public response to what came to be known as the Dreyfus Affair. The excerpt above actually breaks down how the wanton use of falsehoods worked psychologically, thus encapsulating much of the thematic discussions in this book—namely, by misleading public opinion, using deception to create a "delirium," exasperating the "passions of reaction and intolerance," sheltering behind the "odious anti-Semitism," and exploiting patriotism for "works of hate," all of which destroy "truth and justice." As a result of the letter, Zola himself was brought to trial on February 7, 1898, and sentenced to a one-year imprisonment and a fine of 3,000 francs for libel. But Zola's letter achieved results nonetheless, since it led to a new trial for Dreyfus. Although he was still found guilty, Dreyfus was pardoned by the president of the Republic. Only in 1906 was Dreyfus finally cleared of all wrongdoing.

The Dreyfus Affair to which Zola is referring is a horrific example of how a single lie can mutate into a dangerous discourse, dividing an entire society deeply along racial lines, remaining one of the most notable examples of anti-Semitism and of the miscarriage of justice to this day. As mentioned, the affair began in 1894 when Dreyfus, a thirty-five-year-old artillery officer of Jewish descent, was convicted of treason for allegedly communicating French military secrets to the German Embassy in Paris. Two years later, evidence came to light which identified the real culprit as a French army major named Ferdinand Walsin Esterhazy. But high-ranking military officials suppressed the new evidence, and a military court unanimously acquitted Esterhazy. The army then laid additional charges against Dreyfus. It was right after that Zola wrote his letter, which fueled broad support for Dreyfus, putting pressure on the government to reopen the case. A new trial resulted in another conviction, as mentioned, but Dreyfus was however pardoned and released, likely to avoid further civil unrest, given that riots had broken out in cities across France. The point to be emphasized here is that a single false accusation was the spark that ignited hatred that was likely harboring just below the social surface.

Adding credence to the perceived plausibility of the falsehood was the fact that the document offering military secrets to the Germans was found in a bin and sent to the French Secret Service. This supposed happenstance discovery injected an air of treachery into the affair, turning it into a conspiratorial narrative with shifting boundaries between truth and lies, politics and everyday life. It is not coincidental that it was in France in the same period that a member of the Russian secret police concocted the *Protocols of the Elders of Zion* (Chapter 2), used to promote the false claim of a Jewish conspiracy to take over the world. The dovetailing of the Dreyfus Affair with such blatant anti-Semitic conspiracism was arguably the key factor that ignited the riots in the streets.

Dreyfus became the symbolic dark Jewish figure in the purported conspiracy, reinforced by caricatures in posters, depicting a snake-headed Dreyfus (a common anti-Semitic metaphor), and labeled a "*traître*" ("traitor"). Even before the Nazis adopted snake symbolism as an anti-Semitic trope, the portrayals of Dreyfus already associated Jews with snakes to suggest cunningness and untrustworthiness. In effect, the poster depicts Alfred Dreyfus as a hydra—a many-headed snake in Greek mythology whose heads grew again after they were cut off. This image thus encapsulates in visual-symbolic form the perceived treason and disloyalty of Jews.

The Dreyfus case emphatically illustrates, in sum, how a dangerous discourse, described in this book as a form of discursive representation (verbal and nonverbal) based on a code that is delivered through a semiotic network of sign types (rhetorical, imagistic, etc.), can arise when even a single lie is connected to the code—the cabalistic one in this case. Conspiratorial codes loosen people's relationship with reality, provoking the suspension of any rational analysis of a situation. It is in decoding dangerous discourses, such as the Dreyfus one, that semiotics can help, perhaps, restore rational ethical discursivity broadly, or at the very least provide a framework for understanding the semiotic structure of the dangerous ones. This is actually a theme in Liszka's (2022) comprehensive discussion of Charles Peirce's amalgam of ethics and aesthetics, which, he claims, provides a path toward the pursuit of ethics in sign use. The key aspect here is the aesthetic one—given the power of art to affect understanding. The same type of conclusion was reached by Barthes, as discussed several times—namely that it is through the use of different semiotic forms, including artistic ones, that a way to restore ethical communication can be envisioned. The publication in 2002 of his preparatory notes for his lectures at the Collège de France (Pieters and Pint 2008) shows that he was aiming to actually start a semiotic project in "social ethics," which was left unrealized due to his death shortly after. Semiotics with a conscience is just one response to such pleas. Remarkably, in one of the lectures Barthes identifies the mass of information to which people are exposed, which blocks any critical extraction of meaning from it, as a major cause for the collapse of ethical behavior—an observation that came well before the advent of the Internet (Pieters and Pint 2008):

> Today, information: pulverized, nonhierarchized, dealing with everything: nothing is protected from information and at the same time nothing is open to reflection. Encyclopedias are impossible. I would say: the more information grows, the more knowledge retreats and therefore the more decision is partial (terroristic, dogmatic). "I don't know," "I refuse to judge": as scandalous as

an agrammatical sentence: doesn't belong to the language of the discourse. Variations on the "I don't know." The obligation to "be interested" in everything that is imposed on you by the world: prohibition of noninterest, even if provisional.

This final chapter will tie together some theoretical and methodological threads so as to address in a summary way the underlying question motivating this book: Can semiotics help thwart the dangerous effects of the meaning collapses due to conspiracism, communication dysfunctions based on big lies, and the like? The right to speak out publicly or privately, through any medium, is a fundamental one of free democratic societies. But the master liar (individual or group) can take advantage of this very right to twist people's minds, violating ethical speech. Historians have put forth a variety of explanations for the downfall of civilizations. One of these is certainly the emergence of unethical forms of discourse since the dawn of history. Understanding how these have come about and what semiotic structures are used to construct them is the ultimate goal of an ethics-based semiotics.

Inter-Codability

However one conceives of semiotics as a discipline, tool, doctrine, etc., ultimately it can be characterized as a study of how meaning (sense, understanding, thought patterning, etc.) is perceived and how it unfolds in terms of how it is represented via signs and sign systems. Needless to say, the word "meaning" is a problematic one, as Ogden and Richards argued cogently in their famous book, *The Meaning of Meaning* (1923). To resolve the problem, the two authors suggest a model that is highly consistent with the network model proposed here whereby, as they put it, meaning can only be achieved via sign forms and "through their occurrence together with things, their linkage with them in a 'context' [as they] come to play that important part in our life the source of all our power over the external world" (Ogden and Richards 1923: 47).

The term *code* has been used in reference to how the sign linkages deliver meaning unconsciously by revolving around a core meaning system (the code). Without a code or set of codes signs have no external referentiality. As Jakobson (1960) suggested, a code allows users to consistently reference meanings by means of the particular forms that derive from it. In the semiotic method adopted here, the notion of inter-codability implies that there are various codes (or subcodes) that are derived from, or connected to, each other in terms of sharing the same meaning. This notion encompasses the well-established notion of intertextuality, since it is inherent in it—intertexts emerge within the coded-based network itself as T-nodes. So, a code such as the cabalistic one is intertwined with other codes (such as the code of racial purity), which deliver the same meaning in different ways in different contexts, including via texts that reference each other either directly or implicitly. This isomorphism of meaning shows up, in effect, in the actual sign and textual forms in the relevant networks (as discussed throughout this book).

As Barthes emphasized (e.g., 1968), and as discussed briefly, meaning unfolds on two levels—denotative (uncoded) and connotative (coded). This implies that signs always extend into connotative, suggestive, latent, and other modes of coded meaning, which are largely unconscious. What makes discourses dangerous, such as those that are connected with Nazism or Fascism, is the fact that the coded meaning is below the threshold of consciousness, whereby it can be manipulated for ideological purposes. Inter-codability reinforces the danger because one overarching code (as, e.g., Aryanism) is then connected to subsidiary codes, such as the cabal one of a Jewish plot to control the world.

It is relevant to note that the term *codability* was forged within structural linguistics as a means to explain the relation between language, thought, and perception. It designated any lexical system which allowed people to name specific things and the effects of such naming on their cognition and behavior. In 1954, Roger Brown and Eric Lenneberg carried out a series of experiments to show how codability in one specific domain of reference (color) affected perception and understanding in particular ways. In one experiment, speakers of English and Zuñi were asked to name specific color stimuli. The researchers found that, in naming colors, the length of the name, the rapidity in naming, and the agreement in naming between the two languages were good indices of codability. The colors with the highest degree of cross-linguistic codability occupied central positions on the color spectrum, named in English as *red, orange, yellow, green, blue, purple, pink,* and *brown*, while colors with the lowest codability fell within transitional areas between any two such segments on the spectrum—say, between English green and blue. As it turned out, the Zuñi speakers showed lexical differences with regard to this region, given that they had one lexeme that covered the same hue range of English green and blue. As Brown commented in a later work (1958: 241): "the more codable categories of experience are also more available and that more codable stimuli are centrally located in available categories."

As suggested in Chapter 1, the semiotic network model used here is somewhat similar to connectionist (artificial) models of mind, whereby there is an input layer that flows through a hidden layer to produce an output. In the semiotic model, the hidden layer is the code or set of inter-codes, while the input layer is the system of signs that passes through the code to produce the intended meaning (the output). The connectionist diagram below is a generic one that can be applied to semiotic network theory as well, since it shows the different layers as consisting of nodes in a network (Figure 6.1).

The central principle in models of connectionism is that mental states can be described by interconnected networks of conceptual units. The structure of the connections among the units is what assigns meaning to the utilizations of the networks. At any time, a node in the network can be activated semiotically, which then spreads to all the other nodes connected to it. As Anna Aragno (2019: 212) has pointed out, the mind itself may be construed as a blend of nodes of information that are "based on progressive stages in the development

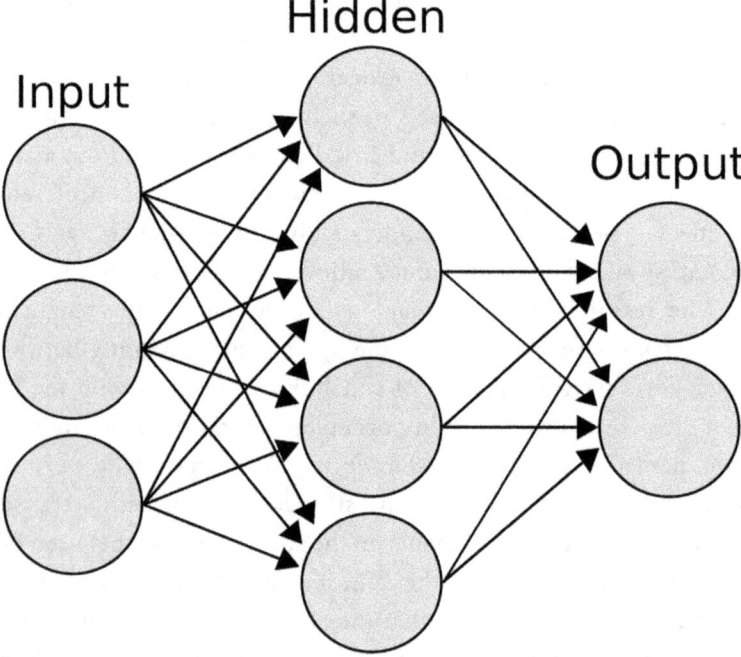

Figure 6.1 Connectionist Model.

Source: https://en.wikipedia.org/wiki/File:Artificial_neural_network.svg. "Permission is granted to copy, distribute and/or modify this document under the terms of the GNU Free Documentation License, Version 1.2 or any later version published by the Free Software Foundation."

of symbolization, a cerebral faculty unique to our species, distinguishing us from all other animals, without which we could neither speak nor conceive of 'Mind' at all." Similarly, Georgij Somov (2016) sees the role of the interlinkages of semiotic codes as the core pattern in semiosis (meaning production and meaning extraction):

> Codes can be viewed as mechanisms that enable relations of signs and their components, i.e., semiosis is actualized. The combinations of these relations produce new relations as new codes are building over other codes. Structures appear in the mechanisms of codes … Hence, codes can be described as transformations of structures from some material systems into others, which reflects the way typical semiotic formations emerge in mind based on the interrelations of various codes.

It can be argued, therefore, that "meaning" is a result of inter-codability and of the sign structures that derive from the overall connective system. One could even claim that our sense of conscience itself is developed from the assemblages of sign forms designed to convey truth-based referentiality. Without these there would be no conscience in the usual ontological sense, just instinctive feelings. The aim of semiotics would be not to raise up conscience, but to unravel how it has been coded and thus understood. This constitutes one way to expose how discourses become unethical, namely how they can redirect the mind to regions in the brain that bear negative images of people and things, as they have developed over time. To use the connectionist model, dangerous discourses manipulate the input nodes that flow through an embedded code to produce outputs that can be twisted to induce hatred or false beliefs. At the very least, this approach provides a way for discussing dangerous discourses in concrete semiotic terms. For instance, it can be used to provide an explanation of why Nazi propagandists branded Jews as a "biological threat" to Germany, a metaphor that flows through the anti-Semitic code that Jews are a threat, producing a meaning output that allowed the Nazis to denounce Jews as "parasites" threatening the "health" of Nazi society, and responsible for Germany's social and economic "ills." This rhetorical circuitry in the semiotic network was used, clearly, to make persecution and violence acceptable, thus neutralizing ethical conscience and behavior.

The "cleansing" of the parasites included the burning of books by Jewish writers, the banning of musical compositions and works of art by Jews, and ultimately the Holocaust. Depictions of Jews as parasites on posters abounded throughout the Nazi realm, suggesting that they were bearers of disease. The Nazis even implemented a policy of "racial hygiene," passing laws to protect

Aryans from the Jews. In occupied Poland, the Nazis confined Jews to ghettos in quarantine because, as German "educational" films proclaimed, "the Jew" was a carrier of lice and typhus.

In various works, Alfred Korzybski stressed that human beings are limited in what they know by the structure of their nervous systems, and the structure of their sign systems, especially their languages. In other words, humans do not experience the world directly, but through their signs, which sometimes mislead humans about what is the truth. That is, sign-based understanding sometimes lacks similarity of structure with what is actually happening. Dangerous discourses can thus be seen as distorting experience by distorting the meaning of signs. Korzybski (1921, 1933) actually provided the same type of plausible solution to the problem of unethical discourse and behavior as the type implied in this book by suggesting that people could easily be trained to become aware of the power of signs to affect thought. He used techniques that he had derived from his study of mathematics and science. In this book the techniques are derived from semiotics. He called the resulting awareness a "consciousness of abstracting," which here can be called a "consciousness of semiosis," a consciousness of how semiotic systems cohere into a code of meaning that affects how we think and behave.

Neuroscience has actually documented that ethical behavior may be beneficial to mental health since it is hardwired in a specific region of the brain. The gist of the relevant research is explained by Eva Ritvo (2014) as follows:

> The altruism center of the brain is considered a "deep brain structure," part of the primitive brain. Humans are social animals, so it is no surprise that we are wired to help one another ... While the brain is remarkably complex, the neurochemical drivers of happiness are quite easy to identify. Dopamine, serotonin, and oxytocin make up the Happiness Trifecta. Any activity that increases the production of these neurochemicals will cause a boost in mood. But the benefits don't stop at moods ... Bonding increases, social fears are reduced and trust and empathy are enhanced.

So, the aim of semiotics would be to "re-activate" those "altruistic centers" through raising awareness of how these have been disrupted and diverted to "hate centers," as neuroscientists Semir Zeki and John Paul Romaya termed these other neural regions in a 2008 study. Using functional magnetic resonance imaging (fMRI), the researchers presented subject images of people whom they hated. They found that regions in the right putamen, medial frontal gyrus, medial insula, and the premotor cortex were activated. They then found that this "hate circuit" is involved in stimulating aggressive behavior, as well as fear and anger. The researchers concluded that activity in these regions indicates that the brain is primed for violence. This type of research can thus be seen to lend neuroscientific substance to semiotic network theory, since it implies that sign forms can be mapped onto the differentiated neural circuitry associated with altruism or hatred, as the case may be. The goal is to divert the mind away from the hate circuitry to the altruistic one by deconstructing the semiotic networks involved in one and the other, presenting them to people by illustration, as this book has attempted to do. Recalling the #MeToo semiotic network (Chapter 1), it can be inferred that its circuitry is directed to the altruistic regions, while the Aryan semiotic network is directed instead to the hate regions. However, it cannot be ascertained that the redirection from hate to altruism can be achieved in exactly this way. On the other hand, there is no reason to doubt that it might be able to do so at some level—as Peirce, Barthes, and other semioticians have suggested in their own way.

According to the authors of the abovementioned study, there are striking similarities between love and hate. The regions of the putamen and insula that are "switched on" by hate are also the same as those for romantic love. As they observe: "This linkage may account for why love and hate are so closely linked to each other in life" (Zeki and Romaya 2008). As discussed throughout this book, the main strategy of a mendacious political discourse is to activate the hate centers by distorting the view of others, by implementing an us-versus-them semiotic network, commuting altruistic circuitry into hate circuitry, both neurologically and semiotically. Follow-up neuroscientific studies found that people feel more aroused, threatened, and inclined toward violence when experiencing hate. The goal of semiotics with a conscience is to potentially help us understand the semiotic and corresponding neural roots of hate and conflict, as well as the ways in which these might be effectively reduced.

Overall, the claim made here is that hate and false beliefs become embedded in neural circuitry by the presence of inter-codability patterns in hate speech, which are instrumentalized for nefarious purposes. As these are spread constantly and broadly through social media systems, it is becoming ever more urgent to find ways to counteract the hate speech that saturates many platforms. One proposal comes from the so-called *Dangerous Speech Project*, founded and led by Susan Benesch (2021). Benesch starts by noting that the term "hate speech" can take on different levels of meaning that produce different consequences. But at any level, the term means that a group is targeted hatefully because of its identity. The goal of the Project is to expose how and why hate speech is effectuated. Above all else, Benesch identifies the speaker or writer as someone who has influence over an audience. This has been the pattern throughout history, from Cleon to Hitler and Trump. The audience puts its faith in the speaker, who breaks down the reasons why a targeted group is hateful, tapping into resentments and grievances that are directed to the hate centers of the brain. What is especially significant is how she defines hate speech itself, alluding indirectly to the exact same techniques of deconstruction that are part of semiotic network theory (Benesch 2021):

> Any form of expression (e.g. speech, text, or images) that can increase the risk that its audience will condone or commit violence against members of another group. Importantly, the definition refers to increasing the risk of violence, not causing it. We generally cannot know that speech caused violence, except when people are forced by others to commit violence under a credible threat of being killed themselves. People commit violence for many reasons, and there is no reliable way to find them all or to measure their relative importance. Often, even the person who commits violence does not fully comprehend the reasons why. To say that speech is dangerous, then, one must make an educated guess about the effect that the speech is likely to have on other people. Speech may take any number of forms, and can be disseminated by myriad means. It may be shouted during a rally, played on the radio as a song, captured in a photograph, written in a newspaper or on a poster, or shared through social media. The form of the speech and the manner in which it is disseminated affect how the message is received and therefore, how dangerous it is.

By referring to "speech, text, or images" as the modes through which hate speech is constructed and delivered, Benesch is intuitively locating her project within the domain of semiotic theory, albeit without naming it as such. She also points to the power of the usage of different media to embed hatred, including rallies, music, photographs, and posters. And she emphasizes the power of repetition to further entrench the hate forms:

> A second question is whether the speech was transmitted in a way that would reinforce its capacity to persuade. For example, was it repeated frequently? Repetition tends to increase the acceptance of an idea ... In the same way that an influential speaker lends legitimacy to a message, a media source that is trusted by a particular audience gives credibility to the messages it spreads.
>
> (Benesch 2021)

What semiotics would add to this approach is the notion of inter-codability, which is the conceptual mechanism that holds hate speeches together. Inter-codability collates the dispersion of meaning, concentrating it into a centralized position in a semiotic network. It is relevant to note that the term "inter-coding" is used as well in computer science to indicate agreement of the extent to which programmers assign the same codes to the same set of data.

By extension semiotic inter-coding can be characterized as the use of different codes that will ultimately produce the same output, in different ways. This can be seen in how the Aryan code and the Jewish cabal code became intertwined to produce the same hatred-based output, namely hatred of non-Aryans and especially Jews.

The use of a semiotic approach as a way to counteract hate speech is also implied indirectly (i.e., without calling it semiotic) by a report by UNESCO, titled *Addressing Hate Speech on Social Media: Contemporary Challenges* (2021). Its overall approach of detecting hate speech is encapsulated in the following statement from the report, which emphasizes sign-based analysis ("keyword filters") and the effect of "context" on meaning, suggesting that collating the relevant linguistic and contextual data can be best done with algorithms:

> Detection methods can be broadly grouped into two categories: more comprehensive efforts that have initially relied on keyword filters and crowd-sourcing methods, and those that rely on human content moderators who review content that has been flagged as hate speech by users and decide on whether it classifies. Whilst manual approaches have the distinct advantage of capturing context and reacting rapidly to new developments, the process is labour-intensive, time-consuming and expensive, limiting scalability and rapid solutions. Many newer initiatives use a variety of methods in combination.

Among the techniques suggested are the following, all of which can be co-opted by semiotics to carry out the phase of data collection and classification related to dangerous discourses:

- *Machine learning*: Techniques that utilize computer algorithms can facilitate the collection and thematic organization of relevant data. In the case of semiotic network theory, it would be used to direct the process of mining the Internet so as to find hate-based discourses and conspiratorial narratives.
- *Natural language processing*: Techniques that process and analyze large amounts of natural language data can be used to help deconstruct the relevant codes and semiotic nodes in hate-based discourses.
- *Keyword-based approaches*: Techniques able to identify hateful keywords and conspiratorial metaphors are of obvious relevance to the study of dangerous discourses.
- *Distributional semantics*: Techniques able to quantify and categorize similarities between words, phrases, and sentences based on how they are distributed in large samples of data are of obvious utility to semiotic analysis, aiding in the construction of the relevant semiotic network.

- *Sentiment analysis*: Techniques able to identify what kind of attitudes are conveyed in relation to a subject in a given text are especially critical in determining what code or set of codes are involved in a discourse.
- *Source metadata*: Techniques able to model information, such as data about the users associated with the messages, number of followers, etc., allow for an identification of the motives of the promoters of falsehoods.
- *Deep learning*: This involves a class of machine learning algorithms that employ multiple layers of signifying structures so as to be able to progressively extract higher-level features from the input—which is clearly important in helping describe the whole meaning network.
- *Perspective API (Application Programming Interface)*: This uses machine learning to score phrases based on their potential toxicity in a discourse.

Practical uses of AI in semiotics have produced intriguing results, such as allowing scholars to extract hidden layers of meaning from texts (Neuman, Danesi, and Vilenchik 2022), whereby the algorithm fleshes out nodes in the hidden layer that connects inputs to outputs. It has also been used to identify core meanings (codes) in texts, as a result of connecting the nodes in holistic ways. The interpretive process can then be completed by the human analysts.

Effects of Dangerous Discourses

The use of the notion of inter-codability as a diagnostic tool for unraveling the sources of dangerous discourses is, to reiterate, a concrete way to develop a semiotics with a conscience, as it has been labeled here. It provides a straightforward method for showing how thoughts and beliefs are shaped via the semiotic action of unconscious codes generating a semiotic network infrastructure. Take, one more time, the foundations of Nazism. First, there is a primary code, namely of racial purity (Aryanism); this is then linked to the code of a Jewish cabal as a threat to the hegemony of Aryanism. From this inter-codability system, specific types of sign forms are used to create the discourse, including rhetorical nodes in the system (metaphors such as those based in biology), symbolic nodes (such as the swastika and the color red), visual nodes (photos, caricatures, etc., of Jewish individuals and their symbols), and narrative-textual nodes (such as the myths connected to Aryanism). The congealment of the constituents of this semiotic network constitutes the dangerous discourse. This can be represented diagrammatically in Figure 6.2 below.

The effect of the manipulation of such meaning networks is that "truth" is snatched from language and symbols allowing a group, such as the Nazis, to construct their own self-serving semiotic network, from which further lies were devised and alternative facts manufactured. Orwell (1949: 313) describes this process as follows:

> You believe that reality is something objective, external, existing in its own right. But I tell you, Winston, that reality is not external. Reality exists in the human mind, and nowhere else. Not in the individual mind, which can make mistakes, and in any case soon perishes; only in the mind of the Party, which is collective and immortal. Whatever the Party holds to be truth is truth. It is impossible to see reality except by looking through the eyes of the Party.

The mind control that dangerous discourses enable is also a shield against any opposing argument or factual evidence that reveals its falsity. Logical counter-arguments are typically ineffectual because they are perceived as the words of the "cabalistic enemy," and thus easily dismissed as conspiratorial. As the master liar knows, this kind of control even impels members to shelter and protect him, almost robotically, from adversities of all kinds. It is a mindset that is tribal and typical of village-type congregations, as French writer Jean de La Bruyère pointed out (1608: 13):

> The town is divided into various groups, which form so many little states, each with its own laws and customs, its jargon and its jokes. While the association holds and the fashion lasts, they admit nothing well said or well done except by one of themselves, and they are incapable of appreciating anything from another source, to the point of despising those who are not initiated into their mysteries.

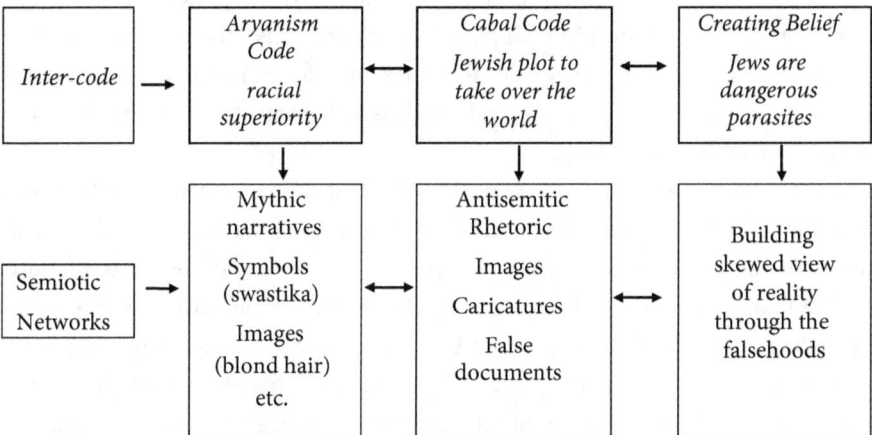

Figure 6.2 Inter-Codability Model.

Conspiracy theories fabricated to support political causes have (as discussed in Chapter 5) occurred throughout history, constituting prototypical examples of how dangerous discourses evolve through connectivity among the parts of a semiotic network. As Massimo Leone (2017) has argued, in reference to Umberto Eco's *Foucault's Pendulum*, and in contrast to a similar novel of conspiracism, Dan Brown's *Da Vinci Code*, it is in exposing the "internal dynamics" of the conspiracy narrative that gives Eco's novel its semiotic cogency:

> *Foucault's Pendulum*, arguably, the best piece of fiction ever written on conspiracy theories, their internal dynamics, and social absurdities. Umberto Eco is also renowned as one of the fiercest critics of Dan Brown. Apparently, indeed, the two authors' works resemble each other: they both draw on historical and cultural erudition in order to design intricate investigative plots. In reality, Eco's and Brown's approaches to mystery and conspiracy could not be more different. Eco narratively represents conspiracy theories so as to ridicule them, and encourage his readers to discard them as mere nonsense. Dan Brown, on the contrary, does not satirize conspiracy theories but fuels them, promoting their wider circulation in society and, what is even more disquieting, enhancing their epistemic status. Cooperative readers of Eco's *Foucault's Pendulum* are prompted to laugh at conspiracy theories; followers of Brown's *The Da Vinci Code* are titillated into believing them and spreading their contagion.

As Leone concludes (2017: 229), the spread of conspiracism is the reason why semiotics has become such an urgent tool of analysis: "Here lies the main role of semiotics: singling out the rhetorical and argumentative lines though which conspiracy theories are created and maintained in the social *imaginaire*." This book has been devoted to exemplifying this role in a specific way. Conspiracy theories work psychologically because they activate the pattern-seeking part of the brain whereby nothing happens by accident. It is this part that activates apophenic thinking, on the basis of the clues (sign forms) that are felt to cohere into a network of meaning. The end result is a firm, unshakeable belief in the veracity of a false conspiracy.

In a relevant article, Otto English (2021) also sees a semiotically based apophenia as having repeated itself in the same way across time—that is, in terms of the same pattern of inter-codability. For example, the assassinations of Abraham Lincoln and John F. Kennedy have been perceived as motivated by political actors belonging to the same type of cabal. The apophenic clues used to connect the two conspiracies included the "observation that both men were elected 100 years apart, that both fought for the rights of black Americans, and both were succeeded by Vice-President Johnsons, that Kennedy was assassinated while travelling in a Ford Lincoln, Lincoln was killed while seated in a theatre called Ford's." These are hardly perceived as coincidences, but rather as commonalities based on the same conspiratorial pattern. The religious code was also evoked (as an inter-code) in the development of the conspiracy theory, given the suggestion that many of the conspirators were Catholics, and that JFK was, ironically, himself a Catholic. English (2021) concludes that conspiracy theories empower people to survive emotionally by allowing them to control meaning:

> It is understandable that when a big and terrifying event shakes our certainties, people become afraid. Conspiracy theories and apophenia are a coping mechanism for people seeking to offset their cognitive dissonance against the terrifying and random nature of world events. They give the illusion of knowledge and the illusion of control.

Machiavelli saw the concoction of false ideas and stories as a critical tactic in gaining and maintaining political power, writing several treatises to emphasize their important role in the repertoire of mendacity that the ruler must exploit to shape minds. As Alessandro Campi (2018) notes, Machiavelli had essentially developed a practical manual for how to plot a successful coup d'état through the construction of falsity, which he understood would generate paranoia among some people, which then has the ability to spread more broadly, even among those who do not believe the conspiracy but may find themselves needing to confront it, thus adding to the cumulus of paranoia that the conspiratorial discourse is designed to evoke. From this, the Machiavellian prince emerges as a political savior who has come out of nowhere to the rescue (to drain the swamp). Philosopher Karl Popper (1945) also argued cogently that totalitarianism is founded on the spread of such paranoia, through strategic lies and conspiracy theories that aim to pit people against each other.

Although he does not label it as inter-codability, psychologist Sander van der Linden (2015) also argues that conspiracy theories are effective because they have the ability to interlink with each other to produce an illusion of truth:

> Conspiracy theorists rarely simply endorse a single conspiracy theory. Rather, belief in one often serves as evidence for belief in others, and this quickly turns into a worldview, i.e., a lens through which we view the world, with new information about world events processed not according to the weight of the evidence but rather in terms of how consistent it is with one's prior convictions. For example, studies have shown that people who believe in conspiracy theories often espouse mutually contradictory explanations about the same event, and

are even eager to endorse entirely made-up conspiracy theories. In sum, it's not really about the actual evidence anymore, but rather about whether a theory is consistent with a larger conspiratorial worldview.

It can be suggested that in generating a false sense of purpose, a dangerous discourse produces paranoia in the process. Research on QAnon by Bloom and Moskalenko (2021) actually bears this out. The two psychologists studied QAnon followers, finding that they were far more likely to have serious mental illnesses, including bipolar disorder, depression, anxiety, and paranoia. This finding was based on an examination of the court records of QAnon followers arrested in the wake of the January 6 Capitol insurrection, which showed that over two-thirds reported they had received mental health diagnoses. By contrast, less than 20 percent of all Americans have a similar mental health diagnosis. Colby (1981) had defined paranoia earlier in terms of persecutory delusions and false beliefs whose content clusters around thoughts of persecution brought about by malevolent others. He suggested that the tendency of blaming others for one's own problems serves to alleviate the distress produced by the feeling of helplessness. This psychological explanation certainly applies to many of Trump's followers, who may feel that they have been persecuted by the liberalism that they see as rampant in the United States. Trump mobilized this feeling by cunningly assuming their persecution as his own.

QAnon members have been recorded as talking about alienation from family and friends, but think that this is temporary and primarily the fault of others. They firmly believe there will be a moment of vindication that will prove their beliefs to be right. After this, not only will their relationships be restored, but people will turn to them as leaders who understand what is really going on. The inauguration of Joe Biden as president was a major disappointment for QAnon followers, who were convinced that Trump would remain or be restored to power. Many explained the event as actually being part of the Plan, which they believed was still unfolding.

Restoring Ethics

According to various scholars of mythology (e.g., Campbell 1969, Heinberg 1989) the emergence of conscious social activity is based on fears related to unexplained events, which constitute the source of our early myths and symbols. Fear of otherness (the foreigner or stranger), in particular, may well be the residue unconscious mode of thought that underlies the construction of hate codes, such as the ones described in this book. One could also argue that codes of ethical behavior emerged at the same time as a basis to negotiate the meaning of otherness and to develop behaviors that ensured the safety of the clan—hence the use of inter-clan agreements and territorial allotments. It is only when such ethical patterns are violated by mendacity that conflicts arise and social balance becomes endangered. As Ralph Waldo Emerson aptly observed: "Every violation of truth is not only a sort of suicide in the liar, but is a stab at the health of human society."

Since antiquity we have been fascinated by stories of deceit, betrayal, and cunning, which clearly reveal that we have always been aware of the destructive effects of lying and of the power of the master liar to wreak havoc on everyone. In his widely cited 1982 book, *Chimpanzee Politics*, Frans de Waals quoted Machiavelli to support his theory that lying emerged in human evolution, in fact, through social competition, whereby the more successful liars enhanced their survivability. Although it has been critiqued on various fronts, de Waals's derivative idea that political success is dependent on the skillful use of mendacity is a plausible one, as has been discussed throughout this book. What is missing from his analysis is how lying is grounded on processes of semiosis. This implies that some people are more "talented" than others at manipulating these processes, gaining trust through the strategic use of words, symbols, and images. However, as far as can be told, there is no evolutionary explanation as to why the human brain is so vulnerable to mendacious discourse. That same brain has, paradoxically (in terms of de Waals's view), created ethical codes to guard against the talented liar. When these codes crumble under the weight of mendacious semiotic systems, it is logical to deduce that, as Eco and Leone also suggest, the only way to restore them is to expose the semiotic maneuvering behind mendacity. In a similar vein, Madisson and Ventsel (2022) see the semiotic deconstruction of the strategic devices in conspiracy theories as a means to counteract what they call a "hermeneutics of suspicion," a hardened skepticism of public authorities.

The primary goal of this book has been to describe a specific semiotic method for interpreting (decoding) dangerous discourses. Whether or not it can realistically help restore ethics in a world of constant lies, conspiracy theories, and other mendacious discourses, spread through cyberspace, it is still worth considering seriously. Mendacity triggers a collapse of meaning; restoring meaning to signs is the ultimate goal of an ethics-focused semiotic analysis. Among the first to suggest the deployment of semiotics as a "science of ethics" was Roland Barthes, who, in his final lectures, as mentioned previously, aimed to develop a semiotic project for such a science (in Pieters and Pint 2008). Among his concrete proposals was the elimination of binarism from discourses, which he saw as being at the core of the attack on otherness (us-versus-them). Any attempt to escape from binaries, Barthes claimed, would help bring about change by eradicating them from the mind. But it is not clear how he intended to realize this. Moreover, as Barthes himself showed in *Mythologies*, the human brain may be entangled in its own binary sign structures, such as mythological ones, from which there may truly be no escape.

Today, mendacity has become a kind of global metalanguage. Maybe artificial intelligence can eventually be the filter for detecting falsity (Neuman, Danesi, and Vilenchik 2022). In a fascinating study, Tangherlini (2021) showed how AI has the potential to decipher conspiracy theories outright. Deep Learning AI operates in ways that are similar to how the brain distributes and connects information throughout its neural circuitry. The key idea here is that such artificial networks can help disentangle the layers of meaning that produce a dangerous discourse. As Tangherlini (2021) notes, conspiracy theories are the result of collective storytelling, and AI is adept at identifying the elements in the collective narrativity.

The answer to the dilemma of dangerous discourses is not, however, to be found in censorship or in any form of state control of media and information, as some have suggested. This is actually what totalitarian regimes carry out. Even if it were possible in a global society to control the contents of discourses, this would invariably prove to be counterproductive. To reiterate, one plausible approach to resolving the dilemma is to become aware of the semiotic networks that are enlisted in the creation of dangerous discursivity. When the human mind is aware of the malicious intent hidden in such networks, it will be better able to fend off the undesirable effects that they may cause. As Eco (1989) asserts through Casaubon, the idea is to deconstruct the code (the Plan) that is so persuasive to the point that it even might convince people to die on its behalf:

> We invented a nonexistent Plan, and They not only believed it was real but convinced themselves that They had been part of it for ages, or rather They identified the fragments of their muddled mythology as moments of our Plan, moments joined in a logical, irrefutable web of analogy, semblance, suspicion. But if you invent a plan and others carry it out, it's as if the Plan exists. At that point it does exist. Hereafter, hordes of Diabolicals will swarm through the world in search of the map. We offered a map to people who were trying to overcome a deep private frustration. What frustration? Belbo's first file suggested it to

me: There can be no failure if there really is a Plan. Defeated you may be, but never through any fault of your own. To bow to a cosmic will is no shame. You are not a coward; you are a martyr.

In his subsequent 2012 novel, *The Prague Cemetery*, Umberto Eco returned to the theme of conspiracism, tracing its roots to anti-Semitism and providing a different semiotic angle from which to view its emotional power. The story is recounted by the main character, Simone Simonini, through his autobiographical diary, as well as a narrator who guides the flow of the narrative as if in a historical documentary. We find out that Simonini is a cynical man whose mother died when he was a child and whose father was killed in 1848 fighting for a united Italy. Simonini is raised by his grandfather, an old reactionary who hates the Jews and who dwells in all kinds of nonsensical fantastic conspiracy theories, such as the belief that the French Revolution was planned by a cabal led by the Jews and consisting of the Knights Templar, the Bavarian Illuminati, and the Jacobins. Simonini is educated at home by Jesuits at the behest of his grandfather. One priest, Father Bergamaschi, teaches him about the ubiquity of evil secret societies. Simonini becomes obsessed by imaginary conspiratorial plots, which he believes have dictated the course of history. He turns to the works of conspiratorial writers, aspiring to emulate the fictions in his own life. At this point Eco presents a conspiracy theory of a conspiracy theory, thus exposing the absurdity and inanity of conspiracisim itself. He does this by recounting that Simonini had composed what would become *The Protocols of the Elders of Zion*, documenting a conspiratorial meeting for world domination that had supposedly taken place at the Old Jewish Cemetery of Prague. After this document is handed over to the Czar's Secret Police, they pressure Simonini to put a bomb in the newly dug tunnel of the Paris Metro, which could then be blamed on the Jews, to corroborate the plot delineated in *The Protocols*. Simonini obtains a bomb from an old Italian expatriate revolutionary living in Paris, whereupon his diary is abruptly cut off, implying that Simonini likely blew himself up with the bomb, even though the narrator remains silent on this.

Eco infuses his novel with intertextual allusions to nineteenth-century novels which, it is suggested, were plagiarized by the writer of the *Protocols*, including Alexandre Dumas's novel *Joseph Balsamo* (1846), which revolves around the exploits of the Italian occultist, Giuseppe Balsamo, who used the alias of Count Alessandro di Cagliostro, a charlatan who duped many into believing that he had psychic powers. In several passages, Eco refers to the term used by various nineteenth-century anti-Semites, namely the "Final Solution," alluding to the total extermination of the Jews. After finishing *The Protocols*, Simonini asserts with certainty that his book would eventually lead to the extermination. Such explicit allusions anticipating the Nazi Holocaust are part of the deconstruction of how hate is spread by words. What Eco suggests is that influential groups and movements in the nineteenth century are largely to blame for the proliferation of anti-Semitic narratives, whereupon the Jewish people are framed as the orchestrators of global events and running the world behind the scenes. These dangerous narratives are still widely promoted today, which was likely Eco's inherent warning in writing the novel, showing the power of confabulation to generate its own self-sustaining alternative reality. This stubborn form of hate is even more embedded today because of the Internet, where conspiracy groups or networks, such as QAnon, no longer need texts such as *The Protocols*, because they create their own false narratives, radicalizing individuals toward violent action.

Perhaps Eco had the right idea after all in how to deconstruct conspiracism—namely, write a conspiratorial novel about conspiracism. In this way, he does not directly ridicule conspiracists or attempt to provide counter-arguments; rather, he emulates their form of thinking to reject the whole enterprise as a fictional fabulist mode of thinking that serves no purpose other than to generate hate and which leads to the self-destruction of conspiracists themselves. As David Ben Efraim (2021) points out, the value of Eco's novel lies in highlighting the sources of conspiracy theories and how they spread through words and related actions:

> Ultimately, *The Prague Cemetery* doesn't answer all our questions about conspiracy theories and their place in society, but I think it does provide some valuable insight on what is necessary for them to spread. They thrive on peoples' ignorance, on their need to explain the woes of their existence by the evil actions of unstoppable outsiders hidden in the shadow, and most of all, it thrives on peoples' need to absolve themselves of responsibility for their own life failures.

Epilogue

The Dreyfus Affair was not sparked solely by an accusation of treason; it became a full-fledged dangerous anti-Semitic discourse after it was connected to the cabalistic code used against the Jews for centuries. It is a prototypical case-in-point of how a dangerous discourse emerges via the linkage of sign structures, including conspiratorial texts and symbols. A semiotics with a conscience approach would study these structures, so as to illustrate how they cohere into networks that deflect meaning away from their normal referential system, redirecting it to an illusory system intended to generate hate. This collapse of meaning is the cognitive-emotional source of hatred of others, and of the ensuing forms of delusion that emerge from it.

But this approach is not a magic pill; it is simply a method that provides a particular analytical lens through which discourses such as the Dreyfus, Aryan, and MAGA ones, among others, can be decoded and exposed for what they are—semiotic strategies to manipulate thoughts and beliefs in a destructive, unethical way. During the height of the Dreyfus Affair, the entire French political class was divided into two groups—the Dreyfusards (who supported Dreyfus) and the anti-Dreyfusards (who did not). The former represented progressive elements in France and the latter conservative, reactionary ones, who used the Dreyfus Affair as an opportunity to promote anti-Semitic propaganda. It is distressing to note that the same type of situation has repeated itself throughout history, indicating that facts are less persuasive or even believable than signs and symbols designed to distort the facts themselves. But, in the end, facts will ultimately win out, as history also records; the goal of semiotics is to show that this coincides with the dismantling of the very semiotic systems used to construct the falsehoods. The two correlate with each other, as the neuroscientific research cited in this book clearly shows (e.g., Samir and Romaya 2014). As Martin Luther King, Jr. (1965) once put it, in response to the lies that were being hurled at him, "No lie can live forever." The falsehoods on which dictatorships, autocracies, and totalitarian regimes were based were eventually exposed as their attendant false discourses came apart.

The Machiavellian liar is someone who can evoke and manipulate hidden fears, hatreds, and resentments so as to gain support and backing by disgruntled segments of a society. His rallying cries become theirs; his transgressions are seen as necessary to bring about change; his attacks on others are perceived as elements in an ongoing political-cultural-racial war. It is in this way that the liar-prince gains control over minds, often distorting history by distorting the true meaning of its events. It is ironic to note that Trump portrayed his MAGA movement as a counterculture one, alluding to the hippies in the 1960s and 1970s, portraying the government as the "establishment" and the liberal democratic state as the enemy of freedom and true American values. This is a clear example of how truth and history can easily be distorted and meaning reversed, given that the hippie revolution was spearheaded by liberal thinkers, and was mainly against radical conservatism.

It is truly remarkable how the masterful liar can change minds through a manipulation of meaning. As diverse studies in *The Routledge Handbook of Semiosis and the Brain* (2023) edited by García and Ibáñez show, the brain may itself be a semiotic organ, constantly involved in creating and searching for meaning. The Estonian biologist-semiotician Jakob von Uexküll (1909) posited the presence of a *Bauplan* in the brain that routinely converts the external world of information into an internal one of representation through semiosis. The result is that there is little distinction between the sign structures in the *Bauplan* and our understanding of reality, and even our reaction to it, given that the two are coincident. A well-known anecdote told about Alfred Korzybski (cited in Derks and Hollander 1996: 58) brings this interrelation out dramatically, and is thus worth revisiting here for the sake of illustration. It is reported that one day, as he was giving a lecture to a group of students, he suddenly stopped talking to retrieve a packet of biscuits from his briefcase, telling the audience that he was hungry and needed to eat something right away. He then asked several individuals in the front row if they would also like a biscuit. A few took one each, eating in front of him. Korzybski then asked: "Nice biscuit, don't you think?" He then ripped the white paper that enveloped the packet which contained the biscuits, revealing a picture of a dog's head and the tagline *Dog Cookies*. The students were visibly upset, and a few put a hand in front of their mouths running to the toilet. Korzybski then remarked: "You see, I have just demonstrated that people don't just eat food, but also words, and that the taste of the former is often outdone by the taste of the latter."

The effects of one single phrase, as showcased by the anecdote, can be extended to entire semiotic codes, which are constantly at work affecting how we come to understand and react to the world. This might explain why so many put their personal stakes in nefarious philosophies such as Nazism—their reactions were activated by specific semiotic signs within a hidden code of meanings. When signs are manipulated, the view of, and reaction to, reality become altered, especially if the liar frames his mendacious discourse as one that promises change and improvement. Machiavelli (1513) put it as follows: "Men are quick to change ruler when they imagine they can improve their lot." While he was writing *The Prince*, Florence was immersed in corrupt politics. Machiavelli witnessed how clever politicians were able to gain power by lying strategically. From his observations, he wrote the playbook from which many subsequent powerful rulers have taken their cues.

Hopefully, we can go beyond the Machiavellian portrayal of politics and keep the world largely free from dangerous mind manipulation. This might involve using semiotics as an epistemic tool which, despite its limitations, deserves greater attention in this area. As a science of signs and symbols, and how they function in all modes of representation and communication, semiotics has obvious ethical implications, since it can expose the illegitimate uses of signs in a concrete way. The central reason why it is able to do this is encapsulated by W. C. Watt (1998) as follows: "Semiotics takes as its central task that of describing how one thing can mean another. Alternatively, since this philosophical problem is also a psychological one, its job could be said to be that of describing how one thing can bring something else to mind." It is precisely in examining how lies bring something deceitful to mind that semiotics can play an important role in the world.

It is fitting to end with the words of Zola who, in his powerful letter, *J'accuse*, encapsulates an implied subtext that has been threaded throughout this book, namely that it is everyone's duty to expose dangerous falsehoods, otherwise, as he puts it, they will lead to the "shut up of truth" and "resounding disasters." The only way out of this semiotic quagmire, Zola emphasizes, is to "hasten the explosion of truth and justice."

> Certainly, the military courts have a singular idea of justice. This, then, is the simple truth, Mr. President, and it is appalling; it will remain a stain for your presidency. I suspect you have no power in this matter, that you are the prisoner of the Constitution and those around you. You still have a human duty, which you will think about, and which you will fulfill. It is not, moreover, that I have the least despair of triumph. I repeat with more strident certainty: the truth is on the move and nothing will stop it. It is only today that the business begins, since today only the positions are clear: on the one hand, the culprits who do not want the light to be shed; on the other, the vigilantes who will give their lives to make it happen. I have said it elsewhere, and I repeat it here: when we shut up the truth underground, it accumulates there, it takes on such a force of explosion that, the day it bursts, it blows everything up. We'll see if we don't just prepare for the most resounding disasters for later. As for the people I accuse, I do not know them, I have never seen them, I have no resentment or hatred against them. They are for me only entities, spirits of social evil. And the act I am doing here is just a revolutionary way to hasten the explosion of truth and justice.

References

Albright, Madeleine (2018). *Fascism: A Warning*. New York: HarperCollins.
Aragno, Anna (2019). Semiotic Realms: Codes, Language, Mind: A Psychoanalytic Perspective. *Biosystems* 182: 21–9.
Arendt, Hannah (1951). *The Origins of Totalitarianism*. New York: Harcourt.
Arendt, Hannah (1972). *Crises of the Republic: Lying in Politics, Civil Disobedience on Violence, Thoughts on Politics, and Revolution*. New York: Harcourt Brace Jovanovich.
Aristotle (1952). Rhetoric. In: *The Works of Aristotle*, Vol. 11. Oxford: Clarendon Press.
Aristotle (2009). *The Nichomean Ethics*. Oxford: Oxford University Press.
Arnheim, Rudolf (1969). *Visual Thinking*. Berkeley: University of California Press.
Baijayanti, Roy (2016). Friedrich Max Müller and the Emergence of Identity Politics in India and Germany. *Publications of the English Goethe Society* 85: 217–28.
Bain, Alexander (1855). *The Senses and the Intellect*. London: Longmans.
Bakhtin, Mikhail (1981). *The Dialogic Imagination*. Austin: University of Texas Press.
Barkun, Michael (2003). *A Culture of Conspiracy: Apocalyptic Visions in Contemporary America*. Berkeley: University of California Press.
Barreneche, Sebastián Moreno (2023). *The Social Semiotics of Populism*. London: Bloomsbury.
Barthes, Roland (1957). *Mythologies*. Paris: Seuil.
Barthes, Roland (1964). Rhetoric of the Image. In: C. Handa (ed.), *Visual Rhetoric in a Visual World: A Critical Sourcebook*. New York: St. Martin's.
Barthes, Roland (1968). *Elements of Semiology*. New York: Hill and Wang.
Barthes, Roland (1970). *S/Z*, trans. by R. Miller. New York: Hill and Wang.
Barthes, Roland (1977). *Image, Music, Text*. New York: Hill and Wang.
Barthes, Roland (1980). *Camera Lucida: Reflections on Photography*. New York: Hill and Wang.
Baudrillard, Jean (1981). *Simulacra and Simulations*. New York: Semiotexte.
Beasley, Ron and Danesi, Marcel (2003). *Persuasive Signs: The Semiotics of Advertising*. Berlin: Mouton de Gruyter.
Beattie, Geoffrey (2022). *Doubt: A Psychological Exploration*. London: Routledge.
Bein, Alexander (1964). The Jewish Parasite—Notes on the Semantics of the Jewish Problem, with Special Reference to Germany." *Leo Baeck Institute Year Book* 9: 3–40.
Beinart, Peter (2006). *The Good Fight: Why Liberals—and Only Liberals—Can Win the War on Terror and Make America Great Again*. New York: HarperCollins.
Benesch, Susan (2021). *Dangerous Speech: A Practical Guide*. https://dangerousspeech.org/.

Ben-Ghiat, Ruth (2016). An American Authoritarian. *The Atlantic*, August 20, 2016. https://www.theatlantic.com/politics/archive/2016/08/american-authoritarianism-under-donald-trump/495263/.

Benveniste, Émile (1939). *Problèmes de linguistique générale*. Paris: Gallimard.

Berger, Jonathan (1972). *Ways of Seeing*. Harmondsworth: Penguin.

Blackburn, Simon (2008). Structuralism. In: *Oxford Dictionary of Philosophy*. Oxford: Oxford University Press.

Bloom, Alan (1987). *Closing of the American Mind: How Higher Education Has Failed Democracy and Impoverished the Souls of Today's Students*. New York: Simon & Schuster.

Bloom, Mia and Moskalenko, Sophia (2021). *Pastels and Pedophiles: Inside the Mind of QAnon*. Stanford: Stanford University Press.

Bobic, Igor (2014). Shelley Moore Capito Says Climate Is Changing because It's 'Raining' Outside. *Huffpost*, https://www.huffpost.com/entry/capito-climate-change_n_5953796.

Boria, Edoardo (2008). Geopolitical Maps: A Sketch History of a Neglected Trend in Cartography. *Geopolitics* 13: 278–308.

Boroditsky, Lera (2001). Does Language Shape Thought? Mandarin and English Speakers' Conceptions of Time. *Cognitive Psychology* 43: 1–22.

Bort, Christopher (2022). Why the Kremlin Lies: Understanding Its Loose Relationship with the Truth. *Carnegie Endowment for National Peace*, https://carnegieendowment.org/2022/01/06/why-kremlin-lies-understanding-its-loose-relationship-with-truth-pub-86132.

Bouissac, Paul (1985). The Potential Role of Semiotics for the Advancement of Knowledge. *Semiotic Inquiry* 5: 339–46.

Bouissac, Paul (1989). What Is a Human? Ecological Semiotics and the New Animism. *Semiotica* 77: 497–516.

Bouissac, Paul (2010). *Saussure: A Guide for the Perplexed*. London: Bloomsbury.

Boulenger, Véronique, Shtyrov, Yury, and Pulvermüller, Friedemann (2012). When Do You Grasp the Idea? MEG Evidence for Instantaneous Idiom Understanding. *NeuroImage* 59: 3502–13.

Bradbury, Ray (1953). *Fahrenheit 451*. New York: Ballantine Books.

Brinkhof, Tim (2022). History Is a Story: Here's How Putin Rearranged the Plot. *Big Think*, https://bigthink.com/the-present/putin-history-narrative-ukraine/.

Bronner, Simon J. and Dundes, Alan (2007). *Meaning of Folklore*. Logan: Utah State University Press.

Brooke, Donald (2016). Stanford Researchers Find Students Have Trouble Judging the Credibility of Information Online. Stanford Graduate School of Information November 22, 2016, https://ed.stanford.edu/news/stanford-researchers-find-students-have-trouble-judging-credibility-information-online.

Brown, Charles Bockden (1798). *Wieland*. New York: H. Colburn.

Brown, Roger (1958). *Words and Things: An Introduction to Language*. New York: The Free Press.

Brown, Roger and Lenneberg, Eric (1954). A Study in Language and Cognition. *Journal of Abnormal and Social Psychology* 49: 454–62.

Bruner, Jerome (1991). The Narrative Construction of Reality. *Critical Inquiry* 18: https://www.sas.upenn.edu/~cavitch/pdf-library/Bruner_Narrative.pdf.

Bruyère, Jean de la (1885). *Characters*. New York: Scribner & Welford.

Buckley, William F. (1954). *McCarthy and His Enemies: The Record and Its Meaning*. Washington, DC: Regnery.

Burke, Kenneth (1939). The Rhetoric of Hitler's Battle. *The Southern Review* 5: 1–21.

Burke, Tarana (2006). The Inception justbeinc.wixsite.com/justbeinc/the-me-too-movement-cmml.

Buxton, Madeline (2018). With Me Too Rising, Google Maps The Spread of a Movement. *Refinery29*, Vice Media Group. www.refinery29.com/en-us/2018/04/196748/me-too-google.

Byrne, Richard (1995). *The Thinking Ape: Evolutionary Origins of Intelligence*. Oxford: Oxford University Press.

Cairo, Alberto (2009). *How Charts Lie*. New York: W. W. Norton.

Cairo, Alberto (2020). Foreword: The Dawn of a Philosophy of Visualization. In: M. Engebretsen and H. Kennedy (eds.), *Information Visualization in Society*, 17–18. Amsterdam: Amsterdam University Press.

Cameron, Deborah (2012). *Verbal Hygiene*. New York: Routledge.

Campbell, Joseph (1969). *Primitive Mythology*. Harmondsworth: Penguin.

Campi, Alessandro (2018). *Machiavelli and Political Conspiracies*. New York: Routledge.

Canefield, Teri (2023). *A Firehouse of Falsehood: The Story of Disinformation*. London: Macmillan.

Caputi, Theodore L., Nobles, Alicia L., and Ayers, John W. (2019). Internet Searches for Sexual Harassment and Assault, Reporting, and Training since the #MeToo Movement. *JAMA Internal Medicine* 179: 258–9.

Carey, Nessa (2013). *The Epigenetics Revolution*. New York: Columbia University Press.

Carroll, Lewis (1871). *Through the Looking-Glass and What Alive Found There*. London: Macmillan.

Carson, Thomas L. (2010). *Lying and Deception: Theory and Practice*. Oxford: Oxford University Press.

Castells, Manuel (1996). *The Information Age: Economy, Society, and Culture*. Oxford: Blackwell.

Chandler, Daniel (2022). *Semiotics: The Basics*, 4th edition. London: Routledge.

Chow, Kat (2018). What the Ebbs and Flows of the KKK Can Tell Us about White Supremacy Today. *Code Switch*, https://www.npr.org/sections/codeswitch/2018/12/08/671999530/what-the-ebbs-and-flows-of-the-kkk-can-tell-us-about-white-supremacy-today.

Cialdini, Robert (1984). *Influence: The Psychology of Persuasion*. New York: HarperCollins.

Cobbett, William (1798). *Detection of a Conspiracy*. Philadelphia: William Cobbett.

Cohen, Richard (2022). Vladimir Putin's Rewriting of History Draws on a Long Tradition of Soviet Myth-Making. *Smithsonian Magazine*, https://www.smithsonianmag.com/history/vladimir-putins-rewriting-of-history-draws-on-a-long-tradition-of-soviet-myth-making-180979724/.

Cohn, Norman (1967). *Warrant for Genocide: The Myth of the Jewish World Conspiracy and the Protocols of the Elders of Zion*. London: Serif Books.

Colby, Kenneth Mark (1981). Modeling a Paranoid Mind. *The Behavioral and Brain Sciences* 4: 515–60.

Coleman, John (2007). Weather Channel Founder: Global Warming Greatest Scam in History. *Icecap*, http://icecap.us/index.php/go/joes-blog/comments_about_global_warming/.

Collomb, Jean-Daniel (2014). The Ideology of Climate Change Denial in the United States. *European Journal of American Studies* 9: https://doi.org/10.4000/ejas.10305.

Conrad, Klaus (1958). *Die beginnende Schizophrenie. Versuch einer Gestaltanalyse des Wahns*. Stuttgart: Georg Thieme Verlag.

Conrad, Klaus (1959). Gestaltanalyse und Daseinsanalytik. *Nervenarzt* 30: 405–10.

Cook, Guy (1992). *The Discourse of Advertising*. London: Routledge.

Corner, John (1980). Codes and Cultural Analysis. *Media, Culture and Society* 2: 73–86.

Crichton, Michael (2003). Environmentalism as a Religion. *Hawaii Free Press*. http://www.hawaiifreepress.com/Articles-Main/ID/2818/Crichton-Environmentalism-is-a-religion.

Crichton, Michael (2004). *State of Fear*. New York: HarperCollins.

Cutrera, Antonino (1900). *La mafia e i mafiosi*. Palermo: Reber.

Czech, Brian (2022). Ukraine: Putin's Lebensraum. *Steady State Herald*. https://steadystate.org/ukraine-putins-lebensraum/.

D'Souza, Dinesh (2017). *The Big Lie: Exposing the Nazi Roots of the America Left*. Washington, DC: Regnery Publishing.

Danesi, Marcel (2008). *Why It Sells: Decoding the Meanings of Brand Names, Logos, Ads, and Other Marketing and Advertising Ploys*. Lanham: Rowman & Littlefield.

Danesi, Marcel (2022). *Warning Signs: The Semiotics of Danger*. London: Bloomsbury.

Davenport, Coral (2017). Climate Change Denialists in Charge. *The New York Times*, https://www.nytimes.com/2017/03/27/us/politics/climate-change-denialists-in-charge.html.

Deacon, Terrence W. (2021) How Molecules Became Signs. *Biosemiotics* 14: 537–59.

Deely, John (2001). *Four Ages of Understanding: The First Postmodern Survey of Philosophy from Ancient Times to the Turn of the Twentieth Century*. Toronto: University of Toronto Press.

Deely, John (2005). *Semiotic Animal*. South Bend: St. Augustine's Press.

Deferrari, Roy J. (1952). *Treatises on Various Subjects*. New York: Fathers of the Church.

Derks, Lucas and Hollander, Jaap (1996). *Essenties van NLP*. Utrecht: Servire.

Derrida, Jacques (1967). *Of Grammatology*. Baltimore: Johns Hopkins University Press.

Derrida, Jacques (1972). *Margins of Philosophy*. Chicago: University of Chicago Press.

Diethelm, Pascal and McKee, Martin (2009). Denialism: What Is It and How Should Scientists Respond? *European Journal of Public Health* 19: 2–4.

Dodds, Joseph (2021). The Psychology of Climate Change. *British Journal of Psychology Bulletin* 45: 222–6.

Doland, Cheryl (1999). *Repeating Is Believing: An Investigation of the Illusory Truth Effect*. Albany: State University of New York.

Dor, Daniel (2017). The Role of the Lie in the Evolution of Human Language. *Language Sciences* 63: 44–59.

Dostoyevsky, Fyodor (1863). *Winter Notes on Summer Impressions*. London: Alma Classics.

Duits, Rufus (2017). *Semiotics of Conscience*. Intertech Publication.

Dumas, Alexandre (1846). *Joseph Balsamo*. London: Simms & McIntrye.

Dunlap, Knight (1944). The Great Aryan Myth. *The Scientific Monthly* 59: 296–300.

Durkheim, Émile (1912). *The Elementary Forms of Religious Life*. New York: Collier.

Eco, Umberto (1976). *A Theory of Semiotics*. Bloomington: Indiana University Press.

Eco, Umberto (1989). *Foucault's Pendulum*. New York: Mariner Books.

Eco, Umberto (1990). *The Limits of Interpretation*. Bloomington: Indiana University Press.

Eco, Umberto (2010). Aristotle, Poetics and Rhetoric. In: T. A. Sebeok and M. Danesi (eds.), *Encyclopedic Dictionary of Semiotics*, 57–8. Berlin: Mouton de Gruyter.

Eco, Umberto (2012). *The Prague Cemetery*. New York: Vintage Publishers.

Efraim, David Ben (2021). "The Prague Cemetery" by Umberto Eco—No Rest for the Jews. *Bookwormex*, https://bookwormex.com/prague-cemetery-umberto-eco-review/.

Emerson, Ralph Waldo (2022). *Essays*, The Project Gutenberg EBook of Essays, by Ralph Waldo Emerson, https://www.gutenberg.org/files/16643/16643-h/16643-h.htm.

Emery, David (2018). Was 'America First' a Slogan of the Ku Klux Klan? *Snopes*, https://www.snopes.com/fact-check/america-first-ku-klux-klan-slogan/.

English, Otto (2021). The Apotheosis of Apophenia: Conspiratorial Minds. *Byline Times*, https://bylinetimes.com/2021/04/26/the-apotheosis-of-apophenia-conspiratorial-minds/.

Esh, Shaul (1963). Words and Their Meanings: Twenty-Five Examples of Nazi Idiom. *Yad Vashem Studies* 5: 133–67.

Esleben, Jorg, Kraenzle, Christina, and Kulkarni, Sukanya (eds.) (2008). *Mapping Channels Between Ganges and Rhein: German-Indian Cross-Cultural Relations*. Newcastle: Cambridge Scholars Publishing.

Espes Brown, Joseph (1992). Becoming Part of It. In: D. M. Dooling and P. Jordan-Smith (eds.), *I Become Part of It: Sacred Dimensions in Native American Life*, 1–15. New York: Harper Collins.

Evans, Alfred B. (1993). *Soviet Marxism-Leninism: The Decline of an Ideology*. Westport: Greenwood.

Fairclough, Norman (2003). *Analysing Discourse: Textual Analysis for Social Research*. London: Routledge.

Fauconnier, Gilles and Turner, Mark (2002). *The Way We Think: Conceptual Blending and the Mind's Hidden Complexities*. New York: Basic.

Fazio, Lisa K., Payne, B. Keith, Brashier, Nadia M., and Marsh, Elizabeth J. (2015). Knowledge Does Not Protect Against Illusory Truth. *Journal of Experimental Psychology* 144: 993–1002.

Feldman, Jerome (2006). *From Molecule to Metaphor: A Neural Theory of Language*. Cambridge: MIT Press.

Feldman, Jerome and Narayanan, Srinivas (2004). Embodied Meaning in a Neural Theory of Language. *Brain and Language* 89: 385–92.

Festinger, Leon (1957). *A Theory of Cognitive Dissonance*. Evanston, IL: Row, Peterson.

Festinger, Leon, Riecken, Henry W., and Scachter, Stanley (1956). *When Prophecy Fails*. London: Printer & Martin.

Fichte, J. G. (1808). *Reden an die deutsche Nation*. Leipzig: Verlag von Philipp Reclam jun.

Foss, Sonja K. (2005). Theory of Visual Rhetoric. In: Ken Smith, Sandra Moriarity, Gretchen Barbatsis, and Keith Kenney (eds.), *Handbook of Visual Communication: Theory, Methods, and Media*, 141–52. London: Routledge.

Foucault, Michel (1969). *L'Archéologie du savoir*. Paris: Éditions Gallimard.

Foucault, Michel (1971). *Hommage à Jean Hyppolite*. Paris: Presses Universitaires de France.

Foucault, Michel (1972). *The Archeology of Knowledge*, trans. by A. M. Sheridan Smith. New York: Pantheon.

Foucault, Michel (1978). *The History of Sexuality*, 2 volumes. Edinburgh: Edinburgh University Press.

Gallop, David (1984). *Parmenides of Elea: Fragments*. Toronto: University of Toronto Press.

Gambetta, Diego (1993). *The Sicilian Mafia*. Cambridge: Harvard University Press.

García, Adolfo M. and Ibáñez, Augustín (eds.) (2023). *The Routledge Handbook of Semiosis and the Brain*. New York: Routledge.

Geertz, Clifford (1973). *The Interpretation of Cultures*. New York: Basic.

Genosko, Gary (2016). *Critical Semiotics: Theory, from Information to Affect*. London: Bloomsbury.

Gilbert, Daniel (1991). Hoe Mental Systems Believe. *American Psychologist* 46: 107–19.

Gillette, Aaron (2012). *Racial Theories in Fascist Italy*. London: Routledge.

Gilman, Sander and Rabinbach, Anson (2013). *The Third Reich Sourcebook*. Berkeley: University of California Press.

Girard, Rene (1974). The Plague in Literature and Myth. *Texas Studies in Literature and Language* 15: 833–50.

Giroux (2016). Challenging Trump's Language of Fascism, *Truthput*, January 9, 2016, https://truthout.org/articles/challenging-trumps-language-of-fascism/.

Godfrey-Smith, Peter (2009). *Darwinian Populations*. Oxford: Oxford University Press.

Goebbels, Joseph (1941). Aus Churchills Lügenfabrik. In: *Die Zeit ohne Beispiel*, 364–9. Munich: Zentralverlag der NSDAP.

Gramigna, Remo (2020). *Augustine's Theory of Signs, Signification, and Lying*. Berlin: Mouton de Gruyter.

Greenfield, Susan (2015). *Mind Change*. New York: Random House.

Grice, H. Paul (1975). Logic and Conversation. In: P. Cole and J. Morgan (eds.), *Syntax and Semantics*, vol. 3, 41–58. New York: Academic.

Group μ (1970). *A General Rhetoric*. Paris: Larousse.

Habermas, Jürgen (1973). *Erkenntnis und Interesse*. Frankfurt: Suhrkamp.

Halliday, M. A. K. (1978). *Language as Social Semiotic: The Social Interpretation of Language and Meaning*. Baltimore: University Park Press.

Halliday, M. A. K. (1985). *Introduction to Functional Grammar*. London: Arnold.

Hannah, Matthew N. (2021). A Conspiracy of Data: QAnon, Social Media, and Information Visualization. *Social Media + Society*, https://journals.sagepub.com/doi/full/10.1177/20563051211036064.

Hanne, Michael, Crano, William D., and Scott Mio, Jeffery (eds.) (2014). *Warring with Words: Narrative and Metaphor in Politics*. Oxfordshire: Psychology Press.

Harmon, William and Holman, C. Hugh (1999). *A Handbook to Literature*. Englewood Cliffs: Prentice Hall.

Hart, Christian L. and Curtis, Drew A. (2023). *Big Lies: What Psychological Science Tells Us about Lying and What You Can Do about It*. Washington, DC: APA Life Tools.

Hasher, Goldstein, and Toppino (1977). Frequency and the Conference of Referential Validity. *Journal of Verbal Learning & Verbal Behavior* 16: 107–12.

Hassan, Aumyo and Barber, Sarah J. (2021). The Effects of Repetition Frequency on the Illusory Truth Effect. *Cognitive Research* 6, https://cognitiveresearchjournal.springeropen.com/articles/10.1186/s41235-021-00301-5.

Hay, Mark (2022). Covid Truthers Have Found a New "Pandemic" to Freak Out About. *The Daily Beast*, https://www.thedailybeast.com/conspiracy-theorists-are-already-freaking-out-about-the-next-pandemic-as-part-of-the-so-called-great-reset.

Heinberg, Richard (1989). *Memories and Visions of Paradise*. Los Angeles: J. P. Tarcher.

Herder, Johann Gottfried (1791). *Ideen zur Philosophie der Geschichte der Menschheit*. Halbleinen: G. Freytag.

Herdy, Rachel (2014). The Origin and Growth of Peirce's Ethics. *European Journal of Pragmatism and American Philosophy* 6, https://doi.org/10.4000/ejpap.1060.

Herman, Edward S. (1992). *Beyond Hypocrisy: Decoding the News in an Age of Propaganda Including A Doublespeak Dictionary for the 1990s*. Montreal: Black Rose Books.

Hertwig, Ralph, Gigerenzer, Gerd, and Hoffrage, Ulrich (1997). The Reiteration Effect in Hindsight Bias. *Psychological Review* 104: 194–202.

Hitler, Adolph (1925). *Mein Kampf*. Munich: Franz Eher Nachfolger.

Hjelmslev, Louis (1959). *Essais Linguistique*. Copenhagen: Munksgaard.

Hobbs, Dick and Antonopoulos, Giorgios A. (2013). Endemic to the Species: Ordering the 'Other' Via Organised Crime. *Global Crime* 14: 27–51.
Hobbes, Thomas (1656). *Elements of Philosophy*. London: Molesworth.
Hodge, Robert and Kress, Gunther (1988). *Social Semiotics*. Cambridge: Polity.
Hofstadter, Richard (1964). *The Paranoid Style in American Politics*. New York: Alfred A. Knopf.
Hoggan, David (1961). *Der erzwungene Krieg*. Zustand: leichte Gebrauchsspuren.
Hoggan, David (1969). *The Myth of Six Million*. Los Angeles: Noontide Press.
Housen, Abigail (2002). Aesthetic Thought, Critical Thinking and Transfer. *Arts and Learning Journal* 18: 99–130.
Hübscher, Monika and Mering, Sabine von (eds.) (2020). *Antisemitism on Social Media*. New York: Routledge.
Hutton, Christopher M. (1999). *Linguistics and the Third Reich*. London: Routledge.
Huxley, Aldous (1942). *The Art of Seeing*. London: Harper & Brothers.
Im, Soo-hyun, Varma, Keisha, and Varma, Sashank (2017). Extending the Seductive Allure of Neuroscience Explanations Effect to Popular Articles about Educational Topics. *British Journal of Educational Psychology* 87: 518–34.
Jacob, Frank (ed.) (2020). *War and Semiotics: Signs, Communication Systems, and the Preparation, Legitimization, and Commemoration of Collective Mass Violence*. Chaim: Routledge.
Jacobson, Zachary Jonathan (2018). Many Are Worried and the Return of the 'Big Lie.' *The Washington Post*, https://www.washingtonpost.com/news/made-by-history/wp/2018/05/21/many-are-worried-about-the-return-of-the-big-lie-theyre-worried-about-the-wrong-thing/.
Jakobson, Roman (1960). Linguistics and Poetics. In: T. A. Sebeok (ed.), *Style and Language*, 34–45. Cambridge, MA: MIT Press.
Johnson, Anne (2020). Examples of Semiotics in Advertising. *Chron*, October 5, 2020, https://smallbusiness.chron.com/examples-semiotics-advertising-38593.html.
Johnson, Mark (1987). *The Body in the Mind: The Bodily Basis of Meaning, Imagination and Reason*. Chicago: University of Chicago Press.
Joseph, John (2006). *Language and Politics*. Edinburgh: Edinburgh University Press.
Kafka, Franz (1915). *Die Verwandlung*. Leipzig: Kurt Wolff.
Kant, Immanuel (1781). *Critique of Pure Reason*. New York: St. Martin's.
Kant, Immanuel (1797). *Der Metaphysik der Sitten*. Königsberg: Hofenberg.
Kaufman, Frederick (2020). Pandemics Go Hand in Hand with Conspiracy Theories. *The New Yorker*, https://www.newyorker.com/culture/cultural-comment/pandemics-go-hand-in-hand-with-conspiracy-theories.
Kelly, John (2016). What's with All Trump's Talk about "Draining the Swamp? *Slate*, October 26, 2016, https://slate.com/human-interest/2016/10/why-do-trump-and-his-supports-keep-talking-about-draining-the-swamp.html.
Keyword Search (2020). #MeToo. Twitter. Twitter, April 29, 2020, https://twitter.com/search?q=#MeToo&src=typed_query.

King Jr., Martin Luther (1965). Speech in Montgomery, Alabama (25 March 1965).
Knight, Peter (2021). Conspiracy Theories: Linked to Literature. *The UNESCO Courier*, https://en.unesco.org/courier/2021-2/conspiracy-theories-linked-literature.
Knudson, Cory Austin (2018). QAnon's Pendulum: On Umberto Eco's Fiction and Right-Wing Conspiracism. *Full Stop*, www.full-stop.net/2018/08/15/blog/cory-austin-knudson/qanons-pendulum-on-umberto-ecos-fiction-and-right-wing-conspiracism/.
Korzybski, Alfred (1921). *Manhood of Humanity: The Science and Art of Human Engineering*. New York: Dutton.
Korzybski, Alfred (1933). *Science and Sanity: An Introduction to Non-Aristotelian Systems and General Semantics*. Brooklyn: Institute of General Semantics.
Kosslyn, Stephen, Ganis, Giorgio and Thompson, William L. (2001). Neural Foundations of Imagery. *Nature Reviews Neuroscience* 2: 635–42.
Krampen, Martin (2010). Code. In: T. A. Sebeok and M. Danesi (eds.), *Encyclopedic Dictionary of Semiotics*, volume 1, 3rd edition. Berlin: Mouton.
Kress, Gunther and Leeuwen, Theo van (1996). *Reading Images: The Grammar of Visual Design*. London: Routledge.
Kuper, Leo (1981). *Genocide: Its Political Use in the Twentieth Century*. New Haven: Yale University Press.
Kurlansky, Mark (2022). *Big Lies: From Socrates to Social Media*. Thomaston: Tilbury House.
LaFollette, Hugh (2000). Pragmatic Ethics. In: High LaFollette (ed.), *The Blackwell Guide to Ethical Theory*, 400–19. Oxford: Wiley-Blackwell.
Lai, Vicky T., Howerton, Olivia, and Desai, Rutvik H. (2019). Concrete Processing of Action Metaphors: Evidence from ERP. *Brain Research* 1714: 202. DOI: 10.1016/j.brainres.2019.03.005.
Lakoff, George (1979). The Contemporary Theory of Metaphor. In: A. Ortony (ed.), *Metaphor and Thought*, 202–51. Cambridge: Cambridge University Press.
Lakoff, George (2004). *Don't Think of an Elephant*. Chelsea, VT: Chelsea Green Publishing.
Lakoff, George (2008). *The Political Mind: Why You Can't Understand 21st-Century Politics with an 18th-Century Brain*. New York: Viking.
Lakoff, George (2014). Mapping the Brain's Metaphor Circuitry: Metaphorical Thought in Everyday Reason. *Frontiers in Human Neuroscience* 8, https://doi.org/10.3389/fnhum.2014.00958.
Lakoff, George (2016). *Moral Politics: How Liberals and Conservatives Think*, 3rd edition. Chicago: University of Chicago Press.
Langer, Susanne K. (1948). *Philosophy in a New Key*. New York: Mentor Books.
Langer, Walter C. (1972). *Mind of Adolf Hitler*. New York: Basic.
Lapouge, Vacher de (1889). *L'Aryen*. Paris: Fontemoing.
Laub, Zachary (2019). Hate Speech on Social Media: Global Comparisons. Council on Foreign Relations, https://www.cfr.org/backgrounder/hate-.

Lee, Graciela E. (2021). Populist Authoritarian Readings of Machiavelli's *Prince*: From Interwar to the Present. *Inquiries Journal* 13, http://www.inquiriesjournal.com/a?id=1912.

Lee, Jason (2018). *Nazism and Neo-Nazism in Film and Media*. Amsterdam: Amsterdam University Press.

Leeuwen, Theo (2005). *Introducing Social Semiotics*. New York: Routledge.

Leone, Massimo (2017). Fundamentalism, Anomie, Conspiracy: Umberto Eco's Semiotics against Interpretive Irrationality. In: T. Thellefsen and B. Sørensen (eds.), *Umberto Eco in His Own Words*, 221–9. Berlin: Mouton de Gruyter.

Lévi-Strauss, Claude (1962). *La pensée sauvage*. Paris: Plon.

Lévi-Strauss, Claude (1987). *Introduction to Marcel Mauss*, trans. by F. Baker. London: Routledge.

Lewandowsky, Stephan and Cook, John (2020). *The Conspiracy Theory Handbook*, http://sks.to/conspiracy.

Li, Yiyi and Xie, Ying (2019). Is a Picture Worth a Thousand Words? An Empirical Study of Image Content and Social Media Engagement. *Journal of Marketing Research* 57: 1–19.

Linden, Sander van der (2015). The Surprising Power of Conspiracy Theories. *Psychology Today*, August 24, 2015, https://www.psychologytoday.com/ca/blog/socially-relevant/201508/the-surprising-power-conspiracy-theories.

Linsroth, J. P. (2018). Myths on Race and Invasion of the Caravan Horde. *Counterpunch*, https://www.counterpunch.org/2018/11/09/myths-on-race-and-invasion-of-the-caravan-horde/.

Lippmann, Walter (1922). *Public Opinion*. New York: Macmillan.

Liszka, James (2022). *Charles Peirce on Ethics, Esthetics and the Normative Sciences*. New York: Routledge.

Locke, John (1690). *An Essay Concerning Humane Understanding*. Oxford: Clarendon Press.

Loebs, Bruce (2015). *Hitler's Rhetorical Theory*. relevantrhetoric.com/Hitler%27s%20Rhetorical%20Theory.

Lombardo, Robert M. (2002). Black Hand: Terror by Letter in Chicago. *Journal of Contemporary Criminal Justice* 18: 394–409.

Lotman, Yuri (1991). *Universe of the Mind: A Semiotic Theory of Culture*. Bloomington: Indiana University Press.

Lovell, Julia (2019). *Maoism: A Global History*. New York: Vintage.

Lowry, Rich (2017). Trump Can't Quit the Victim Act. *Politico*, https://www.politico.com/news/magazine/2022/11/23/how-trump-plays-the-victim-card-00070763.

Lucy, John A. (1997). Linguistic Relativity. *Annual Review of Anthropology* 26: 291–312.

Lund, Frederik H. (1925). The Psychology of Belief. *The Journal of Abnormal and Social Psychology* 20: 183–91.

Lunde, Paul (2004). *Organized Crime: An Inside Guide to the World's Most Successful Industry*. London: Dorling Kindersley.

Machiavelli, Niccolò (1513). *The Prince*. The Project Gutenberg EBOOK of the Prince, http://www.gutenberg.org/files/1232/1232-h/1232-h.htm.

Machiavelli, Niccolò (1517). *Discourses*. Harmondsworth: Penguin Cassics.

Machiavelli, Niccolò (1521). *The Art of War*. Createspace, 2010.

Macknik, Stephen L., King, Mac, Randi, James, and Robbins, Apollo (2008). Attention and Awareness in Stage Magic: Turning Tricks Into Research. *Nature Reviews Neuroscience* 9: 871–9.

Madison, Caleb (2021). How We Swallowed Redpilled Whole. *The Atlantic*, https://www.theatlantic.com/newsletters/archive/2021/12/pilled-suffix-meaning/620980/.

Madisson, Mari-Liies and Ventsel, Andreas (2022). *Conspiracy Theory Narratives: A Semiotic Approach*. New York: Routledge.

Marger, Martin N. (2008). *Race and Ethnic Relations: American and Global Perspectives*. Boston: Cengage Learning.

McCarthy, Ellen (2021). #MeToo Raised Awareness about Sexual Misconduct. Has It Curbed Bad Behavior? *The Washington Post*, August 20, 2021, https://www.seattletimes.com/nation-world/metoo-raised-awareness-about-sexual-misconduct-has-it-curbed-bad-behavior/.

McKenzie-McHarg, Andrew (2018). Conspiracy Theory: The Nineteenth-Century Prehistory of a Twentieth-Century Concept. In: Joseph E. Uscinski (ed.), *Conspiracy Theories and the People Who Believe Them*. New York: Oxford Academic.

McLuhan, Marshall (1968). *Through the Vanishing Point*. New York: Harper & Row.

Mercieca, Jennifer (2018). The Denials of Donald Trump. *Houston Chronicle*, December 11, 2018. https://www.houstonchronicle.com/local/gray-matters/article/donald-trump-robert-mueller-rhetorical-strategy-13458032.php.

Messaris, Paul (1994). *Visual Literacy: Image, Mind and Reality*. Boulder: Westview Press.

Milano, Alyssa (2017). Twitter post. October 15, 2017, 4:21pm. https://twitter.com/Alyssa_Milano/status/919659438700670976.

Milner, Ryan M. (2016). *The World Made Meme: Public Conversations and Participatory Media*. Cambridge: MIT Press.

Moeschberger, Scott L. and Phillips, DeZalia, Rebekah, A. (eds.) (2014). *Symbols That Bind, Symbols That Divide: The Semiotics of Peace and Conflict*. Chaim: Springer.

Monmonier, Mark (1996). *How to Lie with Maps*. Chicago: University of Chicago Press.

Mooney, Peter and Juhász, Levente (2020). Mapping Covid-19: How Web-Based Maps Contribute to the Infodemic. *Dialogues in Human Geography* 10: 265–70.

Moskalenko, Sophia and Bloom, Mia (2021). Why QAnon Followers Are Like Opioid Addicts, and Why That Matters. *Think*, nbcnews.com/think/opinion/why-qanon-followers-are-opioid-addicts-why-matters-ncna1277323.

Müller, Friedrich Max (1859). *A History of Ancient Sanskrit Literature so far as It Illustrates the Primitive Religion of the Brahmans*. London: Williams and Norgate.

Müller, Friedrich Max (1866). *Lectures on the Science of Language*. London: Longmans, Green.

Müller, Friedrich Max (1883). *India: What Can It Teach Us?: A Course of Lectures Delivered before the University of Cambridge*. London: Longmans, Green.

Müller, Friedrich Max (1888). *Biographies of Words and the Home of the Aryas*. London: Longmans, Green.

Musolff, Andreas (2004). *Metaphor and Political Discourse*. New York: Palgrave.

Musolff, Andreas (2010). *Metaphor, Nation and the Holocaust: The Concept of the Body Politic*. London: Routledge.

Mussolini, Benito (2018). *Selected Speeches of Benito Mussolini*. Amazon Digital Services.

Neiwart, David (2020). *Red Pill, Blue Pill*. Lanham: Rowman & Littlefield.

Neuman, Yair, Danesi, Marcel, and Vilenchik, Dan (2022). *AI for Dialoguing with Texts*. New York: Routledge.

Nicaso, Antonio and Danesi, Marcel (2020). *Organized Crime: A Cultural Perspective*. London: Routledge.

Nicolaou, Elena and Smith, Courtney E. (2019). A #MeToo Timeline to Show How Far We've Come & How Far We Need to Go. *Refinery29*, Vice Media Group, 7 October 2019, www.refinery29.com/en-ca/2019/10/8534374/a-metoo-timeline-to-show-how-far-weve-come-how-far-we-need-to-go.

Nie, Jing-Bao (2020). In the Shadow of Biological Warfare: Conspiracy Theories on the Origins of Covid-19 and Enhancing Global Governance of Biosafety as a Matter of Urgency. *Journal of Bioethetical Inquiry* 17: 567–74.

Nietzsche, Friedrich (1873). *On Truth and Lies in a Nonmoral Sense*. CreateSpace Independent Publishing Platform.

Nöth, Winfried (2021). Charles Peirce's Philosophy of Value. *Language and Semiotic Studies* 7: 55–67.

Nuessel, Frank (2013). Lying: A Semiotic Perspective. In: *Semiotics 2013*, 151–62. Semiotic Society of America.

Nunberg, Geoffrey (2018). Why the Term 'Deep State' Speaks to Conspiracy Theorists. *NPR*, https://www.npr.org/2018/08/09/633019635/opinion-why-the-term-deep-state-speaks-to-conspiracy-theorists.

Nyyssönen, Heino and Humphreys, Brendan (2016). Another Munich We Just Cannot Afford: Historical Metonymy in Politics. *Redescriptions: Political Thought, Conceptual History and Feminist Theory* 19: 173–90.

O'Connor, Joseph F. (1975). Odysseus the Liar. *The Classical Outlook* 53: 41–3.

Ofen, Noa, Gabrieli, Susan, Whitfield, Chai, Xiaoqian, J., Schwarzlose, Rebecca F., and Gabrieli, John D. E. (2017). Neural Correlates of Deception: Lying about Past Events and Personal Beliefs. *Social Cognitive and Affective Neuroscience* 12: 116–27.

Ogden, Charles and Richards, I. A. (1923). *The Meaning of Meaning*. New York: Harcourt, Brace and World.

O'Halloran, Kay L. and Tau, Sabine (2023). Discourse Analysis and Semiotics. In: Jamin Pelkey and Paul Cobley (eds.), *Bloomsbury Semiotics*, vol. 4, 231–52. London: Bloomsbury.

O'Meara, Lucy (2013). *Roland Barthes at the Collège de France*. Liverpool: Liverpool University Press.

Orwell, George (1940). Review of Adolph Hitler's Mein Kampf. *New English Weekly*, March 21, 1940, https://gutenberg.net.au/ebooks16/1600051h.html.

Orwell, George (1945). *Animal Farm*. London: Secker & Warburg.

Orwell, George (1949). *Nineteen Eighty-Four*. New York: Harcourt, Brace, and Company.

Orwell, George (1968). *The Collected Essays*, vol. 3. London: Secker and Warburg.

Orwell, George (2017). *Orwell on Orwell*. London: Harvell Secker.

Oswald, Laura (2012). *Marketing Semiotics*. Oxford: Oxford University Press.

Oswald, Laura (2015). *Creating Value: The Theory and Practice of Marketing Semiotics Research*. Oxford: Oxford University Press.

Ozubko, Jason D and Fugelsang, Jonathan (2011). Remembering Makes Evidence Compelling: Retrieval from Memory Can Give Rise to the Illusion of Truth. *Journal of Experimental Psychology: Learning, Memory, and Cognition* 37: 270–6.

Padesky, Christine A. (1991). Schema as Self-Prejudice. *International Cognitive Therapy Newsletter* 6: 6–7.

Parsons, Elaine Frantz (2005). Midnight Rangers: Costume and Performance in the Reconstruction-Era Ku Klux Klan. *The Journal of American History* 92: 811–36.

Pavlov, Ivan (1902). *The Work of Digestive Glands*. London: Griffin.

Paxton, Robert (2004). *The Anatomy of Fascism*. New York: Vintage.

Peirce, Charles S. (1877). *Illustrations of the Logic of Science*. Chicago: Open Court.

Peirce, Charles S. (1931–1958). *Collected Papers of Charles Sanders Peirce*, vols. 1–8, ed. by C. Hartshorne and P. Weiss. Cambridge, MA: Harvard University Press.

Pelc, Jerzy (1992). The Methodological Status of Semiotics: Signs, Semiosis, Interpretation and the Limits of Semiotics. In: M. Balat and J. Deledalle-Rhodes (eds.), *Signs of Humanity*, 247–59. Berlin: Mouton de Gruyter.

Pelkey, Jamin and Cobley, Paul (eds.) (2023). *Bloomsbury Semiotics*, 4 volumes. London: Bloomsbury.

Petrilli, Susan (2014). *Sign Studies and Semioethics. Communication, Translation and Values*. Berlin: Mouton de Gruyter.

Petrilli, Susan (2019). *Signs, Language and Listening: Semioethic Perspectives*. Ottawa: Legas.

Petrilli, Susan and Ponzio, Augusto (2005). *Semiotics Unbounded*. Toronto: University of Toronto Press.

Petrilli, Susan and Ponzio, Augusto (2007). Semiotics Today. From Global Semiotics to Semioethics, a Dialogic Response. *Signs—International Journal of Semiotics*, 1: 29–127.

Pierre, Joe (2020). Illusory Truth, Lies, and Political Propaganda. *Curious*, medium.com/curious/illusory-truth-lies-and-political-propaganda-6810953a6553.

Pieters, Jürgen and Pint, Kris (2008). Introduction: An Unexpected Return. Barthes Lecture Courses at the Collège de France. *Paragraph* 31: 1–8.

Piltz, Rick (2018). Michael Crichton, Author of State of Fear, Leaves global Warming Disinformation Legacy. *Government Accountability Project*, https://whistleblower.org/politicization-of-climate-science/global-warming-denial-machine/michael-crichton-author-of-state-of-fear-leaves-global-warming-disinformation-legacy/.

Polidoro, Piero (2018). Post-Truth and Fake News: Preliminary Considerations. *Versus* 127: 189–206.

Polikov, Léon (1974). *Aryan Myth*. New York: Basic.

Popper, Karl (1945). *The Open Society and Its Enemies*. London: Routledge.

Poulsen, Bruce (2012). Being Amused by Apophenia. *Psychology Today*, https://www.psychologytoday.com/us/blog/reality-play/201207/being-amused-apophenia.

Priniski, J. Hunter, McClay, Mason, and Holyoak, Keith J. (2021). Rise of QAnon: A Mental Model of Good and Evil Stews in an Echochamber. In: T. Fitch, C. Lamm, H. Leder, and K. Teßmar-Raible (eds.), *Proceedings of the 43rd Annual Meeting of the Cognitive Science Society*. Cognitive Science Society.

Proust, Marcel (1913). *Remembrance of Things Past*, vol. 3. Harmondsworth: Penguin.

Putin, Vladimir (2022). Full Text: Putin's Declaration of War on Ukraine. *The Spectator*, February 24, https://www.spectator.co.uk/article/full-text-putin-s-declaration-of-war-on-ukraine/.

Rajan, Anjana, et al. (2021). *Countering QAnon*. Limbik: The Soufan Group.

Randviir, Anti (2004). *Mapping the World: Towards a Sociosemiotic Approach to Culture*. Tartu: Tartu University Press.

Ranta, Michael (2016). The (Pictorial) Construction of Collective Identities in the Third Reich. *Language and Semiotic Studies* 2: 107–24.

Rassinier, Paul (1964). *The Drama of the European Jews*. Silver Spring, MD: Steppingstones.

Rauschning, Hermann (1940). *Hitler M'a Dit*. Paris: Coopération.

Reddy, Michael J. (1979). The Conduit Metaphor: A Case of Frame Conflict in Our Language about Language. In: Andrew Ortony (ed.), *Metaphor and Thought*, 284–310. Cambridge: Cambridge University Press.

Renan, Ernest (1882). *What Is a Nation?* New York: Columbia University Press.

Riehl, W. H. (1857). *Land und Leute*. Stuttgart: Verlag Cotta.

Ritvo, Eva (2014). The Neuroscience of Giving. *Psychology Today*, https://www.psychologytoday.com/us/blog/vitality/201404/the-neuroscience-giving.

Robison, John (1798), *Proofs of a Conspiracy*. Philadelphia: T. Dobson.

Rodríguez-Ferrándiz, Raúl (2019). Faith in Fakes: Secrets, Lies and Conspiracies in Umberto Eco's Writings. *Semiotica* 227, DOI:10.1515/sem-2017-0137.

Roos, Daniel (2014). *Julius Streicher und "Der Stürmer" 1923–1945*. Paderborn: Schöningh.

Rothkopf, David J. (2003). When the Buzz Bites Back. *The Washington Post*, May 11, 2003, p. B.01.

Roy, Marina (2000). *Sign after the X*. Vancouver: Advance Artspeak.

Russell, Bertrand (1950). *Unpopular Essays*. New York: Simon & Schuster.

Sandoval, Chela (2000). *Methodology of the Oppressed*. Minneapolis: University of Minnesota Press.

Sapir, Edward (1921). *Language*. New York: Harcourt, Brace, and World.

Saussure, Ferdinand de (1916). *Cours de linguistique générale*. Paris: Payot.

Sauter, M. R. (2017). The Apophenic Machine: The Conspiratorial Mode and the Internet's Data Hoard Were Made for Each Other. *Real Life*, https://reallifemag.com/the-apophenic-machine/.

Schliemann, Heinrich (1875). *Troy and Its Remains*. Cambridge: Cambridge University Press.

Schulman, Jeremy (2018). Every Insane Thing Donald Trump Has Said about Global Warming. *Mother Jones*, www.motherjones.com/environment/2016/12/trump-climate-timeline/.

Searle, John (1990). The Storm over the University. *The New York Review of Books*, December, 6 1990.

Sebeok, Thomas A. (1984). *Communication Measures to Bridge Ten Millennia*. Columbus, Ohio: Battelle Memorial Institute, Office of Nuclear Waste Isolation.

Seitz, Frederick (1996). A Major Deception on Global Warming. *The Wall Street Journal*, https://www.wsj.com/articles/SB834512411338954000.

Shapiro, Michael (1984). *Language and Politics*. New York: New York University Press.

Shermer, Michael (2008). Patternicity: Finding Meaningful Patterns in Meaningless Noise. *Scientific American* 299: 48.

Sherwood, Harriet (2018). Toxic Christianity: The Evangelicals Creating Champions for Trump. *The Guardian*, 21 October 2018, https://www.theguardian.com/us-news/2018/oct/21/evangelical-christians-trump-liberty-university-jerry-falwell.

Shinar, Chaim (2018). Conspiracy Narratives in Russian Politics: From Stalin to Putin," *European Review* 26L: 648–60.

Silva, Marco and Thomas, Merlyn (2022). How High-Profile Scientists Felt Tricked by Group Denying Climate Change. *BBC*, https://www.bbc.com/news/blogs-trending-61166339.

Silvera-Roig, Marta and López-Varela Azcárate, Asunción (eds.) (2019). *Cognitive and Intermedial Semiotics*. IntechOpen.

Smith, Stephen (2014). Historical Memory. USC Shoah Foundation, https://sfi.usc.edu/news/2014/04/4441-historical-memory.

Somov, Georgij Yu (2016). Interrelations of Codes in Human Semiotic Systems. *Semiotica* 213: 557–99.

Sonnevend, Julia (2020). A Virus as an Icon: The 2020 Pandemic in Images. *American Journal of Cultural Sociology* 8: 451–61.

Sontag, Susan (1978). *Illness as Metaphor*. New York: Farrar, Straus & Giroux.

Stalin, J. V. (1913). Marxism and the National Question. *Prosveshcheniye*, pp. 3–5, March 1913.

Stanton, Gregory (2020). QAnon Is a Nazi Cult, Rebranded. *Just Security*, https://www.justsecurity.org/72339/qanon-is-a-nazi-cult-rebranded/.

Sturrock, John (1986). *Structuralism*. London: Paladin.
Subramanian, Samantha (2017). Inside the Macedonian Fake-News Complex. *Wired*, https://www.wired.com/2017/02/veles-macedonia-fake-news/.
Sun Tzu (2002). *The Art of War*. North Chelmsford, MA: Courier Corporation Reprint.
Svensmark, Henrik (2009). While the Sun Sleeps. *Jyllands-Posten*, https://jyllands-posten.dk/nyviden/article4186842.ece.
Swett, Pamela E. (2014). *Selling under the Swastika: Advertising and Commercial Culture in Nazi Germany*. Stanford: Stanford University Press.
Tacitus, Cornelius (109 CE). *Annals. MIT Classics*, classics.mit.edu/Tacitus/annals.html.
Tangherlini, Timothy R. (2021). Machine Learning Is Helping Decipher Conspiracy Theories Outright. *Nextgov*, https://www.nextgov.com/emerging-tech/2020/11/how.
Telis, Gisela (2012). Metaphors Make Brains Touchy Feely. *Newsbrain & Behavior*, https://www.science.org/content/article/metaphors-make-brains-touchy-feely.
Tench, Watkin (1796). *Letters Written in France: To a Friend in London, between the Month of November 1794, and the Month of May 1795*. London: J. Johnson.
Tharoor, Ishaan (2015). What George Orwell Said about Hitler's "Mein Kampf". *The Washington Post*, www.washingtonpost.com/news/worldviews/wp/2015/02/25/what-george-orwell-said-about-hitlers-mein-kampf/.
Thornbury, Gregory Alan (2020). QAnon's "Messianic Secret." *Religion & Politics*, https://religionandpolitics.org/2020/10/22/qanons-messianic-secret/.
Thucydides (431 BCE). *History of the Peloponnesian War*. Project Gutenberg, https://www.gutenberg.org/files/7142/7142-h/7142-h.htm.
Tillich, Paul (1964). *Theology of Culture*. Oxford: Oxford University Press.
Timberg, Craig and Dwoskin, Elizabeth (2021). With Trump Gone, QAnon Groups Focus Fury on Attacking Coronavirus Vaccines. *Washington Post*, https://www.washingtonpost.com/technology/2021/03/11/with-trump-gone-qanon-groups-focus-fury-attacking-covid-vaccines/.
Toman, Jindřich (1995). *The Magic of a Common Language: Jakobson, Mathesius, Trubetzkoy, and the Prague Linguistic Circle*. Cambridge, MA: MIT Press.
Torbakov, Igor (2022). Russia's Invasion of Ukraine: "It's Worse Than a Crime, It's a Mistake. *Eurasianet*, https://eurasianet.org/perspectives-russias-invasion-of-ukraine-its-worse-than-a-crime-its-a-mistake.
Tracy, Antoine Destutt de (1817). *Projet d'éléments d'idéologie*. Paris: L'Harmattan.
Tromly, Benjamin (2022). 'Denazification,' Putin Style. *The Seattle Times*, https://www.seattletimes.com/opinion/denazification-putin-style/.
Trueman, C. N. (2015). Blood Purity and Nazi Germany. *The History Learning Site*, historylearningsite.co.uk.
Turner, Mark (1997). *The Literary Mind*. Oxford: Oxford University Press.
Tyner, Judith Ann (1974). *Persuasive Cartography*. Los Angeles: University of California.
Uexküll, Jakob von (1909). *Umwelt und Innenwelt der Tierre*. Berlin: Springer.

Umiker-Sebeok, Jean (ed.) (1987). *Marketing and Semiotics*. The Hague: Mouton de Gruyter.
Unesco (2021). *Addressing Hate Speech on Social Media: Contemporary Challenges*. Paris: United Nations Educational, Scientific and Cultural Organization.
United Nations (2021). *Hate Speech Is Rising across the World*, https://www.un.org/en/hate-speech.
United Nations (2022). *Social Media Feeds Holocaust Denial and Distortion*, https://www.un.org/en/delegate/un-report-social-media-feeds-holocaust-denial-and-distortion.
Uspenskij, Boris (2001). *La pala d'altare di Jan van Eyck a Gand: La composizione dell'opera (la prospettiva divina e la prospettiva umana)*. Milano: Lupetti.
Viganò, Carlo Maria (2022). Open Letter to President Donald Trump. *Apisteia*, https://aristeia.news/archbishop-carlo-maria-vigano-open-letter-to-president-donald-trump/.
Viroli, Maurizio (1998). *Machiavelli*. Oxford: Oxford University Press.
Voltaire (1764). *Dictionnaire Philosophique*. Amsterdam: Varberg.
Vygotsky, Lev S. (1962). *Thought and Language*. Cambridge, MA: MIT Press.
Vygotsky, Lev S. (1978). *Mind in Society*. Cambridge, MA: Cambridge University Press.
Waals, Frans de (1982). *Chimpanzee Politics*. Baltimore: Johns Hopkins University Press.
Wachowski, Lana (2012). Interview. In: David Poland (ed.), *Movie City News*, moviecitynews.com.
Walcott, Peter (1977). Odysseus and the Art of Lying. *Ancient Society* 8: 1–19.
Wasniewska, Malgorzata (2017). The Socio-parasite and Bio-parasite Metaphorical Concepts in Racist Discourse. *Crossroads: A Journal of English Language Studies* 10: 46–61.
Watson, Lyall (1990). *The Nature of Things*. London: Houghton and Stoughton.
Watt, W. C. (1998). Semiotics. *Routledge Encyclopedia of Philosophy*, doi:10.4324/9780415249126-U056-1.
Weber, Max (1922). *Theory of Social and Economic Organization*. New York: The Free Press.
Weddig, Catherine (2022). Climate Change Denial & Skepticism: A Review of the Literature. *Mediawell*, https://mediawell.ssrc.org/literature-reviews/climate-change-denial-skepticism-a-review-of-the-literature/versions/1-0/.
Wegner, Daniel M. (1989). *White Bears and Other Unwanted Thoughts: Suppression, Obsession, and the Psychology of Mental Control*. New York: Viking.
Weiss, Andrew (2022). *Accidental Czar: The Life and Lies of Vladimir Putin*. New York: Macmillan.
Welch, Bryant (2008). *State of Confusion: Political Manipulation and the Assault on the American Mind*. New York: Thomas Dunne Books.
Wheeler, Wendy (2006). *The Whole Creature: Complexity, Biosemiotics and the Evolution of Culture*. London: Lawrence & Wishart.

White, Hayden (1973). *Metahistory: The Historical Imagination in Nineteenth-Century Europe*. Baltimore: Johns Hopkins University Press.

Whorf, Benjamin Lee (1941). The Relation of Habitual Thought to Language. In: Leslie Spier (ed.), *Language, Culture, and Personality: Essays in Memory of Edward Sapir*, 75–93. Menasha: Sapir Memorial Publication Fund.

Wilde, Oscar (2007). *Complete Works*, vol. 4. Oxford: Oxford University Press.

Williamson, Judith (1978). *Decoding Advertisements*. London: Marion Boyars.

Winkler, Martin M. (2009). *The Roman Salute: Cinema, History, Ideology*. Columbus: Ohio State University Press.

Wright, Richard (1995). *The Moral Animal: Why We Are the Way We Are*. New York: Vintage.

Xun, Zhou and Gilman, Sander (2021). *I Know Who Caused Covid-19: Pandemics and Xenophobia*. Chicago: University of Chicago Press.

Yablokov, Ilya (2022). The Five Conspiracy Theories That Putin Has Weaponized. *The New York Times*, https://www.nytimes.com/2022/04/25/opinion/putin-russia-conspiracy-theories.html.

Yenne, Bill (2010). *Hitler's Master of the Dark Arts: Himmler's Black Knights and the Occult Origins of the SS*. Minneapolis: Zenith.

Yu, Xing (2013). *Language and State: An Inquiry into the Progress of Civilization. United States of America*. Lanham: University Press of America.

Zappavigna, Michele (2018). *Searchable Talk: Hashtags and Social Media Metadiscourse*. London: Bloomsbury.

Zeki, Samir and Romaya, John Paul (2008). Neural Correlates of Hate. *PLoS One*, doi: 10.1371/journal.pone.0003556.

Zola, Émile (1996). *The Dreyfus Affair: "J'accuse" and Other Writings*, curated by Alain Pagès and Eleanor Levieux. New Haven: Yale University Press.

Index

adrenochrome 81, 97
advertising ix, 1, 8
aesthetics 101
algorithms 72, 76, 126, 139, 140
Alice's Adventures in Wonderland 52
alien conspiracy theory 20
alienation 98, 144
alt-right 24, 25, 43, 50, 53, 65, 74, 79, 119
alternate reality 53, 90
alternative history 23
alternative truth xi, 90, 91, 92, 93, 96, 97
Animal Farm 110
anomie 98
anti-science xiii, 3, 70, 125
anti-Semitism 4, 81, 129, 130, 147
apophany 26, 124
apophasis 41
apophenia 25, 26, 51, 58, 72, 75, 115, 116, 119, 124, 126, 142, 143
Arendt, Hannah xv, 29, 61, 63
Aristophanes 17
Aristotle 85
artificial intelligence 11, 146
Aryan 19, 21, 22, 23, 24, 28, 43, 35, 46, 47, 48, 49, 50, 54, 55, 65, 94, 95, 104, 106, 107, 108, 109, 111, 113, 121, 122, 124, 125, 126, 133, 136, 137, 139, 140, 141, 149
Augustine of Hippo 87

Bakhtin, Mikhail 9, 15
Barthes, Roland xii, 2, 5, 7, 9, 12, 55, 57, 58, 107, 108, 116, 117, 131, 133, 137, 145, 146
Baudrillard, Jean 53, 64, 91, 118
Benesch, Susan 137, 138
Big Brother 99, 110
big lies x, xi, xii, 19, 21, 22, 83, 84, 85, 86, 87, 89, 90, 91, 92, 93, 94, 95, 96, 97, 98, 99, 100, 101, 111, 132
binarism 2, 146
bioethics 3

biosemiotics 9
Birth of a Nation, The 125
Black Hand 20
blending 35, 40, 41
blood libel 52, 81, 82
blood symbolism 21, 24, 29, 34, 35, 36, 44, 45, 48, 52, 66, 81, 82, 97, 103, 105, 107, 109, 113, 124
Blut und Boden 24, 27, 34, 35, 49, 97
Bouissac, Paul 6
Bradbury, Ray 11
Brown, Dan 78, 79, 142
Burke, Kenneth 27, 28
Burke, Tarana 13
buzzwords 70

cabal xiii, 6, 11, 38, 51, 52, 53, 58, 59, 62, 63, 65, 66, 72, 73, 74, 75, 76, 77, 78, 79, 93, 97, 99, 104, 114, 116, 133, 139, 140, 141, 147
Cagliostro, Count Alessandro di 147
Carroll, Lewis 52, 75, 117
cartographic propaganda 122
Cleon 17, 39, 83, 138
climate change xii, xiii, xiv, 3, 61, 62, 69, 70, 71, 72, 73, 74
Cobley, Paul 6
code xiv, 6, 7, 8, 10, 11, 13, 14, 15, 20, 22, 23, 24, 25, 28, 31, 32, 33, 34, 42, 44, 49, 51, 53, 55, 59, 62, 65, 70, 72, 73, 75, 76, 78, 80, 81, 82, 85, 97, 105, 113, 114, 116, 120, 122, 124, 125, 127, 131, 146, 148
coded meaning 7, 11, 12, 13, 15, 16, 29, 31, 33, 34, 46, 53, 59, 62, 69, 70, 110, 114, 115, 127, 133, 135, 149
cognitive dissonance 107, 143
confabulation 104, 105, 109, 148
connotation 7, 8
Conrad, Klaus 25, 26, 51, 126
conspiracism 43, 72, 80, 115, 116, 117, 119, 120, 121, 122, 126, 130, 142

conspiracy theory 10, 54, 71, 73, 104, 113, 114, 115, 117, 147
contradiction 98, 99
coronavirus 74, 77, 116
Council on Foreign Relations 10
Cours de linguistique générale 7
Covid 50, 74, 75, 77, 78, 79, 116, 125
Crichton, Michael 61, 62, 63, 69, 70, 79, 80
cross symbolism 125, 126
czar 96

Da Vinci Code, The 78, 142
dangerous discourse x, 1, 3, 4, 5, 6, 7, 8, 9, 10, 11, 13, 15, 17, 19, 21, 23, 25, 26, 27, 29, 35, 38, 41, 46, 50, 129, 130, 131, 135, 136, 139, 140, 141, 142, 144, 145, 146, 148
deceit 85, 88
deception 19, 83, 88, 130
decoding xiii, 3, 6, 7, 8, 9, 15, 37, 58, 63, 131
deconstruction 116, 120, 138, 145, 148
Deep Learning 146
deep state 22, 51, 52, 54, 59, 62, 69, 70, 86, 89, 98, 100, 109, 114, 116, 122
defense mechanism 64, 65
denazification 32, 37, 50, 59
denialism 63, 64, 65, 66, 67, 69, 72, 73, 74, 76, 80
denotation 7, 8, 50, 133
Derrida, Jacques 5
disinformation xi, xv, 126, 165
Dostoyevsky, Fyodor 41
doublespeak 22, 39, 40
doublethink 40
Dreyfus Affair 129, 130, 131, 148, 149
Duce, il 95
Dumas, Alexandre 147
Durkheim, Émile 98

Eco, Umberto xi, 7, 51, 86, 115, 142, 147
Edelweiss 37, 40
emoji 13, 16
environmentalism 69
epigenome 78
ethics 3, 8, 9, 84, 101, 131, 145

Fahrenheit 452 xi
fake news 92, 100
false beliefs xiv, 8, 15, 26, 34, 35, 41, 58, 64, 76, 79, 135, 137, 144

false memory 18, 105
false myth 104, 117, 124
false narrative 124
Fascism 31, 54, 93, 96, 99, 107, 108, 111, 114, 133
Festinger, Leon 76
films (propaganda) 29, 54, 104, 136
firehose of falsehoods xi
flag symbolism 48, 54, 58, 89
Foucault's Pendulum 51, 115, 119, 120, 124, 127, 142
framing 16, 65
French Revolution 33, 79, 97, 147
Führer, 95

Garbati, Luciano 13, 14, 15
gaslighting 32, 39, 42
geo-location 28
gesture 46, 47, 96, 108
global warming 61, 62, 63, 69, 70, 71, 72, 80
Gobineau, Joseph Arthur de 22, 108
Goebbels, Joseph 29, 84, 85, 94, 104
Great Awakening 38
great replacement 10, 42
Great Reset 74, 75, 76, 77, 78
Griffith, D. W. 125

Halliday, Michael 10
hashtag 13, 14, 16
hate speech xii, 7, 8, 11, 137, 138, 139
Herder, Johann Gottfried 66
historical memory 37, 68
historiography 109
Hitler, Adolf xiii, xiv, 19, 21, 22, 23, 24, 27, 28, 29, 34, 36, 41, 42, 47, 48, 49, 54, 56, 57, 59, 65, 67, 78, 81, 82, 84, 85, 86, 88, 89, 94, 95, 96, 97, 98, 104, 105, 107, 108, 109, 113, 125, 138
Hoggan, David 64, 65
Holocaust 3, 4, 6, 36, 64, 65, 67, 68, 72, 81, 107, 148
Homer 83, 111
hoods symbolism 44
hyperreality 53, 72, 91

iconicity 12, 33, 46, 49, 50, 55, 66, 80, 110, 121
Iliad, The 111
Illuminati 78, 79, 116
illusory truth effect 18, 25, 43, 72, 100, 125

images 4, 12, 31, 33, 54, 55, 56, 57, 58, 59, 66, 67, 68, 80, 97, 108, 113, 122, 123, 135, 136, 141
indexicality 34, 35, 37, 38, 47, 52
infodemic 75, 76
infrastructure 113, 114, 115, 116, 117, 120, 121, 124, 125
inter-codability 6, 76, 116, 132, 135, 137, 138, 140, 141, 142, 143
Internet xi, 6, 43, 51, 63, 69, 75, 76, 125, 126, 131, 139
intertextuality xiv, 15, 133, 147
irony 41, 70

J'accuse 129, 151
Jacobins 97

Kafka, Franz 36, 37, 66
Kant, Immanuel 85
Kennedy, John F. 103, 142
keywords 139
Korzybski, Alfred 21, 58, 136, 150
Ku Klux Klan 43, 44, 45, 125, 126

Lakoff, George 16, 32, 36, 40, 41
Langer, Susanne 123
Lapouge, Cacher de 106
Lebensraum 31, 33, 42, 46, 106
letter (alphabet) symbolism 23, 46, 50
Lincoln, Abraham 142, 143
Locke, John 8, 43, 99
Ludendorff, Erich 51, 89
lying 18, 29, 39, 61, 69, 83, 84, 85, 87, 88, 89, 90, 91, 93, 145, 150

Machiavelli, Niccolò 17, 18, 19, 21, 28, 29, 32, 37, 39, 40, 51, 68, 84, 87, 88, 89, 100, 101, 105, 143, 149, 150 Machiavelli
Machiavellian intelligence 87
machine learning 140
Mafia 20, 91, 92
MAGA 22, 73, 92, 109, 110, 111, 149
maps 121, 122, 123
marketing 8, 32
Marxism 28, 36, 89, 96, 98, 114
master race 22
Matrix, The 52, 53, 91, 117, 118
McCarthyism 114, 115, 116
media 3, 10, 29, 32, 42, 54, 62, 56, 92, 98, 138, 146

Medusa 13, 14, 16
Mein Kampf xiii, 23, 24, 28, 34, 48, 65, 82, 84, 86, 89, 96, 105
memes 4, 6, 72, 76
Mendelism 24
metaphor 11, 19, 32, 36, 37, 52, 67, 70, 92, 93, 111, 118
metonymy 40
#MeToo 13, 14, 16, 25, 26, 40, 41, 137
mimesis 93
mind control 19, 21, 58, 97, 98, 99, 100, 101, 111, 125, 141
Ministry of Truth 21, 23, 32, 110, 117
misinformation 18, 75, 76, 82, 118
Müller, Friedrich Max 48
Mussolini, Benito 54, 73, 78, 93, 95, 96, 99, 101, 107, 112
mythology 2, 107, 109, 117, 126

narrativity 104, 121, 126, 146
natural language processing 139
Nazis xiii, xv, 19, 22, 23, 24, 25, 29, 31, 32, 34, 36, 38, 42, 47, 48, 49, 52, 58, 64, 66, 67, 68, 76, 86, 94, 95, 101, 104, 106, 107, 108, 109, 122, 125, 131, 135, 136, 140
Nazism xi, 22, 23, 24, 26, 31, 32, 35, 38, 40, 47, 56, 82, 86, 140, 150
Neo-Nazis 24, 25, 34, 43, 52
neuroscience 9, 36, 136
Newspeak 99
Nietzsche, Friedrich 59
Nineteen Eighty-Four xi, 110
Nuremberg 31, 34, 64, 109, 113

Obama, Barack 52, 71, 73, 100
Odysseus 83
Odyssey, The 83, 111
Orwell, George xi, 21, 23, 29, 32, 39, 40, 42, 81, 82, 99, 100, 101, 110, 111, 117, 141
otherness 3, 73, 95, 144, 145, 146

pandemic 63, 73, 74, 75, 76, 77, 116
paranoia 143, 144
parasite metaphor 65, 66, 67
Peirce, Charles S. 6, 7, 9, 10, 35, 58, 101, 112, 123, 137
Pelkey, Jamin 6
Perseus 13
Petrilli, Susan 2, 3, 9

Plantard, Pierre 124
Ponzio, Augusto 2, 9
post-structuralism 5
posters 23, 54, 66, 104, 131, 135, 138
Prague School 5
Prague Cemetery, The 147, 148
Prince, The 17, 18, 19, 84, 88
Priory of Sion 78, 124, 126
projection 85, 89, 92
propaganda x, xi, xiii, 21, 26, 27, 29, 52, 54, 66, 67, 75, 84, 86, 94, 122
Protocols of the Elders of Zion 11, 22, 51, 52, 130, 147
punctum 57, 58
Putin, Vladimir xi, xiii, 31, 32, 33, 37, 40, 41, 42, 43, 45, 59, 78, 90, 95, 96, 110

Q 38, 50, 51
QAnon 38, 42, 50, 51, 52, 53, 54, 56, 57, 74, 76, 77, 78, 81, 82, 97, 115, 116, 117, 118, 119, 121, 122, 126, 144, 148

radio (propagandistic) programs 29, 104, 138
rassenschande 34
Rassinier, Paul 65, 66
red (color) symbolism 23, 27, 44, 49, 105
red pill 52, 53, 91, 118, 119
revisionism 64, 65
rhetoric 11, 21, 22, 24, 25, 28, 31, 32, 33, 34, 35, 36, 37, 38, 39, 40, 41, 42, 43, 46, 50, 55, 56, 58, 50, 55, 56, 58, 59, 66, 67, 72, 73, 76, 93, 94, 96, 97, 109, 113, 122, 131, 135, 140, 142
robes symbolism 44
Robespierre, Maximilien de 97
Rossi-Landi, Ferruccio 9
runic alphabet 23, 46, 47
Russian Revolution 110

sacred geometry 44, 45
Saussure, Ferdinand de 5, 6, 7, 8
Schliemann, Heinrich 48
Schopenhauer, Arthur 86
Sebeok, Thomas 6, 8, 9
semioethics xii, 2, 3, 9
semiosis 136, 145, 150
semiotic network xiv, 6, 8, 11, 12, 13, 14, 15, 16, 22, 23, 24, 25, 26, 27, 32, 37, 42, 43, 45, 46, 47, 49, 50, 54, 56, 58, 63, 65, 68, 70, 78, 81, 85, 87, 101, 105, 125, 131, 134, 135, 137, 138, 139, 140, 141, 142, 146
sign systems 3, 53, 86, 105, 116, 132, 136
slogans 21, 24, 29, 34, 35, 45, 47, 52, 92, 99, 100, 118
social media xi, xiii, 3, 4, 10, 11, 14, 16, 20, 21, 25, 38, 50, 53, 54, 56, 63, 64, 65, 67, 70, 72, 74, 75, 100, 103, 117, 126, 137, 138, 139
social proof theory 64
social semiotics 10
Socrates 19
Soviet Union 123
Stalin, Joseph xv, 29, 78, 95, 96, 98, 99, 101, 110, 11, 114
State of Fear 61, 69, 79, 110
Storm, the 38, 52
structuralism 5
studium 57, 58
superior race theory xiii, 22, 106, 108
swamp metaphor 59, 92, 93, 96, 143
swastika 22, 23, 27, 46, 47, 48, 49, 57, 58, 94, 105, 124, 140, 141
symbolism 1, 23, 26, 43, 44, 45, 46, 50, 51, 52, 53, 57, 58, 81, 105, 124, 125, 131
synesthesia 36, 37

Tacitus 11
texts 7, 12, 13, 15, 56, 109, 113, 133, 140, 148
Thucydides 17, 111
totalitarianism 21, 29, 143, 152
Trojan War 109, 111
Trump, Donald 21, 22, 25, 38, 42, 45, 52, 53, 54, 56, 57, 58, 62, 63, 69, 70, 71, 72, 73, 74, 77, 78, 79, 81, 86, 89, 92, 93, 95, 96, 98, 100, 109, 110, 112, 114, 116, 119, 120, 138, 144, 149, 153

Uexküll, Jakob von 150
uncoded 7, 115
UNESCO 139
United Nations 10, 11, 64

vaccination xiv, 63, 74, 77
Verwandlung, Die 36
victimization 15, 33, 95
Viganò, Carlo Maria 74
visualization 121, 122, 123

völkisch 23, 24
Voltaire 66

Waals, Frans de 145
Wachowski, Lana 53
Wagner, Richard 23
Welby, Lady Victoria 9
white supremacy 20, 29, 34, 43, 44, 46, 47, 50, 65, 113, 125

Wilde, Oscar 93
Williamson, Judith 7, 8

xenophobia 94

Z (letter) 50
Zelenskyy, Volodymyr 31
Zola, Émile 129, 130

www.ingramcontent.com/pod-product-compliance
Lightning Source LLC
Chambersburg PA
CBHW052122300426
44116CB00010B/1771